BLOOD AND GUTS

BLOOD AND GUTS

RULES, TACTICS, AND SCENARIOS FOR WARGAMING WORLD WAR TWO

Heroes and Legends

DAVID W. HALL

iUniverse, Inc.
Bloomington

Blood and Guts
Rules, Tactics, and Scenarios for Wargaming World War Two

iUniverse books may be ordered through booksellers or by contacting:

iUniverse
1663 Liberty Drive
Bloomington, IN 47403
www.iuniverse.com
1-800-Authors (1-800-288-4677)

Because of the dynamic nature of the Internet, any web addresses or links contained in this book may have changed since publication and may no longer be valid. The views expressed in this work are solely those of the author and do not necessarily reflect the views of the publisher, and the publisher hereby disclaims any responsibility for them.

Any people depicted in stock imagery provided by Thinkstock are models, and such images are being used for illustrative purposes only.
Certain stock imagery © Thinkstock.

ISBN: 978-1-4620-2556-5 (sc)
ISBN: 978-1-4620-2555-8 (hc)
ISBN: 978-1-4620-2554-1 (ebk)

Library of Congress Control Number: 2011909305

Printed in the United States of America

iUniverse rev. date: 07/27/2011

www.commandpostproductions.co

CONTENTS

ACKNOWLEDGMENTS

I would sincerely like to thank those who have contributed to the composition of this book. Greg Hall, Associate Professor of History, Western Illinois University, performed a fabulous job as editor. Eric King, illustrator, did a tremendous work in designing the cover art and maps. Daniel Erdman, senior wargame consultant, was a wonderful help in advising on the rules. Monica Hall, my lovely wife, continues to be an incredible supporter of my writing. Finally, I am grateful to my Lord Jesus for giving me the ability to put two sentences together.

INTRODUCTION

I suppose man's fascination with war is nearly as old as man's first steps on earth. Perhaps the thrill of strategizing to kill a prey with a group of men, with a common purpose, was a natural development toward the art of making war. The ages of time are filled with *Heroes and Legends* of war: Alexander the Great, Gaius Julius Caesar, Genghis Khan, Fredrick the Great, Napoleon, Robert E Lee, Patton, and Rommel, just to name a few. There is no doubt that war has interwoven itself into politics in every society throughout history, from the Greeks to the mighty British Empire. It should come as no surprise that man would invent wargaming first as a tool for young officers in training to tools of conquest like the Von Schlieffen Plan of the First World War to tabletop encounters with miniatures to PC warriors hunched over their computers.

This work is dedicated to the likes of miniature heroes slugging it out in pitched battles on terrain-fitted tables of all kinds, from the dining room to the garage, where the only casualties are widow-less plastic or metal soldiers that are gathered up and placed in neatly arranged storage boxes. The rules that follow in the subsequent chapters are applicable for those gamers using 15mm miniatures to those folks battling with 1/72 scale plastic figures. I have struggled to achieve a balance between the competing military arms of tanks, infantry, artillery, and aircraft. Further, the rules can be used for any land theater of combat. However, to achieve such a scope of work, the rules, by design, are not overly complex.

The purpose of this venture in writing is first and foremost to entertain. I truly hope this work can provide a smile or two as I reflect on my own experiences with toy soldiers and wargaming. I trust it will cause the reader to reminisce on his own childhood or gaming exploits. Next, I propose to get the reader to critically think about "wargame theory and methodology," as I will lay out my thoughts. I have deliberately chosen that term because it describes more thought than simply playing with model soldiers. Many of us game because we love history and we want to represent what we have learned, and get a glimpse into the past, by gaming. I sincerely believe that wargaming is the end result and ultimate expression of the vast time spent studying period warfare, tactics, uniforms, personalities, and specific battles, and painting troops and period vehicles. The culmination of our work is displayed on the game table with our works of art locked in nonlife-and-death struggles for victory. Last, I would like to think that some of the readers of this work will take up the rules and game it as their own system. Frankly, I know this is going to be tough. Gamers have particular systems they like and are committed to them. In this endeavor, I hope I can alter some thinking, maybe be a resource, win a few converts, provide a level of entertainment, and then I will have succeeded in my quest.

Wargames of all periods are fantastic spectacles to watch and be encouraged by. It is most enjoyable to go to a friend's house where there is a gang of gamers who are eager to display their recent miniature works of art. To observe the great care and diligence some have put into their figures, buildings, and vehicles; it inspires and excites true gamers. Having been to numerous events and having observed the handiwork of many enthusiasts, it has served to stir my imagination and has propelled me to learn more about uniforms, weapons, and tactics. For example, when I first started wargaming the American Civil War, I thought I would merely paint the rifles, webbing, and flesh of the soldiers because most manufactures have their plastic figures in a base blue or gray. However, when I seriously started gaming I witnessed magnificent regiments sporting colorful weatherworn uniforms marching to engage my pathetically clad troops. Needless to say, I started over.

My journey in wargaming with 1/72 scale figures started the Christmas vacation of my fourth grade year. My oldest brother Greg had bought me a box of Airfix British Waterloo Infantry and one box of Waterloo French Infantry. Zack, my other brother, bought me one box of Airfix Marines and one box of Africa Korps. Soon, I was adding other sets: Romans, Barbarians, and World War One British and German armies. Within a short period of time, I had filled one of my brother's shoeboxes with 12 to 14 boxes of figures.

This is not to say I had no other toy soldiers in my life. I most definitely had the large ubiquitous green fellows of the 54mm type. However, once the little ones were introduced to me, those chaps took a back seat. They later met an unfortunate end at the hands of an older neighbor boy who asked to borrow them for his ninth grade film-making class. My large brown grocery bag of soldiers was returned to me with the contents in charred ruins and busted body parts! I guess he was trying to film his version of *Apocalypse Now*.

Once the little men entered my world, I was hooked. Playing with them became a life's passion. After school, homework, and sports, I was making battles on the floor or furniture, wherever it was conducive to having soldiers stand on their own. (Digging the soldiers into the shag carpet was always an impediment to a good battle.) Sometime later, maybe the fourth or fifth grade, a friend introduced me to gaming with them. The use of dice never occurred to me. Blake Meech and I found a small clearing among the bushes in the front yard. Each combatant had 50 or so troops and a couple of those *Atlantic* plastic tanks. The battle began with two 6-sided dice rolling on the ground; 1, 2, or 3, you're dead. To be sure, we were not gunning for complexity.

Though I cannot recall the outcome of my first *real* battle, it set in motion a childhood filled with collecting and gaming. I was at the local hobby shop every chance I could get. I had to beg a ride from my mom or older brother Greg, which resulted in fewer trips than I would have liked. Occasionally, a friend's mom would relent and take us. Many a time, I found myself sporting tennis shoes and grunting my way on foot or on my bike to get a look at what was new. As my friends and I gathered more, our games became larger and we sought better ways to game. Our simple system was not matching up to those Hollywood movies we so eagerly tried to portray on our fields of battle. At first, we had no rule sets. For that matter, it would be years later before I discovered rules actually existed and that there were whole networks of wargame societies and books written on the subject. What we had were simple ideas about movement for soldiers, differing types of vehicles, and planes. Firing and damage effects were based solely on two 6-sided dice. Such as 2 through 6 were a hit on a tank and a second roll of 9 through 12 was a kill for a tank. We were not too savvy on the types of tanks. I think I recall a Stuart knocking out a King Tiger and not being surprised!

One problem manifested itself early in our gaming. How to cope with 200 figures set up on each side of a game board and allowing all figures to fire per turn. Another friend and I once set up a game: sheets with pillows under them for hills, a blue towel folded for a river and crinkled T-shirts for ridges. He and I had 20 tanks each, with 200 troops apiece. The battle lines were drawn and the firing began. However, our enthusiasm quickly faded as we tried to fire each figure. *Oh the drudgery.* We both realized there must be a better way. It was at that time I settled on a firing point system. Each side would get 50 points per turn: tanks, mortars, bazookas, and anti-tank guns would cost 7 points, heavy machine guns 5, submachine guns 3, grenades and flame throwers 2, and pistols and rifles 1. This allowed a player to choose what was in his best interest in that firing turn. Some may instantly think that firing all your tanks would be the natural outcome. It was not. Such a tactic would leave your infantry exposed while allowing your opponent's infantry free reign to occupy positions of strategic value. Although I have left this facet of my rules behind in favor of what will be described later, I think I may institute it again for a skirmish set of rules.

Within a few years, at about 12 years old, I started writing my own rules for combat. I had picked up a small bookcase game called *Rommel's Panzers*. As I read it, I realized I could convert this into 1/72 scale to meet my needs—and it worked. I was also able to grasp the differences associated with different tanks and guns of the battlefield. I modified movement and firing for tanks and infantry. It gave me a working structure on which to develop and grow. Further, I started studying tank books at the local library and started reading small war books written for kids. This set of rules grew and evolved for 25 years until I decided to stop gaming World War Two. I packed up my troops and tanks and headed for other periods in time: the Thirty Years War, Seven Years War, U.S. Civil War, American Revolution, and Zulu War. I blame my wife for this diversion. We had recently married and she was staring in disbelief at my collection. I have always had the habit of amassing every period of plastic 1/72 or 1/76 scale figure set produced. She said to me "What are you going to do with all of this, if you are not going to use them?" It was truly a frank and honest question to which I had no answer. Hence, I started studying the U.S. Civil War and spent five years on the subject and that grew into the study of other periods.

(A gallant battle between the Union and Confederate forces.)

CHAPTER 1

Influences and Observation
of a Wargamer

The set of rules that I will lay out is entirely different from the set I developed in my childhood and adolescent years. It is a collection of influences and convictions that I have developed over the years. As I have interacted with other wargamers, read different authors, and experienced the games themselves, I have reached my own conclusions about how rules should be designed. I am certainly not advocating that my rules are superior to other sets but simply stating my conclusions has helped me concentrate and produce a set I can call my own.

Wargamers are a very diverse group of people with varying backgrounds, influences, understandings, and interpretations of history. However, there is one commonality that unites them: their time is limited. Many of us are still raising families, are committed to support our children's extracurricular activities, and have demanding jobs. We have spouses that require our time and attention. Therefore, we are barely able to squeeze in "hobby time," let alone spend hours each weekend wargaming one game. I have participated in far too many games that were too large in scope for the allotted time given. Either there was an overabundance of units or the rules themselves were overly complicated to allow a smooth game in a four-to five-hour period. The most frustrating aspect was that a conclusion was never reached. I am sure there are many in this audience of readers that have played an eight-hour game, watched a few gamers come and go with hardly an exciting turn played, only to have the game called a draw. Following that, the "after action reports" from the players were filled with ifs and buts as to the eventual winner. Such things should never happen! This has led me to one of my core principles in game creation and rule design: **Can the game be set up and played, with a conclusion, in 5 hours?**

As for our differences, there are those gamers who relentlessly argue every point. To be kind, it probably stems from an over exuberance and knowledge of period weaponry and tactics. However, the disagreements only add to the length of time needed to play and hopefully reach a conclusion. The best way I have found to solve this issue is to allow each side two objections to either the interpretation of a rule or how the rule should be applied. The player issuing his objection must clearly state his logic and reasoning. Then he will submit to a simple roll of a 6-sided die. If the roll is 1, 2, or 3, then he wins the argument. If he loses, the affair is considered closed and the game moves on. The irony is I have seldom had to use it. I think just knowing a player can object is enough to keep most gamers in check.

It was some time in my mid-twenties that I stumbled on to other wargamers outside of the friends I grew up with, who were long gone in terms of throwing dice. While I was serving in the Marine Corps, I did manage to persuade a few Marines to take up gaming, but not to any great extent. It was at the Keller Show, in the Los Angeles area that I met Larry Squire, a prolific wargamer. He was selling built and un-built 1/72 scale armor kits. He and I started chatting and he told me of an informal group of wargamers with whom he played. I soon met the players and a new chapter in my wargaming life opened up for me. Their World War Two collections were fantastic and their wargaming system was grand. Larry has a great game just waiting to be published. He also introduced me to Mike Creek, a legend in his own right with his massive game board and hobby room. It is his entire two-car garage! I can only dream to have such hobby space. Mike, too, has his own set of rules that should be in print. The experience with this group enriched my wargamer soul. To know there were others contemplating wargame theory and developing systems of play to incorporate historical events into exercisable game simulations that went far beyond watching *The Longest Day* and trying to play a game of soldiers landing on a beach was a great encouragement to my own ideas. To this day I am not immune to being inspired to play a solo game after watching an old war movie, such as *The Devil's Brigade*. I am indebted to Larry for opening his game space and permitting me to invite the group to play a few of my games using my rules. There was one memorable occasion in which we gamed the Thirty Years War. I do not believe anyone at the table had tried this period. The game turned into a very exciting event, with cavalry charges, musketry, and solid shot flying everywhere. As I recall, the Swedes held the field at the conclusion of the game.

(Wargame at Larry's. Author's collection and photo)

It was by chance in the year 2000 that I discovered Donald Featherstone. I was attending a training class to get my stockbroker's license. Near the training center was a used bookstore. At a break, I was browsing the books. I came across

Battles with Model Soldiers. It was a revelation. I had absolutely no idea that there were genuine authors on the subject discussing wargames in hardcover. I was blown away.

I went on to collect numerous books from Featherstone, Charles Grant, Peter Young, Terence Wise, Bruce Quarrie, and C.F. Wesencraft. What inspired me was that their rules did not attempt to achieve absolute realism. Their rules and theories made their games fun, enjoyable, and still they achieved a degree of realism that enabled the player to taste the art of war for the period being played. In the end, I think as wargamers that is all we want to obtain.

It was Wise and Wesencraft that exposed me to the idea that there was an alternative to rolling for every rifleman for the musket period and that troop quality played a large part on the unit's proficiency at firing and morale. This solved a difficult problem for me. During my early teens and later in my early thirties, I flirted with the *Horse and Musket Age.* I was using the idea of rolling an 8-sided die for every six men firing, given the target was in range and morale was very basic. Both writers used the morale or troop quality, plus the number of troops firing to determine the number of casualties inflicted on the opponent, without rolling a die. Of course, there were modifiers to either increase or decrease the number of hits. This process greatly increased the turn sequence thus hurrying the game along without jeopardizing the playability and, more importantly, the essence of the period in question. Further, the use of morale was simple but played a large part in their systems, either through attrition or due to the reactions to opposing units firing or charging. If morale collapsed, it could pull in other units with it. The point of mentioning this is to illustrate that there are ways to approach wargaming that may seem unconventional, such as not rolling for firing infantry, but still present a useful set of rules and thoughts that challenge the mind.

The games have taught me that there is something called tactics on the battle table. I know gamers will huddled in a corner and lay out a strategy for defeating their steely-eyed antagonists. They will make moves and countermoves in the process of the match. But I am referring to something more subtle. Here is an example of what I mean. Years ago I hosted a game featuring Poles vs. Swedes. The inspiration was Gustav Adophlus' campaigns in Poland, his training ground prior to his entry into the Thirty Years War. I was the Game Master. My friend Larry Squire was on the side of the Poles and he had command of three regiments of Winged Hussars. The tactic he employed was that of a feint. He kept his ferocious cavalry on the right flank of the enemy performing mock charges solely to distract and pinned down two Swedish regiments, keeping them from making any rash decisions. It worked. It allowed the rest of the Polish cavalry and infantry to attack and penetrate the left flank and go on to win the game. Admittedly, I painted those Hussars and the entire forces used that day and I was hoping they would majestically charge across the field and smash and destroy anything and everything in their path. All I got to see was a nice looking *Merry-Go-Round*! But tactics are tactics and they do not have to be pretty to be effective.

Once, I was able to exercise the old one, two, three punch on a fellow gamer who was taking up the role as a World War Two German commander. I had recently read in one of Gene McCoy's *Wargamer's Digest* issues an explanation of employing the Attack Element, the Maneuver Force, and the Reserve in a coordinated attack. The game was a small skirmish between the Afrika Korps and British 8th Army. Each side was outfitted with a company of infantry and a platoon of tanks. I had used my infantry as the attack force, piercing the broken ground in the center of the table. The three Panzer III tanks maneuvered to my right flank, skirting the edges of a hill and the board. The Reserve (the troop's support element) contributed by laying down a base of fire for the Attack. The Panzer IIIs successfully engaged his Crusader tanks causing his infantry to fear attack from the left flank. It therefore caused him to split his attention from my infantry assault, resulting in a weakened defense. The Reserve unit moved in behind the Attack and together they carried the day. By keeping this ploy in mind, I was able to exploit his lack of a cohesive battle plan. We had discussed the battle in an "After Action Report," where I discovered his plans were based on an if/then approach, despite his having an overall strategy. He wanted to get his Crusaders into an attack position against my infantry and if I did x, y, or z then he would do a, b, or c. I think that this is a common mistake many wargamers fall into without realizing it. I know I have on many occasions substituted strategy for tactics and gotten my ammunition trailer kicked.

CHAPTER 2

Wargame Theory and Application

A theory, as defined by *Webster's II New Riverside Dictionary*, second definition, states: "a body of principles governing the study or practice of an art or discipline." I think this puts into perspective what designers of wargame rules attempt to achieve. The body of principles is two-fold. One, we have a set of facts or presumed facts relative to historical events. Two, we are confined to time and space in terms of what a game board is representing. These principles are funneled into a set of rules governing the practice of our discipline. Like any theory, it is subject to human interpretation. For instance, here is a classic example: How far can a regiment charge? Assume we are discussing the U.S. Civil War. Some designers will allow a charge to go far beyond a normal move. Let's say the normal in-ranks move is 6 inches, which represents 150 yards, the charge may allow for a movement of up to 12 inches or more. We now are talking 300 yards, which is a mighty long run in any combat gear and still remain combat-effective. Certainly, modifiers can be allocated to diminish the effectiveness if the entire course is run. However, that is not my point. Conversely, one could argue that a charge can only be carried out when the opponents are within 100 yards (4 inches) of each other. Most infantry-to-infantry engagements in the civil war were within 100 to 200 yards of each other before a running charge was committed. I am not writing to pass judgment on which approach is correct. I want to demonstrate what a designer has to rationalize in his mind when creating a system. In this instance, whether a man can cover more ground running than a man walking in a given segment of time. Should his rules necessarily grant a charging unit a move at twice the distance of a walking unit? On the other hand, if history reveals charges were short bursts of energy to force a reaction from an enemy, should the charge movement be restricted to a shorter move than a normal one? I can almost certainly hear a few readers howling at my logic on both sides. If so, I am pleased. Wargaming is a thinking man's game. **Finally, I submit that the definition of Wargame Theory is a set of principles and rules reflecting historical events on a three-dimensional field governing the discipline of wargaming.**

The Relationship Between Time and Space

The next step in the theory is the application of time and space. How long should we say a turn represents: 1 minute, 5 minutes, 30 seconds? Let's use 5 minutes. How far can a U.S. Civil War regiment march while the officers are dressing the ranks and the troops are presumably under fire? Perhaps 150 yards is reasonable. But what about a charge given the same time period, did that change the dynamic? Does the unit actually run for 5 minutes or do we revert back to the historical discussion above? Keeping these thoughts buzzing about and reflecting on the problem, if the designer is developing rules for mechanized warfare, how much ground can an infantry squad cover in 5 minutes relative to a Sherman M4 moving at full tilt, particularly if 1 inch is representing 25 yards? I think it is fair to say that the squad might get 10 inches, but the Sherman probably fell off the board. One lesson in game design is that the rules should provide enough movement for units to elicit a reasonably quick response from an opponent and those movements need to be in relationship to the size of the game board. I recently played a game where a British MkVI was able to move 48 inches. The game table was only 54 by 60 inches. I do believe that game designer has changed his movement charts. However, it does illustrate my point.

On the subject of time and space per turn, the turns of these rules to follow are broken down into 4 phases: Player A moves, Player B moves, Player A fires, and Player B fires. It is not quite that simple, but for this brief discussion we will assume it is. The complete turn will be defined as 5 minutes, 2½ minutes for moving and 2½ minutes for firing. The time specified may strike some as long for mechanized warfare, because some gamers play a 30-second turn. Using 5 minutes as the length of time allows for rates of fire particularly for infantry, which will be explained later. Of all wargame theory aspects, this is probably the least important and least relevant. Once the game starts, very few players ever think twice about the time component. I do not think I have ever encountered a gamer making a stink about such and such move taking too long or there is no way X can happen in that amount of time. Frankly, all that matters is that the relationship between movement and firing feels reasonable given the size of the game board.

The heart of wargame theory is to develop a set of principles that effectively deal with competing factors both relationally and historically. In this set of rules, I have chosen to represent 1 inch as 10 yards. This will of course pose a few problems. If the game board is 6ft. by 5ft., that is 72 by 60 inches, than any weapon save a pistol or a Japanese knee mortar can hit any target on the battlefield, thus restricting any kind of skillful maneuvering. The solution to this is to "dumb down" the ranges to be proportional to the field. For example, a U.S. bazooka's range is 14 inches and a tank's maximum gunnery range is 60 inches. A medium machine gun can reach out to 40 inches where as small arms can reach out to 30 inches. There are, of course, the obligatory modifiers, which makes hitting those maximum ranges extremely difficult in practice. Therefore, maneuvering can be obtained without getting chewed to pieces before getting into position.

The Dynamics of Spatial Relationships

I could have selected an alternative method that is fairly common, which is to use millimeters to represent yards or meters. This does make using ranges much easier, so that the maximum effective range for a heavy machine gun, such as a .50 caliber, might be 1000 yards. This reduces the scale down to 40 inches. However, this system presents some terrain distortion, which can pose another set of challenges. Suppose a tank is crossing a 4-inch bridge over a 4-inch river, does this match the scenario? A 100-yard bridge and river might be an objective in and of itself, not to mention that only one 1/76 or 1/72 scale tank can cross at a time and they too are 75 to 100 yards long. Therefore, I have stuck with maintaining the spatial relation between units and terrain and have sacrificed the range dynamic. In doing so, I have still kept the weapons systems' dissimilarities intact. Quite honestly it probably does not matter much once the dice are rolling, provided the rules meet the desired effect. I personally like to think that what is representing a squad in a house is not theoretically occupying a massive factory because the model is 75mm by 150mm which translates into 75 yards by 150 yards.

Continuing on the subject of spatial relationships, the next area to discuss is the size or scope of the game relative to the dimensions of the battlefield. As gamers, we get excited about having a "big game" where all the guys come over; the players confirm the time commitment, the chips and sodas are prepared, and maybe some beers are ready to go. The game finally gets set up, sides are matched, and the dice let loose. However, "there's no action" to quote Telly Savalas in *Kelly's Heroes*. The game takes on a slow pace because either there are too many units on the board or the game board has been enlarged beyond the rules' subconscious intent. I believe most sets of rules are designed with an average-sized game board in mind, something in the neighborhood of 5ft. by 8ft. This has a huge impact on the nature of the relationship between movement, firing, and ranges. Imagine the 5ft. by 8ft. board crowded with 50 tanks on each side. This would cause a huge traffic jam. One might even have to call out the *Airfix U.S.A.F. Personnel* and employ a few of those MPs to direct traffic. Conversely, envision a nice 9ft. by 16ft. board to play on where the average movement of a tank is 12 inches, not to mention the infantry. If the average turn takes an hour to play out, maybe more if 6 to 8 players are involved, it would take 4½ hours just to clash in the middle of the table, crossing by means of the width. The significance of all this is that it would be advisable to take this into account before signing the call to arms that a battle is coming. In the former case, simply look at what number of units is reasonable given the table in question. In the latter case, one might want to increase the movement and firing ranges somewhere between 10 and 25 percent to allow for a more fluid game.

Why Roll for Initiative?

One of the aspects of these rules is that I utilize rolling for initiative at both phases throughout the game. There is a roll to see who moves first and a roll to see who fires first; in both instances the high roll wins. The roll is played out using a 6-sided die. At first this may seem odd. I have never come across a system that employs this tactic. However, this is not to say it is not out there. I have some very specific reasons for using this particular wargame method. First, it does require that a player assume some risk. If you are the one that must move first you have two courses of action to pursue: play it defensively and make no bold movements or make some provocative shift to force your opponent to react to you. The former allows the player to play a bit of a cat-and-mouse game with his opponent to get him to reveal a piece of his strategy. The latter puts the player in the driver's seat by causing his foe to react to his actions. Suppose the player that moved first advanced with a brave dash toward his enemy to close the distance, leaving in his wake his support units, then rolls the initiative to fire first: the RISK paid off! Imagine in the next turn our "General Patton" rolls a repeat both times. He is now starting to develop some momentum and the poor opponent is starting to feel a little like "General Ambrosio" during the Sicily Campaign. He has seen his counter efforts smashed and the tightening grip of defeat is tugging on his dice. "Patton" is starting to feel and taste an easy victory. Pleased with himself and his brilliance, a bit of arrogance is detected on his lips as he explains his dazzling moves. For a third time he gets to move first, further pressuring "Ambrosio" to fill the hole developing in his line. The third roll bounces on the table and our poor general wins the initiative to fire first. Now the tables are turned and "General Ambrosio" blasts away, making "Patton's" efforts look like a thrown Roman Pilum. The use of this approach causes the momentum to shift throughout the game. This helps to simulate the natural ebb and flow of a real battle and puts the player in a position to take risks. The attempt is also to try and elicit real emotion in the play sequence. Instead of the cool methodical detachment associated with most rule systems' sequence of play, which in and of itself has the potential to rob the game from building momentum, I want players to feel some passion about what is occurring on the battlefield and feel the frustration of things moving against them despite their best efforts. It should be remembered a wargame is attempting to replicate a battle. Why not introduce an emotional aspect to the game? I have played this aspect out many times and experienced the elation and frustration of the shifting momentum. Many times it has left me with some great memories of fantastic battles. For example, I recently played a game with my friend and neighbor, Ernie Hoeffner. Ernie is not a wargamer, but he is willing to entertain me from time to time. The setting was Sicily and I was trying to move a platoon of M3 Lee tanks up a road. In the distance was a concealed Pak 40 75mm anti-tank gun with a Rate of Fire of 2. The son of a gun won the initiative twice before I was able to silence it. I lost two tanks and one was immobilized. I was certainly perturbed by the course of events. However, would not a real platoon commander be hacked off, to say the least, about having tried to get his tanks in position but having events happen too quickly to get the jump on that gun?

Additionally, I have two other motives for using this method, which are a little more practical. First, using initiative rolls like this does speed the game along. Some systems have players use orders either written on a sheet of paper or by placing special counters upside down with certain markings that indicate an order to a specific unit. Though these are not bad ideas, they do slow down the game considerably. If each order segment takes 10 minutes and I know that is giving the benefit of the doubt, a 6-hour game loses 1 hour to disseminating commands. Second, the initiative rule absolutely eliminates cheating, or even the suspicion of it. Once a player starts moving, he is observed the entire time. There will be no question of what move was made. This can happen when orders are written or the rules call for simultaneous movement. But, of course, what am I talking about? Wargamers never bend their movement orders, not even a little bit.

Saving Throws

Another factor that is incorporated into the rules is saving throws. I know this issue may stick in the craw of some readers. But I do use them. Some argue that once something is knocked off, bringing it back only makes the player repeat the action and it slows down the game. I argue that the use of the method smoothes out unrealistic casualty results and prevents some weapon systems from dominating the game. I first started using this practice when I developed my U.S. Civil War rules. Before I employed it, the casualty rates in the game seemed too unrealistic relative to historical accounts. For example, Union troops attacking a Confederate regiment behind a stone wall appeared to have an easier time defeating the rebels than history portrayed. Thus, I made it harder to score hits. Then it became impossible. The happy medium was using saving throws to assist the reduction of hits and render a more acceptable casualty rate. In these rules saving throws are mainly used, but not limited to, minimizing the effects of high explosive rounds. I selected this approach because I did not want mortars and artillery to dominate the game. As a reminder, part of wargame theory is striking a balance between competing factors.

Assault Factor (AF)s and Armor Class (AC)s

Next, I want to discuss my use of the tank charts for these rules and give the reader some understanding of my rationale behind their creation. Each tank listed has an Assault Factor (AF) and an Armor Class (AC). The AF is its ability to penetrate an opposing tank's armor. In the Tank Combat Chart, I have listed the AF and the associated gun it represents. There are a few that do not fit neatly into the table. For example, the Panzer IVc armed with a short 75mm gun did have the ability to fire armor piercing shells, but it was definitely not equal to a mid-war Sherman's 75mm gun. This is why it was given an AF of 8, which is equivalent to a 40mm anti-tank gun. Some tanks get an asterisk beside their AF, which means it has a slightly better accuracy and the user gets a –1 die roll modifier to hit. Moreover, I do want to make a point on the 75mm and 76mm guns and why I have a few different categories. As the war progressed, so too did calibers and munitions. An AF of 11 represents the gun used on the M3 Lee/Grant and the AF 12 represents the Sherman gun. AF 13 is for the early T34 and KV1 tanks. The AF 14 is designed for the later Panzer IVs and greater caliber 76mm guns. Next, the AC is essentially the tank's armor protection. I have listed next to the ACs an approximation of the number of millimeters of armor it corresponds to. The base number represents the maximum armor strength of the tank. I do make allowances for those that have slightly better armor than listed by placing an asterisk next to the AC, which causes a +1 to be added to the die roll of the opponent to try to punch the armor. There are modifiers that reduce the AC if it is a side or rear shot. The angle of the shot also comes into effect but that will be covered later.

Last, it is important to note the rules are designed to cover the whole of World War Two. I want any player to pick up the set of rules and be able to game France 1940, North Africa, North West Europe, the Eastern Front or the Pacific. However, this does create some challenges in one set of rules. Not every tank's AC and AF will fit neatly into the Tank Combat Chart (Table 8.3). I am trying to keep the dice used simple and the game playable. I originally used a 12-sided die with 10 columns in the chart but it could not adequately account for the varying guns used so I expanded it to 16 columns and introduced a 20-sided die. This was a great help. It achieved the degree of flexibility required without overcomplicating the game. Further, the chart system is limited by intent. I purposely did not want to take into account each tank's varied armor statistics and cause the player to become a tank expert, nor did I want overly detailed tank hits for each angle. These factors would only serve to lengthen the game. This system is intended to be a combined arms game, not exclusively an armored one.

In conclusion, wargame theory and its application are a quest to find balance between competing elements in a game and how to best apply them in a given set of rules. This also implies the designer's intent for the level of complexity of the rules. The rules that follow are not intended to be vastly difficult. To the contrary, I want the game to move at a reasonable pace. Therefore, I have tried to keep the complexity to a modest level. I hope the reader will keep this in mind as he reads through these rules.

CHAPTER 3

Blood and Guts

This chapter lays out the rules that the player can use to game this system. It is broken down into infantry and tank composition, morale, movement, and firing. The reader should not feel compelled to take copious notes. Chapter 4 is a summary of these rules. I have tried to envision nearly all basic and most complex situations a gamer could find trying to simulate World War Two combat. However, I am sure there will be something I have overlooked or that has not come up during this system's play testing. If a player should find an oversight, I encourage the player to create a simple method for accomplishing the task.

Basing Your Infantry

I have selected this game to represent at least an infantry company but not more than a battalion to be engaged in combat, which can be supported by a few platoons of tanks or other armored fighting vehicles, with indirect weapons in support, such as mortars, artillery, or aircraft. The basic unit for the game is a platoon of infantry. The platoon's composition, depending on national origin and time period, can vary. In Chapter 5, I provide a listing of units and their company level structure. Most platoons are made up of 3 squads and some support elements. For example, a British platoon consists of 3 squads and a headquarters (HQ) element. To represent the squad, I chose to have two figures mounted on a 1½ by 1½-inch base. The HQ section is a little more complicated. It contains a 2-inch mortar team, an anti-tank rifle (ATR) or PIAT (Projector, Infantry Anti-Tank) team, and the command unit. These have been broken out to allow the tactical dimension to be played. I still mounted 2 figures but they are mounted on a 1¼ by 1¼-inch base. This allows there to be a visual distinction within the platoon. Therefore, each platoon consists of 12 figures.

The Tactical Label

There are a few important points that need to be made about these stands. The reader can change these mountings to meet his own preference. One figure can be used for those players pressed for time, though I do not recommend more than 3 figures to a squad stand. But the number of figures is not important nor for that matter the exact size of the base. What is important is what is written on the back of the squad or fire team. There are 3 platoons to a company and the company level HQ structure is also represented. For the British, this is a section made up of 13 men, which I portray on one stand with 2 to 3 figures. The bases have a small strip of paper pasted to them with paper cement. I refrain from using white glue because it will stick to the wood and it cannot be fully removed. The paper cement, like tacky glue, is not permanent. The paper can easily be removed and the glue rubbed off. This comes in handy when it becomes necessary to replace the tactical information on the label. On the base is written the tactical and game component information. The tactical data can be anything that a gamer can easily recognize. The label above lists platoon, squad, and company. It is written like this: 1a♣. It reads as such: first platoon, *a* squad of the listed company symbol. The company symbol color can be changed as new companies of the same battalion are created, though I have limited myself to 1 to 2 companies for different theaters of action. The only exception to this are my Japanese troops. I do have a full battalion. My Marines occasionally need to be outnumbered, especially if I am going to recreate a Banzai charge, which I have and it was a fantastic learning exercise. (I was able to watch the charge form and smash into the Marine line. One platoon was overrun but the company held with the support of the mortar team.) National flags can also be used to help identify squads and it also looks great. I have flags on my German infantry, German paratroopers, Gurkhas, and Australians. The flags have been downloaded from the Internet and shrunk down via my PC to fit on the label. All the information on the labels is sized up using Excel.

The base material can be purchased at any local hobby store. The bases are made from 3/32-inch balsa wood. Most of the bases are 1½ inch square. I do make the platoon support bases a little smaller: 1¼ inch square. I like there to be a visual distinction between squad and support. The company level support bases vary in size depending on what I am representing. As an example, a medium machine gun section might be on a 1¾-inch square and an 80mm mortar platoon could be affixed to a 1½ by 2-inch base. The back of the base comes from a 28 by ¼-inch triangle balsa wood strip. I cut these down to fit the bases. The slope of the triangle makes reading the labels much easier.

After the figures are based, I like to make the base into a tiny diorama. Having already painted the base in either a medium green or desert tan, I add grass, dirt, rock, and brush to match the terrain of the theater of war being developed. For those portraying North Africa, I do still add an olive drab piece of shrub just to give it a little color. For those bases representing more of a wooded climate, I add more greenery. But I have to be mindful that I do not want the base to appear too cluttered. The intent is to make the bases seem more realistic.

For those wishing to experiment with these rules, I suggest not going through the trouble of detailed basing. I recommend simply taking some thin cardboard, perhaps a box from a built model kit or poster board, and cutting it up into squares. If there are some loose painted or unpainted figures sitting around waiting for their next mission, muster them up and mount them on the squares. However, be sure that enough room is left to note the needed information on the back of the base or label them first.

Morale

There are 3 elements making up the label: Morale (M), number of Strength Points (S), and Rate of Fire (R). The morale can range from 1 to 4; 1 being the worst and 4 being the best. The typical morale is a 2. This is used for all major combatants. The 1 is reserved for inferior troop quality, though I rarely have all units saddled with a 1. Depending on what is being played it is usually a mix of 1s and 2s, with 1 making up 50% to 75% of the stands in the assembled force. This is usually for Italians, Poles, French, Romanians, and Hungarians, or for Americans if the Kassarine Pass is being played. The 3 is used for elite troops like U.S. Rangers and Marines, German paratroopers, Waffen SS, etc. However, the units should be a mixture of 2s and 3s in order not to overly weight the morale unless specifically gaming a particular scenario, such as Marine Raiders hitting the beaches in Tulagi. The 4 is exclusively set aside for commandos or elite special forces. This too should be mingled with 3s unless there is a specific action being played like St. Nazaire.

Strength Points

The (S) factor in this game is a very key element in establishing the squad's ability to take casualties. I have assigned the average squad-sized unit with 3 Strength Points. With this in mind, it becomes the benchmark for assigning point values to other stands. The average number of men in a squad in World War Two was 10 men. Therefore, anything less is assigned a lower value. The platoon support elements are typically given a 1. For example, the British platoon has a 2-inch mortar team with a crew of 2. Thus, it is assigned a Strength Point of 1. The same is true for the platoon's anti-tank rifle and the platoon commander. When the company support elements are reviewed, one has to consider the size and composition of the unit. The medium machine gun section of a British medium machine gun platoon is made up of two guns and 13 troops. Accordingly, the base represents one gun and 6 or 7 men and is given a 2 for Strength. The player can deviate from this for different games and scenarios, such as an Afrika Korps delaying action after the Battle of El Alamein. In that case, it would certainly not fit to assign full Strength Points to all the squads of a company.

Rate of Fire

Determining Rates of Fire is a bit more problematic. The equipment carried by different squads of different nations was not always equal and so their relative firepower is open to interpretation. Continuing with the British squad, the troops were armed with rifles and one Bren light machine gun. This gives them an (R) of 2, one for the machine gun and one for the rifles. This is a fairly common set up for the Soviets, French, Japanese, and Poles. In contrast, the German squad has a Rate of Fire of 3 even though it has a slightly smaller squad. One point is for the rifles and two are given for the belt feed MG34 or MG42. Obviously, the MG34 could outperform a Bren gun and hence it carries more value. The Americans also get a Rate of Fire of 3 but for a different reason. One point goes toward the BAR (Browning Automatic Rifle) and two go to the rifles. The rifles are significant because the M1 Grand was a semi-automatic weapon with a higher rate of fire than bolt action rifles. Submachine guns in this game count as Small Arms fire as do hand grenades and are not broken out from the squad's (R). It is the same term given to the rifles. The idea is that the squad's weapons are firing as a team and not individually. The (R) for the support teams of a platoon or company is usually a 1 for its small arms or specific weapons. This can range from the platoon anti-tank rifle (ATR) or bazooka to a light machine gun. However, this can be altered depending on the weapon the team is employing. The platoon mortar typically gets a 2 as does a German MG34 team, for platoon HQ support.

The challenge comes when trying to rate weapon systems that are very different in the same theater of war. The Japanese Model 92 machine gun vs. a U.S. Browning .30 caliber machine gun is a good example. The fact that the Japanese gun was strip fed with 30 rounds per strip and the Browning was belt fed makes a huge difference in combat comparability. In ideal firing conditions the two guns might have had similar rates of fire. Nevertheless, the Model 92 was known for jamming and could be difficult to load in a stressful situation. The U.S. Browning was far superior in reliability and in rate of fire because of its long cloth belt with 200 or more rounds attached. In this case, it would be wise to give the Browning a Rate of Fire of 2 and the Model 92 a 1. The German MG34 and MG42 will rate a 3 for having the best rate of fire among medium machine guns in the war. The British Vickers will rate a 2 like the .30 caliber. One may ask why the German squad with a rate of 3 (2 for the machine gun and 1 for small arms) is not given a higher fire power because the MG42 is given a 3 when it is in a supporting machine gun section. The logic behind this is in their respective roles. In theory, the support element is going to be more heavily supplied. They would be assigned a cart or truck for movement whereas the squad in combat is relying on their version of the Black Cadillac, i.e., their Jack Boots to get them around.

As with Morale and Strength Points, I will include suggested Rates of Fire, in the Basic Table of Organization and Equipment chapter of the book. I say suggested because I want the player to feel free to change the base detail to fit his own wargame theory. As I stated earlier, historical events are open to interpretation. The key in wargame theory is striking a balance between all the competing factors.

There is one special character on the battlefield that deserves special mention and that is the dreaded sniper. These fellows are based as individuals on a small tray. They get an (R) 1, (S) 1, and a general morale of 3. Their use on the battlefield should be used sparingly unless fighting scenarios against the Japanese, where it was more commonly used as a delaying tactic across a sector of the battle line. In the Infantry Combat table (Table 5.1), there are special modifiers both for sniper fire and firing at a sniper.

Relationship Between the (S) and the (R)

Now the discussion must turn to the relationship between Strength and Rate of Fire. If the Strength Points are equal to or exceed the Rate of Fire before any casualty has been taken then the full Rate of Fire is in effect. Although once a casualty is taken the Rate of Fire must be assessed by a simple rule of thumb. As the stand loses one Strength Point it will lose one Rate of Fire except in cases where the starting Strength Point was greater than the Rate of Fire. That unit will maintain its starting Rate of Fire until it takes another casualty. For example, a British squad will start with an (S)3 and (R)2. The first hit will mean it will have an (S)2, but the (R)2 will remain until a second hit is taken which will result in an (S)1 and (R)1. Of course the next hit means the squad is eliminated. On the other hand, a typical German squad will have an (S)3 and an (R)3. As that unit takes hits, a corresponding Rate of Fire is deducted. In cases where the (R) exceeds the (S), both get reduced together. This can be found in company supporting machine gun sections, where the (S) is a 2 and the (R) is a 3. This may seem confusing at first, but once employed it will feel intuitive.

Tanks and Tank Morale

Unlike the composition of the infantry platoon, tanks, and AFVs (Armored Fighting Vehicles) are played in a one-to-one scale. The average tank platoon size was 4 to 5 tanks with AFV varying in their respective types. In the Basic Table of Organization and Equipment chapter, I list some common formations for AFVs and tank platoons. Depending on the game being played, tanks may not play a significant role. There may only be 2 or 3 panzers supporting an infantry company advance. Because of this, I have created morale for tank crews as an option. The thought behind this is to avoid a game ending prematurely because the tank crews got upset and decide to collect their dice and go home, leaving the poor infantry to fend for themselves. Also, I try to image a real scenario in which the tanks are attached to the ground commander and one of his tanks is destroyed; would the tankers give up or push on? The option states: "Any tank that receives a hit from a 2pdr (AF of 8) or greater on the Tank Combat Chart must roll a morale check." (Morale checks will be covered later.) Of course this hit would have to be unsuccessful; i.e., the round did not penetrate the tank's armor. Morales are noted at the start of the game per tank and should be appropriate for the equipment in use. It is the equipment that dictates the morale levels, which will become clearer once the tank morale check is discussed. Generally speaking, the Germans should have a morale of 3, if in Panzer IVs or heavier. Anything smaller should be a 2. The French crews in French equipment should have a 1 or 2. The Americans and British should receive 2s, and Russians, Italians, and Japanese a 1 or 2.

The Strength Point and Rate of Fire for a tank or AFV is effectively 1 and 1, respectively. Once the vehicle's armor is penetrated it is considered knocked out and combat irrelevant. Naturally, this does not apply to those fighting machines if they become immobilized. They are still able to fire. The reason that the Rate of Fire is limited to one is to achieve balance on the game board. With players rolling for initiative, it would be too easy to destroy an opponent. If a player won the fire-first initiative 2 or 3 times, there would probably not be much of a game left. The opposing player would be left staring at miniature heaps "burning" on the battlefield.

Support Units, (M), (S), and (R)

As in most games, there are those units that support the infantry and tank formations. For this game, support units are defined as "on" and "off" game-board artillery, mortars, aircraft, and anti-tank guns. Each of these is on a one-to-one scale, except the mortar sections. The player can have a single mortar represent 1 to 3 guns. I decided this was a more economical approach. I know from experience it can be difficult to obtain the needed amount of mortars. When on-board artillery is used, the artillery crews will be assigned Morale, Strength Points, and Rate of Fire. Their morale will correspond with their infantry counterparts. The (S) will depend on the size of the crew. They can range from 6 to 12, which will give an (S) of 2 or 3. The (R) is 2 per gun represented. For off-board artillery, no Morale or Strength is needed. The Rate of Fire is still 2. Mortars are very similar. Their (R) is also a 2 per gun. The (S) is determined by the number of guns represented. One Strength point is allotted for each gun. Thus, a British 2-inch mortar, in an infantry platoon, will have an (S) of 1 and a 3-inch mortar section will have an (S) of 3 for 3 guns. Aircraft in this game do not have any of these factors. They buzz in and buzz out so fast that it would be inconsequential to provide them with an (R), (S), or (M). However, I have a special way of dealing with them, which will be covered later. The anti-tank gun stands are similar to the infantry. They can have Strength Points of 2 or 3 depending on the gun. I have decided that guns 75mm or greater get a 3 and those that are lower get a 2. The Rate of Fire is 2 for 50mm and below and 1 for those greater than 50mm. The logic is that the smaller guns are quick and easy to load. The larger caliber guns are powerful and I have decided to follow the same line of thinking presented on tank Rate of Fire. Admittedly, the Rates of Fire can be changed to represent a specific battle. I do not want players feeling confined to specific Rates of Fire. Suppose a game calls for two 88mm guns holding a ridge against two platoons of Sherman tanks. It may make sense to give the 88s an (R) of 2 or 3. Conversely, a game portraying a battle in France in 1940 with four British 2pdr anti-guns as the main defense against a platoon of PzIIs and supporting infantry, it might be necessary to limit the (R) to a 1.

It is important to remind players that one must take into account size, scope, and mission of the game when determining the (M), (S), and (R) of units. As I mentioned, infantry, tanks, and anti-tank guns might be altered as well. The players could decide that a quick armored battle is to be gamed. The scenario could be M24s advancing on two King Tigers. In that case, the American tanks might be given an (R) of 2 and the Tigers a 1. These components are up to the player, to use his imagination and wargame theory to match the game in question. The hope is that the flexibility granted in this set of rules will spark great ideas and games.

Summary of Combat Order

Before diving into the mechanics of the rules, it is important to provide the reader with a quick summary of how the game is played. The outline below reveals how the steps of the game are played out. The first step is to determine which player gains the movement initiative. This is done by using a 6-sided die. The one who rolls the highest number wins the contest and he proceeds with his movement phase. Also, it should be noted that the player cannot cede his movement initiative because he won. Before his units commence movement, those units needing a morale check, because they received fire in the previous fire phase, must check morale first. Once that has been completed and the results carried out, general movement may begin. The player can move any unit he wishes, as long as it is not restricted by the effects of a morale check. While the player is moving, the opponent gets to observe and mark for any opportunity fire. When the player has finished and has stated so, the other player will commence his opportunity fire and determine results. Once this is done, the other player will test the morale of his units needing to be checked. He will then carry out his movements, while the first moving player spots and marks for Opportunity Fire and so on. This completes the movement phase. Next, the players will roll another 6-sided die to determine who fires first. The highest roll wins. The order of firing is aircraft, artillery/mortars, and then general firing of infantry and tanks/AFVs. There is no prescribed order for tanks, anti-tank guns, and infantry units. The player determines the order of firing as he sees fit. Once the player has finished, the next player may repeat the process for his forces. In the event of a tie during any phase, the players will roll again to determine the winner. There are no simultaneous movements or firing phases.

A few final notes before starting: whenever a 10-sided die is used in this book, the 0 number is a 10. Also when the game begins, the opening setup or initial deployment of forces constitutes the first movement phase of turn one. The players will start with the initiative roll for first fire.

Combat Order
1. Roll to see who moves first. (Player A)
    a. Morale checks
    b. General Movement
    c. Player B gets Opportunity Fire
2. Opponent moves second. (Player B)
    a. Morale checks
    b. General Movement
    c. Player A gets Opportunity Fire
3. Roll to see who fires first. (Player A)
    a. Aircraft
    b. Artillery/Mortars
    c. General Firing
4. Opponent fires second. (Player B)
    a. Aircraft
    b. Artillery/Mortars
    c. General Firing

When Morale Checks Apply

Most wargames include some form of a morale check to replicate the behavior of stress-filled men in a combat situation. This game also includes this concept. The composition of this game's morale includes the unit's training, leadership, and veteran status. These factors are summed up in the morale value (M) assigned to the unit at the beginning of the game. Troops, in this game, can react to fire directed at them in several ways. There are four main ways that troops can react. There are two other responses that can be a result of the behavior of the troops around them. First, troops may simply not react at all to being fired upon. They can take it in stride. Second, a unit may be stunned and unable to gather itself up to advance further. Next, due to being fired upon, the squad maybe forced back or retreat. These last two instances can upset adjacent units. If a squad is forced to give ground either by being forced back or retreating, any nearby squads within 4 inches of the fleeing unit must test their morale. In addition, if a squad watched another squad be forced back or retreat and was itself hit by fire, it will roll the morale check for being fired at first. Then the player will roll the reaction to its retreating neighbors. However, the unit is only required to roll once for a withdrawing squad. Furthermore, the squad rolling because of a retreating or forced back squad will roll the worse of the two modifiers. A "forced back" unit requires its friends to take a −1 die roll modifier and a "retreating" unit demands a −2 modifier. Next, units that receive fire during a turn are only required to take *one* morale check for receiving fire, *not multiples*. Last, troops that receive indirect fire from artillery and mortars (including aircraft bombs) are exempt for taking a morale check unless the fire is a *direct hit* or a *near miss*, which will be covered shortly. The reason for this is that the impact points may completely miss the intended target by as much as 12 inches.

At this point, it is well worth walking through an example to get the reader familiar with the process and to introduce Table 1.1 below. Imagine three war-weary squads advancing on line toward a farmhouse. Unbeknownst to them, there is a machine gun section waiting behind a courtyard wall with a Rate of Fire of 3. It rattles away at each squad, but misses each time. The mere shock of having bullets dancing in front of them is enough to make the toughest plastic soldier think twice. The advancing player will have to roll a morale check for each squad. *Therefore, rule number one on morale checks is that any infantry unit that receives fire must check morale.* The player will first review Table 1.1 and its associated modifiers, which will be covered shortly. Then he will roll one 6-sided die and add that number rolled to the unit's (M), in this case two squads have a 2 and one has a 1. The first roll glares with disappointment, a miserable 1. The total morale comes to a 3. The squad is forced back 3 inches, per the scoring in Table 1.1 for morale. The next squad has a 4 rolled for it and shrugs off the machine gun blast. The third squad has a basic morale of a 1 and for reasons that will be revealed momentarily it has a modified morale of a zero. The player rolls another 1, which means it retreats 8 inches. The unit that has already been forced back does not need to roll again for his retreating comrade. The squad that shrugged off the rattling bullets will have to roll again for watching the other unit retreat. He will reroll with a –2 to the die.

Morale Modifiers

I have just laid out a simple morale check process, but there are a few other modifiers affecting the die rolls for morale that are listed under Table 1.1. The second rule of morale is *once a hit is achieved, the owning player must roll a **sergeant's casualty*** for that unit. A 1 or 2 on a 12-sided die means the squad's NCO (noncommissioned officer) was killed. If this occurs, than the unit's morale level is reduced by 1 level, hence the poor squad above had suffered this hit previously. Any unit that has already taken a sergeant's hit does not reroll again. *The third rule is that each hit taken in the current fire turn is a –1 to the morale check.* The fourth rule does allow for a positive modifier. *It states that any squad within 5 inches of its platoon commander gets a +1 to* *its roll. Also, platoon and company commanders give themselves a +1 when rolling their own morale check.*

The next rule applies when a tank is about to overrun an infantry position. This is the only time when a morale check is done separately and is not a result of firing. It will be rolled during the movement phase of the player advancing his tank to overrun an infantry unit. (As an aside, tanks are permitted to overrun light obstacles, brick walls, fox holes, small horizontal logs, etc. without resulting in damage to their tracks.) The rule is stated like this: *if any enemy armor approaches an infantry unit within 5 inches, with the intent to overrun the unit, the infantry must take a morale check to hold that position.* There is no modifier added or deducted to the squad. The player rolls a single 6-sided die and adds the number to the roll: a 5 or better is a pass and 4 or less is a fail. If the unit fails morale, the squad is then overrun with 2 hits and will be marked for a morale check. If the unit passes its morale check, it can move up to 4 inches to escape even if the unit has already moved. To illustrate this process, a player who has already performed morale checks before starting to move his units moves one squad into an abandoned fox hole. During the next player's turn, the player advances a tank to overrun the position. Once the tank is within 5 inches, the unit must roll a separate morale check to see how the unit reacts to this threat. The player will roll a 6-sided die and in this case he rolls a 4. He then adds the 4 to the basic morale, M(2), and the unit escapes by moving 4 inches away, as depicted beneath Table 1.1. The squad is then still capable of firing and should the process need to be repeated on the same squad, it most certainly can.

Effects on Firing

Now the discussion turns to how firing is affected by failing morale and how to mark those units that fail it. Units that score a 4 or 5 are "shaken" and cannot move for that turn. This can be interpreted as temporarily pinned. The effect is a +1 modifier, which is found in the modifier list for infantry firing. To mark this unit, simply use a colored bead to show it is shaken. The color of choice for these rules is yellow. The beads can be purchased at nearly every local arts and crafts store. (While on the subject of beads, red is used for hits, green is used to denote which units were fired on, and black is for those units that have suffered a sergeant's casualty.) All units that are forced back or retreat also receive a "shaken marker" and suffer the +1 modifier for firing. The marker will remain on the unit until the start of the next movement phase; i.e., for one complete turn. Therefore, before morale checks are rolled, the players will remove all previous shaken markers. There are a few special notes on morale. Mortar units that receive a shaken marker cannot fire while they have the marker. Also, crew-served weapons like medium machine guns cannot fire if they have had to retreat or are forced back. This is not to be confused with light machine guns. They can still fire. Gun crews for anti-tank guns or artillery can be forced back or retreat because of morale but for obvious reasons they cannot fire. They leave their guns in place.

Infantry Morale Check: Any unit that took a hit or was fired on. Table 1.1

Effects	Total Morale Points
No effect	6 or more points
Shaken and cannot move	4 to 5 points
Forced back 3 inches	2 to 3 points
Retreat 8 inches	1 or less points

Die Roll Modifiers
−1 for each hit in that turn
−1 for a sergeant's casualty hit
Any squad within 5 inches of its platoon commander gets a +1 to its roll.
Platoon and Company Commanders give themselves a +1 to their roll.

Any unit within 4 inches of a retreating unit takes a morale check

−2 for any retreating unit that pass by

−1 for any unit that is forced back

Overruns by tanks

5 or more the unit passes and moves up to 4 inches

4 or less the unit freezes

Special note reminders:
1. Shaken markers = yellow bead; must stay on until the next morale phase. The yellow marker indicates the troops are shaken and that affects their firing ability.
2. Mortar units that receive a Shaken marker cannot fire while they have the marker. Also, crew-served weapons such as medium machine guns cannot fire if they have had to retreat or were forced back.

Optional Tank Morale

As mentioned earlier, tank crews can be given a morale factor (M) depending on the scenario to be played. However, players should think carefully when it ought to be utilized. Using it in a small game could prematurely doom the venture. The rule states that *any tank that receives fire from a 2pdr anti-tank gun (Attack Factor 8, which is discussed later) or larger, must roll a morale check*. To be clear, this means that the round bounced off and had no effect on the tank, but it may have unnerved the crew. As covered under Tanks and Tank Morale, there are different factors used to assign morale. The process to determine the effect of morale is basically the same as those described above, but Table 1.2 is used. The player takes the base morale and the number rolled from a 6-sided die to determine the results. There is also a separate chart, Table 1.3, for those tanks or AFVs that become immobilized. There is one modifier. That is a −1 for each tank destroyed in the platoon *every time* it is forced to take a morale check. Stated differently, there is an accumulative effect as tanks get knocked out. This is for both ineffective and immobilization shots. If the tank fails morale, a marker will be placed on it until the following morale phase. The tank can still fire but with a +1 to its *to hit* range, even if it is retreating from the board.

Tank and AFV Morale Table 1.2

Effects	Total Morale Points
No effect	5 or more points
Stopped, shaken and cannot advance toward the enemy*	3 to 4 points
Back up one full move to the rear*	2 points
Back up two moves*	1 to 0 points
Retreat from board*	−1 or less

*Place a yellow marker until the next morale phase.

Die Roll Modifier

−1 for each tank destroyed in the platoon every time it is forced to take a morale check.

Immobilized Tanks and AFVs Table 1.3

Effects	Total Morale Points
No effect	5 or more points
Stopped and shaken	3 to 4 points
Crew bails out	2 points
Crew bails out and flees the field	1 or less points

In Table 1.3, the crew can bail out as a result of being immobilized. With 2 points, the crew bails out and moves 8 inches away from the tank. The crew can remount the tank in the next turn by moving an infantry move but it takes an additional turn to be able to fire the main gun. The machine guns in the tank can be fired, and this is true for AFVs, in the turn the vehicle is reoccupied. However, if the crew scores 1 point or less it bails out and flees the field and it is immediately removed from play. Also, the crews can be shot at and destroyed. Each hit on a crew represents 2 to 3 men killed. Since most tank crews were 3 to 5 men, this means that the smaller crews are wiped out with one hit and the larger crews can take one hit and can still somewhat operate the tank. If a partial crew is able to remount its tank it can fire the hull machine gun or fire the main gun/turret machine gun but not both. If a crew is hit by fire or shot at, it will have to undergo a normal morale check like infantry. Tank crews can fire but only at Assault Range with a Rate of Fire of 1.

General Movement

The general movement section of the game is broken down into two basic elements, the movement of vehicles and the movement of infantry stands. In addition, there are several modifiers that restrict the movement of units. For these rules, all movement is denoted in inches, except aircraft. They come into the battlefield during firing and the defender gets a general strike first before the plane can inflict its damage. But this will be covered later.

Tank and AFV Movement

As players start to think about moving their vehicles on the board, there are a few issues they need to keep in mind. Generally speaking, tanks and AFVs can move plus or minus 12 inches. Players will not have to worry about moving turrets as a part of movement; turreted vehicles can fire in any direction. Self-propelled guns, however, must face their enemy within a 45-degree zone of fire. There will be a listing of AFVs and tanks by nation in the Tank Charts and it will catalog among other things their movement. Below is a list of modifiers affecting their movement. The units get no penalty for turns under 45 degrees. AFVs turning greater that than 45 degrees will get a

2-inch deduction from their movement. Some of these modifiers are accumulative and therefore some slow infantry tanks, like the Churchill, will have a tough time traversing difficult ground. Naturally, some are mutually exclusive. A tank cannot be off road and in designated rough terrain. It is either one or the other. But a hill slope can be uphill and rough. This would produce a minus 5 inches of movement. Of course, games can consist of terrain impassable to AFVs or tanks or both. The one setting up the game must designate this before the game starts.

For those units that are not moving, it is important to note which units moved. This can be done with any small bead or marker. For small games, it is not as much of an issue as it is for larger games. The reason it is important is that there are die roll modifiers making it harder to fire and hit moving targets.

Furthermore, this list is not all-encompassing. Terrain modifications can be endless. The idea is to get the gamer to think of those factors that are either accumulative or mutually exclusive. Before a game can begin any changes or additions to the list must be provided at the onset of the game for each player to review.

AFV and Tank Movement Modifiers

–3 inches off road
–3 inches for snow or mud
–2 inches per 45 degree turn
–5 inches for fording
–3 inches for designated rough ground to include lightly wooded areas
–2 inches for going uphill at each contour and/or light obstacles
½ movement lost for loading or unloading troops; limbering or unlimbering a gun; vehicles going in reverse

Infantry Movement

Infantry movement is divided into two categories: those stands with crew-served weapons like heavy machine guns (HMG), and medium machine guns (MMG) and basic infantry stands. Those stands with crew-served weapons move 6 inches and regular stands move 8 inches. However, a Japanese MMG section can move 8 inches due to the number of men in the section. They were generally much larger than a western equivalent. One important aspect for the crew-served weapons is that they can move and fire in the same turn. Last, players ought not to concern themselves with facing. The units can fire in any direction. The only exceptions are MMGs and HMGs in fixed positions or in buildings.

There is **one optional rule for infantry movement**, which restricts a unit's ability to advance. Infantry stands outside of a 10-inch radius from their respective platoon commander to include the company commanding officer (CO) cannot advance toward the enemy. The idea here is to give the player the option to represent very nervous infantry in particular scenarios. This can be used in representing Soviet or Italian infantry unwilling to advance on an enemy without the near presences of their commander, although this can also be applied to untried U.S. troops, such as at the Kassarine Pass.

The movement modifier list below is not meant to be all-encompassing and the same logic and procedures that apply to the tanks and AFV's movement apply here as well.

Infantry Movement Modifiers

–2 inches for wooded terrain, no movement penalty for light wood
–2 inches for snow or mud
–4 inches for rough terrain and streams
–3 inches for walls and obstacles
–2 inches for uphill at each contour

–4 inches for infantry loading (and unloading) into a vehicle or mounting/dismounting a tank

Opportunity Fire

The movement initiatives in this game could allow units to escape being fired on unrealistically. For instance, an infantry unit might dash from one building to another across the line of sight of a light machine gun (LMG) team. Therefore, an opportunity fire phase was created to counter this occurrence. *Opportunity fire is defined as fire directed against a unit that attempts to move from a concealed position to another concealed position across the line of sight of an enemy unit.* Though this does not happen often, it does come in handy when dealing with wooded or urban environments. Also, those units wishing to "close assault" a vehicle that moves past their position, either dug in or concealed, can perform an opportunity fire. The rules for that attack are outlined in the Close Assault section following the Tank Combat Chart (Table 8.3).

The process for opportunity fire is a simple one. While player A is moving, after having checked morale, player B gets to sit back and observe any movements that cross the line of sight of his units and the enemy movements meet the definition of opportunity fire. If this occurs, he can choose to fire on them. He will mark the spot where the units passed. The units will complete their moves. After player A completes all his moves, player B can fire those specific units using the normal fire rules. If the firing unit needs to take a morale check, this must be done first. If the unit fails, it cannot fire. Hence, no unit having failed a morale check is permitted to fire an opportunity fire. Further, once they fire, the units cannot fire again in the fire phase. The moving unit will suffer regular casualties and morale unless destroyed and removed from play.

Fire Phase

As mentioned earlier, the fire phase is similar to the movement phase in that both players roll a 6-sided die to determine who fires first. Once it has been determined which player will begin firing first, the player will lead with his aircraft if he has any. Next, his artillery and mortars will give it a go, followed by his infantry. Just in case there is any question, the 2-inch mortar carried in a platoon is to be fired during the artillery or mortar section of the turn. Finally, as in the case of Movement, the initiative winner cannot cede firing first.

Aircraft Firing

When a plane attempts to attack the battlefield, whether it is by strafing or bombing, it must endure a general defensive fire from the opponent before its damage can be assessed. Should the aircraft be hit and destroyed by enemy fire first, the plane is said to be knocked out and is unable to continue its mission. If the plane is hit but not destroyed, it continues its run but cannot return to the field for the rest of the game. Planes are limited to two turns of attack on the battlefield unless specified at the onset of a game. The intention is to restrict the impact a plane may have on the game relative to the other units. Again, the need for balance in the game is paramount.

Table 2.1 below reveals the different types of defensive fire. The defending player gets to roll his anti-aircraft fire first. Small Arms are one generic die roll for *all* the infantry units on the ground and the die is rolled one time. The other four categories are for specific anti-aircraft cannons. It should be noted that machine guns must be mounted for that purpose in order to fire.

The process to bring an aircraft into attack is simple. The player first declares his target and endures anti-aircraft fire first. In the first numbered row, the defending player rolls the listed number or less for a hit using one 20-sided die. Since not all hits equal a destroyed plane, the defending player rolls for a kill on the italicized row. For the second numbered row he rolls a 10-sided die to score that number or less.

Aircraft Strafing

Anti-Aircraft Fire Table 2.1

Small Arms	Machine Gun	Single	Double	Quad
2	3	3	4	5
2	*3*	*4*	*6*	*8*

Assuming the plane made it through the onslaught of anti-aircraft fire, the player will run the attack. For those planes that have the machine guns mounted in the nose, the player lays down a 12-inch string. Any units within ½ inch of either side of the string are considered affected and must be assessed for damage. For those planes with machine guns in the wings, lay out two 12-inch pieces of strings and anything within ½ inch is considered hit. The obvious question is how far apart should the strings be? If a model of the aircraft is not being used, then players should use 3 inches as the distance. When an actual model is being used, the player should measure the actual distance between the guns on the wings and use that for the space between the strings. Once the string(s) are laid out, the player must roll to see if the "pilot" deviated from the prescribed attack run. Using the table below (Table 2.2), the player will roll an 8-sided die to determine if the plane squarely attacked the target. If he did not, the string(s) will be adjusted accordingly.

Pilot Deviation Table 2.2

1,2	3,4,5,6	7,8
3 inches to the left	On target	3 inches to the right

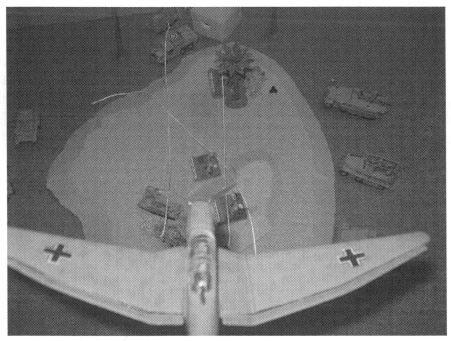

(String has been laid out for this attacking JU87)

Assessing Hits by Aircraft

The infantry units being hit by the aircraft fire take one hit and it is automatic. However, there is a saving throw of a 1 or 2 on a 6-sided die. There is, of course, the obligatory –1 for soft cover and a –2 for hard cover. Buildings are to be treated as soft cover unless otherwise stated before the game begins. Hard-roofed bunkers and dugouts are considered impervious to machine gun fire. Whether or not the unit is saved from a hit, the owning player must perform a morale check on the infantry units affected, except in cases where the unit is in hard cover with a solid roof, such as a concrete bunker. Soft-skin vehicles (trucks and jeeps) hit by machine gun fire are automatically hit and destroyed. *If troops are inside, they take 1 hit with no saving throw.* If they occupy an armored vehicle, the unit gets the saving throw. All other AFVs and tanks take a hit and it is assumed to be a top hit. Thus, it reduces their armor by 3 levels and the Assault Factor is a 2. (see Tank Combat Chart, Table 8.3)

As the war progressed, some planes were fitted with anti-tank guns or rockets to further enhance their anti-tank prowess. When aircraft enter the board with these weapons and have endured the anti-aircraft fire, Table 2.3 is used to determine if they score a hit. To see if a hit is achieved the player must roll a 10-sided die and roll that listed number or less for a hit, the 3 or 4 respectively. It will be assumed that the hit occurs on the top deck of the vehicle and the player must still roll for the placement of the hit. This too must be done for machine gun hits. The placement of the hit will be covered under Table 8.2. Also, the corresponding AF number will be used in the Tank Combat Chart (Table 8.3) to assess whether the hit penetrated the armor of the AFV. All soft skins are considered destroyed with a hit and the player does not need to roll for the placement of the hit, for it is destroyed automatically. If troops are being transported in a truck, the unit takes an automatic hit but gets no saving throw. Also, one note needs to be made regarding rockets. The high explosive (HE) rating is defined as a 75mm howitzer. This can come into play when firing at bunkers. Last, there is only one die modifier and that is for attacking a moving target.

Should a player use a plane with a larger caliber gun, use the same chart but use the corresponding caliber in the Tank Combat Chart (Table 8.3). The one in the chart below uses one for a JU87 Stuka Dive bomber with twin 37mm guns. To be clear, each gun or rocket rolls for a hit and damage. For example, a Stuka with twin 37mm guns blazing away would roll twice to hit and potentially twice for damage. The same would be done if a P47 Thunderbolt fighter launches 4 rockets against a Panther tank. The player would roll 4 times to hit and up to 4 times for damage.

Aircraft Assault Chart Table 2.3

Rockets	ATGs
−3 per rocket	−4 per ATG, (Stuka)
AF 11	AF 7

<u>Die Roll Modifier:</u>
+1 for moving target

Planes and Bombs

Of course planes coming to the aid of the ground forces not only used rockets and machine guns, but bombs were used in abundance. This game uses the common 250-and 500-pound types. The player can select which type of attack, but both cannot be done in the same turn. When a player uses aircraft to drop ordnance on the enemy, the chart below is used to access where the bomb falls on the table. The player will roll an 8-sided die to see if the attack was successful. Numbers 1, 2, 5, and 6 are in line with the plane's bombing run. Numbers 3 and 4 are perpendicular to the plane's attack path. For the effects of the bomb or bombs, see the Indirect and Direct HE Fire Blast Results Chart (Table 3.2). There are also two die roll modifiers listed below Table 2.4 to increase or decrease the likelihood of a direct hit. Both are self-explanatory.

Dropping Bomb Chart Table 2.4

1	Overshot the target by 12 inches
2	Undershot the target by 12 inches
3	Left of target; perpendicular to the plane's approach: 8 inches
4	Right of target; perpendicular to the plane's approach: 8 inches
5	Overshot the target by 6 inches
6	Undershot the target by 6 inches
7-8	Hit

Die Roll Modifiers
+1 for dive bombers
−1 for moving targets

Artillery and Mortar Firing

Following the aircraft section of the firing phase is the call for fire using artillery and mortars. Any unit that would naturally have a radio can call for fire. Therefore, all platoon and company command stands can call for fire. Most Armored Fighting Vehicles can likewise call for fire, although that can be tricky when gaming early war scenarios, because many of the French and Russian AFVs lacked communication devices and relied on signal flags. It will be important for the players in that case to note which vehicles have radios. The note can be set aside as not to reveal the worthiness of those targets.

The procedure for calling in indirect fire is simple. During his fire phase, the player announces his target and uses the chart below (Table 3.1). He will roll a 10-sided die to determine where the first round lands. For each successive turn firing at a stationary target the player gets a +1 to his die roll. This will help simulate zeroing in on the target. It is important to note that for those artillery and mortar positions that are on the board, the measurement for misses is made either in line or perpendicular to the gun position. When a player has off-board indirect fire, the measurements are from the player's end of the table, either to his left or right or to him or away from him.

Artillery and Mortar Plotting Table 3.1

1	Overshot the target by 12 inches
2	Undershot the target by 12 inches
3	Left of target; perpendicular to the unit's position: 8 inches
4	Right of target; perpendicular to the unit's position: 8 inches
5	Overshot the target by 6 inches
6	Undershot the target by 6 inches
7	Left of target; perpendicular to the unit's position: 3 inches
8	Right of target; perpendicular to the unit's position: 3 inches
9-10	Hit

Plotting the Shells

The picture below represents a cluster of four shells hitting the game board. There is the initial impact of the first plotting round, as determined in Table 3.1, and three subsequent rounds from the unit's (R). The laying out of impact diameters is fairly easy. Each mortar and gun represented gets two rounds of high explosive (HE) or whatever is determined for the Rate of Fire. The only exception to this are tanks firing HE. They get one round.

When the impact point is determined, lay out the first circle. The numbers 1 to 6 will need to be on the circle. This will be the first round landing and the *number one* will be pointed back in the direction of the firing unit. To determine the second round, roll a 6-sided die. The number rolled will be matched up with the number on the first circle. In the example below, the center burst diameter was laid out first. Note that the center dot is the impact point and can represent a direct hit on a gun or vehicle. This is important in determining whether the hit was a near miss or not. The roll of a 3 brought the next round to its right; the roll of a 6 the upper left and the roll of a 5 the lower left. All rounds will impact off the first round. Rounds will sometimes land on each other, pulverizing anything in the diameter. *Anything in the diameter will suffer the prescribed hits for each diameter laid out.* This can often mean a unit can take multiple hits, particularly from direct hits of the 2-inch mortar. The infantry stand is 1½ inches square and the burst of the 2-inch mortar is ¾ inch. A direct hit is taken at the center of the stand. This will put 2 bursts on the unit. An alternative plotting method is to cascade the impacts, meaning the rounds follow the previous impact and are not centered on the first. Whichever method is used, the player will have to announce it prior to firing.

Indirect Fire Ranges

While on the subject of artillery and mortars, the natural question of effective range needs to be addressed. The indirect guns in this game can range or cover the entire board. The game is designed with a battlefield that is roughly 6ft. by 8ft. Therefore, if the game were to be played on a board that is substantially larger, the players would have to make some allowances on range limitations for 60mm mortars and 75mm infantry guns. The only range limitations are for the 2-inch mortar and howitzers firing indirectly. The maximum range for the 2-inch mortar is 30 inches with the Japanese "knee mortar" being 18 inches. The howitzers have a minimum range of 24 inches. Last, the mortars can theoretically drop rounds on their own position or very close to it. It should be kept in mind that a roll of a 2 or 6 on Table 3.1 will bring those rounds toward the mortar itself; 12 and 6 inches, respectively. Thus, a good rule of thumb is to make the minimum range at least 13 inches.

Assessing Damage from HE

The chart below, Table 3.2, is used to determine the gun type used, burst diameter, hit value, and any potential saving throw. (When I first set up this system, I was fortunate to come across a set of wooden circles at a local arts and crafts store. They became the burst diameters for the different common shells listed below.) It is important to note that not all HE hits get a saving throw. The reader will notice that an 88mm HE round produces 3 hits but the player taking the hits only gets 2 saving throws. This is to at least guarantee the artillery barrage has some effect for the larger caliber guns. As I mentioned earlier, the use of the saving throws help prevent the domination of indirect fire in the game.

The roll for a saving throw is conducted on a 6-sided die and there are a few basic modifiers that affect the outcome of saving throws; these are hard and soft cover. All the modifiers for this chart are listed below the table. Hard cover is defined as anything that can reasonably resist a blast and is designed with that purpose, such as earthworks, sandbag emplacements, or fox holes. Soft cover is defined as anything less likely to resist a blast but provides some cover like a wall, log, or rock outcropping. These definitions are slightly different from those covered during general firing. Here, the soldiers are seeking shelter from the effects of a blast and shockwave as opposed to bullets. For items that might be questionable, the players should discuss the definitions first before starting to play.

Indirect and Direct HE Fire Blast Results Table 3.2

GUN	Burst Diameters	Hit Value	Saving throws
Mortar 45/50mm**$$ 2.8cm, 37mm, 47mm Grenade Launcher	¾ inch	(1 hit)	1 saving throw
Mortar 60mm, 75mm infantry gun, 50mm, 57mm	1 inch	(2 hits)	2 saving throws
Mortar 80mm or 75mm Howitzer, 76 mm	1¼ inches	(2 hits)	2 saving throws
85mm to 90mm	1½ inches	(3 hits)	2 saving throws
Mortar 120mm or 105 mm Howitzer	2 inches	(3 hits)	2 saving throws
120mm Howitzer	2½ inches	(3 hits)	2 saving throws
155mm Howitzer/250lbs. bomb	3 inches	(3 hits)	1 saving throws
500 lbs	4 inches	(3 hits)	no saving throws

Die Roll Modifiers
−2 hard cover
−1 soft cover
+1 troops in a building
−1 Troops in an armored half-track or open top Self-Propelled Gun, Universal Carrier
** Range 30 inches

$$ Japanese knee mortar and rifle grenade launcher; range 18 inches

Table 3.2 is also used when a player is firing HE rounds over open sights on a target. This can mean a tank or howitzer is firing HE on an infantry unit in the open. The player would naturally roll to see if it hits first on the To Hit Chart for Tanks and Guns (Table 8.1), which will be covered later. Since the chart *is not all inclusive*, some judgment calls will have to be made for calibers not listed and for tank HE firing in terms of the impact of the hit. If there is a disagreement, let a roll of a 1, 2, or 3 on a 6-sided die pass in favor of the firer. For instance, a Soviet SU100 is firing a HE round. Because it is closer in size to a 105 howitzer, let the round side there. Should an opposing player object, let the dice determine the issue.

Direct Hits from HE

For direct hits on AFVs, tanks, or other guns, the HE Direct Results Chart (Table 3.3) is used to determine the effects of the impact. Use a 12-sided die and roll the number indicated or less to see if the object in question is destroyed. All soft-skin vehicles (trucks and jeeps) are instantly destroyed. If the round lands inside an open-topped vehicle such as a M10 Jackson or German Hummel, the crew is killed and the vehicle is considered knocked out. Should the round or bomb land inside a half-track or truck with troops being carried, the appropriate number of hits are applied with no saving throws and the vehicle is destroyed. I have included in this section the destruction of anti-tank guns. It is designed for guns that are greater than a 75mm. I do not have a problem imaging a 37mm anti-tank gun being hit and torn up by a 2-inch mortar. However, it is a little different if it hits a German 88mm. I did not want to have small munitions automatically destroying large guns rendering them inoperable. They can still do it. But the player must roll for its demise.

HE and Bunkers

In the HE Direct Results Chart (Table 3.3), there is some allowance for damage to an Earthen Bunker or Concrete Bunker. If a player scores a *direct hit* on the bunker or pillbox as a result of indirect fire, the player will simply cross-reference his munitions with the type of structure and roll appropriately for destroying it. If successful, the defending player will roll for the saving throws for the HE caliber involved from the Indirect and Direct HE Fire Blast Results (Table 3.2). Only the units affected in the burst diameter are subject to the roll. If there was a gun in that section of the bunker it is automatically destroyed.

The logic behind the double roll, the first hit, and the bunker hit is that it is assumed that a bunker is designed with the intent to survive a direct hit from a high explosive round. Therefore, the penetration roll is needed to see if it is destroyed. The resulting saving throws will determine the amount of destruction to the bunker and the troops inside. The key here is that the troops inside *do not* get any hard-cover modifiers and once it is destroyed it cannot be reoccupied.

HE and Buildings

For troops occupying a building, the procedure is essentially the same. If there is a direct hit on a building structure with troops inside, those troops get a +1 to their saving throw. In addition, it is only those troops affected by the burst diameter. For example, two squads are occupying a house and have been seen by their opponent; the attacking player fires his 80mm mortar platoon to quiet their fire. After his second fire for effect, he scores one burst diameter on one of the squads in the building. The defending player gets to roll two saving throws for the 2 hits delivered by the 80mm mortars with a +1 added to the save roll. The other squad is unaffected by the blast. The reason the troops in a building get a saving throw is that there is an assumption that the troops are spread out in the structure and not concentrated under the roof of a bunker.

I would like to take a moment to point out why I chose to address the high explosive effects in both the HE Direct Results chart (Table 3.3) and the Near Miss chart (Table 3.4), which will be covered below. I wanted to create simple charts that would speed up the indirect fire section of the fire turn and that would be different from general firing for tanks. I did debate whether or not to use the Tank Combat Chart (Table 8.3) for the effects of HE on armor. However, I decided that converting each gun into an HE Assault Factor that could penetrate armor would be beyond the scope of this game. I believe it is better to keep this matter simple and stick to generalities. Thus, it would have a speedier result on the game and get to the all important conclusion.

If a player has successfully rolled to hit a target with HE, the HE Direct Results chart (Table 3.3) is used to determine the likely kill of the target. For example, a 25pdr fires and hits a light tank. The player will use this chart below to see if he destroys the tank. In this case, he will need to roll an 11 or less to be successful. The procedure would be the same if a Sherman fires HE at a bunker. The assumption is that the shock and concussion from the blast is what kills or incapacitates the crew and not the penetration of the round.

HE Direct Results Table 3.3

	ATG and Howitzers	Tankette or Armored car Half-Track	Light Tank	Med. Tank/ or Earthen Bunker	Heavy Tank/ or Concrete Bunker
Mortar 45/50mm**$$ 2.8cm, 37mm, 47mm, grenade launcher	7	4	5	NA	NA
Mortar 60mm, 75mm infantry gun, 57mm, 50mm	8	5	6	3	NA
Mortar 80mm or 75mm Howitzer, 76 mm	X	7	8	5	2
85mm to 90mm	X	X	9	6	4
120mm Howitzer	X	X	10	7	5
Mortar 120mm or 105 mm Howitzer	X	X	11	8	6
155mm Howitzer /250lbs. bomb	X	X	X	X	8
500 lbs	X	X	X	X	X

(Note: All soft skin vehicles and guns smaller than a 75 mm are instantly destroyed.

X= means destroyed.)

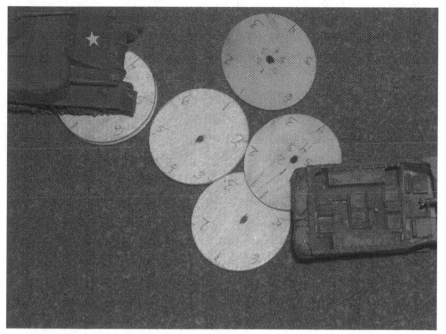

(Notice the two hits on the M3 Lee and Near Miss on the M2 Scout Car)

HE and Near Misses

Now that direct impacts on targets have been discussed, the next topic to cover is near misses. During an aircraft bombing run or an artillery or mortar barrage, the impact of the ordnance can constitute a near miss if a truck, tank, or gun is in the burst diameter and not in the center point. Table 3.4 below lays out the results of a near miss. The simple hyphen (-) indicates no effect. The IM results in the vehicle being immobilized. The X means the vehicle was destroyed while the Xx means the crew is still alive. The Xx* indicates the vehicle is immobilized, but the crew manning the vehicle maybe injured. The crew or troops that are in a half-track or armored car get some protection and the player must roll for their effect (see Indirect Fire Results, Table 3.2). For example, if an 80mm mortar round was used, there would be 2 hits delivered with 2 saving throws and a –1 die roll modifier for being in a half-track. The player will attempt to save his soldiers.

When an AFV is firing HE and misses its target this chart is *not used*. It is said to have missed completely due to the round's trajectory and the round is not tracked. Also, AFVs fire HE during the General Fire section. I mention it here because this is where the charts for using them are to be found. Last, if a vehicle with passengers is destroyed from a near miss, the troops are treated the same as if the round landed inside (see Direct Hits from HE).

Near Miss Table 3.4

Within Kill Zone	45/50mm Mortar Grenade Launcher	60mm mortar	80mm mortar	120mm mortar	75mm	88mm to105mm	120mm	155mm	250lbs bomb	500lbs bomb
Soft Skin	Xx	X	X	X	X	X	X	X	X	X
ATG/Gun	-	-	-	X	X	X	X	X	X	X
Half-Track Armored Car	-	IM	Xx*	X	Xx*	X	X	X	X	X
Tankette	-	-	IM	Xx	IM	Xx	X	X	X	X
Light Tank	-	-	-	IM	-	IM	Xx	X	X	X

55

Med. Tank Earthen Bunker	-	-	-	-	-	IM	IM	Xx	X
Heavy Tank Concrete Bunker	-	-	-	-	-	-	IM	IM	X

(-)—no effect
IM—Immobilized
X—Destroyed
Xx—Destroyed but crew is still alive
Xx*—roll for the effects of the passengers, the vehicle is immobilized, can be applied to universal carrier.

Smoke Rounds

Finally, before moving on to infantry fire, a few details need to be discussed regarding how to employ smoke. The same rules apply for smoke shells as they do for high explosive ones. Therefore, the same procedures are followed. Nevertheless, once the burst diameters are laid out, cotton is laid out to fit the same pattern. The smoke will last for two turns. All units that have their line of sight blocked by the smoke will be prevented from firing through it.

There has been no accounting for the effects of wind on smoke, either to lengthen the duration and expansion of the smoke or its quick dissipation. The reason for this is that it would further complicate and delay the game without materially affecting the outcome of the game. But should the game be played on a much larger game board, it may become necessary to adjust this approach. I suggest the following method. A chosen player will roll a 4-sided die to determine the duration of the smoke: 1 to 4 turns. Then a 6-sided die is thrown to determine the cardinal direction and drift of the smoke. Numbers 1 to 4 are the 4 corners of the board and numbers 5 and 6 represent edges of the mid sections. As the turns go on, the burst pattern is repeated in the direction of the drift.

General Fire

After firing indirectly at the enemy, general firing may begin. There is no actual order here, meaning tanks fire before infantry. The player will determine his own order. What follows here first is infantry fire. This consists of observing enemy units, performing fire, urban fighting, and how to game special weapons. Once the infantry portion is reviewed, there will be a detailed explanation of how tanks and anti-tank guns engage in combat.

David W. Hall

Observing Units

Below are charts that allow the player to ask a set of easy
questions about the nature of the enemy unit. Here it is important
to mention that all units are considered observed if they fired.
Also, any unit that has moved and has crossed the line of sight
of an opposing unit is considered seen or revealed to the enemy.
Therefore, the questions are based on units in certain situations
that have not fired.

1. Is the unit in a wood line or in a firing position in
    building?
2. Is the unit dug in/behind cover or camouflaged?
3. Is the unit in the open, stationary but has not fired?

In the tables that follow (Tables 4.1, 4.2, and 4.3), the player
who is firing is asking the above set of questions about the
intended target. These are placed in the left corner of the chart,
while his unit that is trying to observe the target is listed on the
top. To help keep this in mind, a question is written at the top of
the table: "Observing unit is a ____?" The numbers in the boxes
are inches. This tells the player that his unit is able to observe
an enemy unit at a particular range. For example, an infantry
squad trying to see an enemy anti-tank gun in a wood line must
be within 5 inches of the gun to see it and fire on it. Also, if a tank
is in the open and it is trying to observe another vehicle in the
open that has not fired, it must be within 24 inches.

The reason for listing Recon is to give some merit to having
jeeps and armored cars on the battlefield. Armored or motorized
infantry can count as Recon, but distinctions must be made before
a game starts. Also, other clarifications should be noted so both
sides are clear as to what constitutes what on the battlefield. For
example, a game may call for the Italian CV-33 to be considered
Recon. In addition, some common sense will have to be applied.
The German 88 may be an anti-tank gun, but it should really be
counted as Artillery. Last, supply trucks or minor noncombat
miscellaneous vehicles might be counted as infantry.

Using these charts below puts the players in a risk-taking position during the movement phase. If the player commits his forces, he knows at a particular range his troops will be exposed. However, should he win the initiative to fire, he can then lower the boom!

Sighting an enemy in a wood line or in a firing position in a building
Observing unit is a:_____? Table 4.1

Unit in woods/ building is a:	Recon	Infantry	Tank
Tank?	15	10	7
AFV or Artillery?	12	7	5
Infantry or ATG?	10	5	3

Sighting an enemy camouflaged or dug in
Observing unit is a: _____? Table 4.2

Unit dug in is a:	Recon	Infantry	Tank
Tank?	20	15	10
AFV or Artillery?	15	10	7
Infantry or ATG?	12	7	5

Units in the open can be observed moving. If the unit is stationary, but has not fired see the chart below. If the unit has fired, it is considered observed and thus can be fired upon.
Observing unit is a:_____? Table 4.3

Unit in open, but has not fired is a:	Recon	Infantry	Tank
Tank?	60	42	36
AFV or Artillery?	42	36	24
Infantry or ATG?	36	18	12

Notes on Terrain

Sometimes during a wargame terrain can pose some challenging questions. For instance, how close to an object does a unit need to be to get the cover or block line of sight when units are not on equal ground? Such as, when a unit is on a hill, can it see an enemy on the other side of a building? Here is when the *principle of obstruction* is applied. It is defined as this: when a target is near an obstruction such as a, hill, clump of trees, or building the target must be within 4 inches of it in order for it to block the line of sight. Dive bombers are exempt from this as they are capable of diving down on a target. In determining whether a unit has gained the protection of cover, units must either be fully in it or fully behind it. For example, a squad ends its movement partially entering a wood line. The infantry *would not* get the desired effect. Similarly, if a squad ends a movement turn short of fully coming behind a wall, the wall would not give the unit the beneficial cover.

Hills and Ridges

Hills and ridge lines can also create some potential problems if there is not a clear definition of where the crest line of a hill is located. Many times gamers will collect flat Styrofoam sheets from various packing material to paint and make into hills. Admittedly, they are convenient to create multiple hill and ridge levels. However, unless the players are wargaming a scenario in central New Mexico the features do not do much to block line of sight from one flat hill to the next. Thus, it becomes pertinent to know how the hills and ridges are bisected. If not otherwise stated at the onset of a game, hills are divided into four sections as close to the middle as possible and ridges down the center of the length. Units on either side of a crest have their line of sight blocked by that crest. Units may become visible once they have touched or crossed the crest line. When slightly behind the crest line, the units do get soft cover.

(Notice how the units are on two different sides of the hill.)

Troops in Buildings

All troops that enter a building are considered to be manning firing positions. In other words, it cannot be said that a unit occupying a building was deep within the structure and could not be seen at its seeable range in the Observing Unit distance. However, if a scenario calls for large buildings to be used, then special allowances must be discussed prior to the game. Infantry squads and support teams are capable of firing from all four adjacent walls, except for medium and heavy machine guns. These are restricted to their current facing within the building. Also, troops may not fire through another section of a building. They are limited to firing at adjacent rooms.

Infantry Firing

Having discussed observing units and terrain, infantry firing becomes the next step in the process. The first aspect to address is Rates of Fire (R). Those units with a (R) greater than one can split their fire between multiple targets. The chart below, Table 5.1, specifies the different range categories and weapon types infantry use to fire. Across the top of the table the ranges are denoted in inches. The weapons used are the following: Heavy Machine Gun (HMG), Medium Machine Gun (MMG), Light Machine Gun (LMG), and Small Arms. They are listed in the Weapon Type column. Here are some brief descriptions of these weapon systems. The HMG is any large-caliber belt-feed machine gun, such as an American .50 caliber. The MMG is any standard tripod mountable gun like a German MG42 or Soviet Maxim 7.62mm machine gun. The LMG is for all light portable squad-fired machine guns. This can range from the American BAR to the British Bren or the German bipod-mounted MG42. There may be a question as to why the MG42 would be in both categories and why it is not just counted as an MMG. The logic behind this is that the gun in the German army fulfilled both roles and, more to the point, when it was mounted on a tripod it usually had a scope attached and this increased its effective range capability.

The table is designed to be a simple process. To use the chart, a player will cross-reference the range with the weapon type. He will then roll that number or less to score a hit. For example, if an MMG fires at medium range, the player would need to roll a 5 or less on a 10-sided die. This situation brings up the use of modifiers. It is rarely the case that a target is just standing around waiting to be shot. Hopefully, the poor souls have sought some sort of shelter.

Below the chart is a list of common modifiers which either increase or decrease the likelihood of a hit. Using the previous illustration, suppose our machine gunner, still firing at medium range, is firing from a hill at a squad dug in on an equal level hill. The 5 is the base number. The player would add a +2 to his die roll for troops dug in. On a 10-sided die, a roll of a 3 or less would equal a hit. Had the MMG been on a higher hill than the target squad, the MMG would have needed a 5 or less because the +2 for being dug in and the –2 for firing on lower ground would have cancelled each other out. Some of the modifiers are accumulative and some are not. For instance, a unit cannot be behind a tank and behind brush. But a target can be up a hill and behind rubble. The players will have to make some determinations as to what makes sense in applying these modifiers. There should be no more than a –3 or a +4 applied to a die roll, except when fighting in wooded or jungle terrain.

Infantry Firing Table 5.1

Weapon Type	Assault 0-6	Close 6 + to 12	Medium 12 + to 18	Long 18 + to 24	Extreme 24 + to 30	Machine Gun Extreme 30 + to 40
HMG	8	7	6	5	4	3
MMG	7	6	5	4	3	3
LMG	7	6	5	4	3	—
Small Arms	7	6	5	3	2	—

Die Roll Modifiers
+1 behind tank
+2 behind brick, sand bags, rubble/troops in a building

+1 behind brush (does not apply in wooded terrain described below)

+2 behind hedgerow

+1 target on hill

−2 target fired on from hill to lower ground

+2 target dug in

+2 target behind earthen cover

−2 target fired on by sniper

+1 target is a sniper

+1 for soft cover

+2 for hard cover

+1 firer is shaken

+1 infantry unit moved

+2 darkness or predawn

Fighting in Wooded Terrain

Now that basic infantry firing has been established, the next issue to tackle is how to engage troops in wooded terrain. The first facet to deal with is observation. This is not to be confused with observing enemy units that have not fired. This is about troops fighting in wooded areas against targets that have already been revealed. Displayed below are 4 categories of wooded terrain, which must be designated before the game begins: light wood or shrub bush, medium wood to light jungle, heavy wood to medium jungle, and heavy jungle. These have different rates at which the wood blocks the line of sight. Beyond that distance the engaged units cannot fire either directly or indirectly at one another. Within the prescribed distance the units can fire at each other but the modifier comes into play. For example, two units are slugging it out in heavy wood or medium jungle at a range of 6 inches. Since the units are within the 8-inch limit they can see and fire at each other. But units that are beyond the 4-inch boundary for close assault in the terrain, the players are forced to take a +3 to their die rolls plus any other modifiers. Suppose one of the units being fired on is dug in, the player would get a +3 for being 6 inches from the target in the medium jungle and a

+2 for the target being dug in, resulting in a brutal +5 to his die roll. Therefore, a LMG firing in the Assault column above that starts with a 7 or less on the 10-sided die would need to roll a 1 or 2 to score a hit. (A roll of a 2 +5 modifier = 7 or less in the column.)

Again the discussion goes back to rolling for fire initiative to see who fires first. Players will be compelled to make tough choices in difficult terrain. Wargamers should feel some anxiety about their decisions, and that is the intent. Hopefully in this case, they will get a glimpse into the realities of fighting in the Buna area of New Guinea or the American struggle in the Huertgen Forest.

Modifiers for Combat in Wood and Jungle with Visibility Factors

Light wood/ shrub bush	+1 if outside 6 inches	always observed
Medium wood and Light Jungle	+2 if outside 5 inches	Blocks beyond 10 inches
Heavy wood and Medium Jungle	+3 if outside 4 inches	Blocks beyond 8 inches
Heavy Jungle	+4 if outside 3 inches	Blocks beyond 6 inches

Flame Throwers and AFVs

Flame throwers get a little extra detail as a weapon system because of their uniqueness and the way in which they inflict damage. There are three main categories that can receive damage in wargaming: Tanks and AFVs, Structures, and Infantry/crew. The charts below are simple in nature and require a 10-sided die. The flame thrower may not destroy something immediately. Therefore, it could take up to two turns before it totally engulfs its target. The assumption here is that the fire takes some time to do its work before the troops at risk know what is happening. Vehicles that are not destroyed immediately can still function at full capability and troops occupying a structure not destroyed immediately can still fire. As seen below, this is noted as: X for destroyed, X+1 for destroyed in 1 turn, and X+2 for destroyed in 2 turns. The N means no effect.

The flame thrower unit is represented by one or two figures on a stand. It is assigned a Rate of Fire of 2. However, this means it only gets 2 blasts per game then it reverts to a rifle team. As it is a platoon support unit, the stand is 1 by 1¼ inches. It has a range of up to 3 inches with a minimum range of ½ inch. When targeting a tank or other AFV the player rolls a 10-sided die to determine damage, if any. Table 6.1 constitutes the *to hit* roll. For example, a player is an inch and half away from a tank and rolls a 5. In this instance, there is no effect on the tank. Had he rolled a 2, the tank would have been destroyed the following turn. As a reminder, the zero on the 10-sided die counts as a ten. There are some modifiers included below that either increase or decrease the chance of scoring a destroying number.

Flame Thrower vs. Tanks and AFVs Table 6.1

Tank/AFV	.5-1.0 inch	1.1-2.0 inches	2.1-3.0 inches
X	1 or 2	1	—
X+1	3	2	1
X+2	4	3	2
N	5-10	4-10	3-10

X destroyed
X+1 destroyed in 1 turn
X+2 destroyed in 2 turns
N No Effect

Die Roll Modifiers
If the tank is moving it is a +1
If the target is an AFV or open top tank –1
If the target is a soft skin –2

Flame Throwers and Bunkers

The following table (Table 6.2) is very similar to the above table (Table 6.1) and it also uses a 10-sided die. The main difference is that it is used to fire up a structure such as a pillbox or bunker. There are two modifiers: one for blasting an earthen bunker and the other for a housing structure. It is assumed the earthen bunker is reinforced with flammable logs and the housing structure would naturally burn without too much trouble.

Flame Thrower vs. Structure Table 6.2

Bunker/ Structure	.5-1 inches	1.1-2 inches	2.1-3 inches
X	1-3	1-2	1
X+1	4-6	3-4	2-3
X+2	6-7	5-6	4-5
N	8-10	7-10	6-10

Die Roll Modifiers
−2 for earthen bunkers
−3 housing structures

Flame Throwers and Infantry

Assuming the reason for blasting the structure is to kill or drive the enemy out, Table 6.3 is used to determine the effects on the infantry inside. It is also used for dug in troops or troops in the open or in a wooded area. *If an immediate hit is scored, then the unit takes one hit.* Should there be more than one unit occupying the structure, these other units must abandon the structure during their next movement. If the structure is to be destroyed in a turn or two the player must still roll to see if the infantry are affected.

The player will roll here to see if he scores the hit to the corresponding situation. In both charts a 10-sided die is still used but in this chart, the goal is to roll that number or less. If that number is achieved, then the infantry inside takes one hit.

Flame Thrower vs. Infantry Table 6.3

Infantry	.5-1 inches	1.1-2 inches	2.1-3 inches
In Structure	6	5	4
Dug In	7	6	5
In woods	8	7	6
In the open	9	8	7

To illustrate this situation, suppose a player wants to roast a machine gun team in a bunker. He works his flame thrower up to within an inch and a half of the earthen bunker and lets loose. He must first roll for the structure itself and then the infantry inside the bunker. He wins the initiative to fire first and rolls a 5 with a –2 modifier, which means he gets a modified 3 and the bunker will be destroyed in one turn. He then rolls for the infantry occupying the bunker. Hoping for a 5 or less, because the unit occupies a structure, the player rolls a 6. The infantry escape torching and taking a hit. They will be able to fire back in the current turn but must abandon the position in the movement of the following turn.

It should be noted that the flame thrower is not intended to burn down large buildings and factories. For the purposes of this wargame, it is used on small houses and bunkers. If it is to be used on a larger structure, the player will skip the structure chart and treat the unit being assaulted as dug in. This can occur if the game is to be a large urban fight in which the flamethrower is used inside large buildings trying to expel an enemy. Last, woods for this chart are defined as Heavy Wood to Heavy Jungle. That type of wooded environment is thought to provide some cover from the blast of the flame thrower. Any other wood cover would be considered as "open."

Rifle Grenade Launcher

The next weapon system to examine is the grenade launcher. It acts very much like a 2-inch mortar in that a ¾-inch burst diameter is used, but the range is 18 inches. The same tables are also used (Tables 3.1 to 3.4). The only differences are that the launcher uses one burst diameter instead of two and the player *does not* get a +1 added to his die roll for subsequent rounds on the same target. The reason for this is that there is no bipod mounting for the launcher and it is virtually all estimation by the gunner. Once the first round is fired the gunner will have essentially moved the rifle to reload it, unlike a mortar where the gun stays in place while being reloaded, which makes adjusting easier. Also, players can choose to use anti-tank grenades in the same fashion. Last, grenade launcher firing is conducted in the infantry firing section and not indirect firing.

Shoulder-Fired Rockets and Anti-Tank Rifles

The last infantry weapons to discuss are those used to destroy tanks or other armored fight vehicles. There are 5 systems used in this game; the ATR (anti-tank rifle), U.S. bazooka, the British PIAT, and the German Panzerfaust and Panzershreck. Each of these is assigned their own AF (Assault Factors) values and ranges, which are found below Table 7.1. In the back of the Tank Development of World War Two chapter (Chapter 10), the penetration capabilities are listed. Given the nature of the shoulder-fired rockets, generically speaking the bazooka, they were close-range weapons. For the purpose of achieving balance on the game board, the bazooka has a limited range relative to other weapons. They also have a minimum range, which prevents the team from getting blasted from destroying a tank or AFV. The range is denoted in inches in the chart below and a

10-sided die is used. The player must roll the listed number or less to that corresponding range. Also, the same modifiers found under Table 5.1 still apply to this firing section.

Unlike the above weapons, the ATR will only have one AF assigned to it. It can be argued that there were differences in the performance of the gun from different nations. However, they were of limited value on the battlefield and were mostly abandoned for better weapons soon after the war began.

For those readers perhaps not so familiar with the bazooka story, it may be important to note that it was designed by the Americans and was first used by U.S. forces in North Africa. The Germans were impressed with the device and, of course, like most things German in that era, they made it bigger and more powerful. It was known as the Panzershreck. They later went on to create the Panzerfaust, a more powerful weapon with a reduced range. The British did create their version of an infantry-carried anti-tank rocket known as a PIAT (Projector Infantry Anti-Tank). It was a half-tube device that loaded from the top instead of the rear like the American bazooka.

The composition and movement of a bazooka or ATR stand is similar to a single LMG team or platoon HQ base. The anti-tank team's base is a 1¼-inch square stand and can be represented by one or two figures. The unit moves as a crew-served weapon except the Panzerfaust. It is a lighter and smaller weapon.

Bazooka/ATR Table 7.1

3-6	6.1-9	9.1-12	12.1-14	14.1-18
8	7	6	5	4

Anti-Tank Rifle: AF (3), range 18 inches
PIAT: AF (10), range 10 inches
U.S. Bazooka: AF (10), range 14 inches
Panzershreck 88mm: AF (13), range 10 inches
Panzerfaust: AF (14), range 6 inches

Bazookas and Bunkers

The bazooka (again, this referrers to the generic use of the term to include the U.S., British, and German rocket launchers but not the ATR) can tackle both earthen and concrete bunkers. If a player sends a U.S. bazooka team to try to demolish a log bunker manned by German machine gunners, he will first have to see if he hits using the above chart and then the *bazooka will have to be converted to use the HE Direct Chart* (Table 3.3) where the bunker is found. In this case, the AF is a 10, which on the Tank Combat Chart (Table 8.3) equates to a 50mm to 57mm gun. On the HE Direct Chart, a 50mm would require a roll of a 3 or less on a 12-sided die to score a hit. That may seem a little complicated, but as a player gets familiar with the millimeter size of these weapons, referring to Table 8.3 will become unnecessary. The player will then follow the prescribed method of saving throws for the troops inside. It will be important to remember the troops inside will get no hard-cover modifier.

Tank, AFV, and Anti-tank Firing

Now the time has come to introduce the king of the battlefield, at least in the opinion of some, the tank. In the Tank Chart section of the book, at the end of the Summary of Rules chapter (Chapter 4), the player will find a listing of the most common tanks, AFVs, and anti-tanks guns used by nations during the war. Each one has its corresponding Assault Factor (AF), Armor Class (AC), Movement (MT), Crew, and Miles Per Hour (MPH). The AF is used to cross-reference the opponents AC in the Tank Combat Chart (Table 8.3). There the players will see the number to roll or less for a penetration. The MT shows the movement in inches that the vehicle can move. The crew is used to determine the number of hits it can take before being eliminated. Crews of 2 or 3 men take one hit and crews of 4 to 6 can take two hits. The MPH is primarily used as a reference to compare relative movements in inches between vehicles.

Below is the Tank and Gun Firing chart (Table 8.1) and the associated modifiers. In referring to guns, in generic terms this means the main gun of a tank, anti-tank gun, or the gun mounted on other AFVs. Technically, guns can range the whole chart, 60 inches. However, given the modifiers, this can be nearly impossible. Some guns in the Tank Charts have an asterisk next to them. This means the gun gives the player a slight advantage when firing. It is a –1 to the roll to penetrate the enemy's armor. This is used to help distinguish slightly better guns of the same caliber. For instance, a Soviet 76mm anti-tank gun has the asterisk and a SU-76 does not.

Before moving on to working through the chart, there are a few special notes that need to be made. First, single-man turrets can fire on the move but on an every other turn basis. Also, all tank machine guns get an automatic (R) of 2. Next, when tanks or AFVs shoot HE at infantry, the burst radius and impact results for the millimeter used are listed on the Indirect and Direct HE Chart (Table 3.2).

Using the Tank Firing Chart

The next several paragraphs will deal with the process of using the tables necessary to engage in armored combat. The player will first declare his target and measure the distance starting from the tip of the gun's barrel to the center of the target. As with the other charts in this book, the range is denoted in inches and the player will attempt to roll that number listed or less. Once the player has checked the range, he will review the modifier list to see what can be applied to his roll of a 12-sided die. For example, a Sherman M4 is firing at a Panzer IVh at a range of 32 inches. The panzer is moving on a ridge. Looking at Table 8.1, the player needs to roll a 5 or less. When checking the modifiers, he must add a +1 for firing at a moving target and +2 for the target being uphill. He rolls a lucky 2. Therefore, it is a hit.

Tank and Gun Firing Chart Table 8.1

0-6	6-12	12–18	18–24	24–-0	$\frac{30-}{36}$	$\frac{36-}{42}$	42–48	48–54	54–60
–10	–9	–8	–7	–6	–5	–4	–3	–2	–1

Die Roll Modifiers
–1 The firing unit has an asterisk next to its AF
–2 Firing from a hill to a unit on lower ground
+2 The target is on a hill
+2 Mobile fire
+2 Firing at a dug in target
+2 Target is in the woods
+2 Target is behind earthen cover
+1 For a shaken marker on the firing unit
+1 Firing at a moving target
+2 Target is partially obscured
+2 Darkness or predawn

Location of the Hit

The next obvious question is how a penetration is determined. But, first it must be decided where the round landed. Table 8.2 below requires a 6-sided die to be rolled. If the player rolls a 1, it results in an immobilization shot and the defending player will mark it accordingly for a morale check, should that be in play. If not, it is just marked as an immobilized unit for the rest of the game. In this game, there is no use of recovery vehicles because they were primarily used after the ravages of war had wrecked enough tanks to fill the day.

Location Table: Tanks and AFVs Table 8.2

Tank Shot	AFV, Open Top SP, or Vehicle
1 immobilized	1 immobilized/wheel
2–4 hull	2–4 hull/engine
5–6 turret/SP superstructure	5–6 passenger compartment

Before moving on, it is important to highlight the slightly unique treatment of open-topped self-propelled guns such as a German Hummel, or open-turreted tank hunters such as the American M10. When determining the location of the hit, all regular procedures are taken. However, should it be determined that the top of the SP was hit, the shooting player will roll for the location of the hit under the right hand column of the Location Chart (Table 8.2). If a 5 or a 6 is rolled, the crew compartment is considered hit and the SP is knocked out. Of course, this is not to be confused with shooting at others SPs, such as the Stug. III or SU100.

Continuing with the example of the Sherman M4 and Panzer IVh, assume a hull shot was rolled. The next matter to determine is the penetration of the Sherman's armor-piercing round on the panzer. Before jumping to the armor charts, three issues must be settled. Did the range have an increased or decreased effect on penetration? Did the angle of impact decrease the likelihood of penetration? Last, does the gun being used increase the chances of a kill?

The reader will notice that the ranges in Table 8.1 above are differentiated; 0 to 24, 24 to 42, and 42 to 60. The closer the tank is to its target the greater the chance of penetrating. Conversely, the farther the target the more difficult it is to punch. Of course there is a middle ground added to have no effect on the ability to punch. Therefore, when the player rolls his die, he either gets a −1, no change, or a +1 applied to the roll when rolling on the Tank Combat Chart (Table 8.3). This is merely added for game effect because the chart itself has a limited range and I decided that trying to splice the chart more would skew the chart beyond the scope of the game. Coming back to the tank-to-tank action in question, the range is 32 inches and results in no range modifier.

Following the range determination, the angle of impact must be assessed. The angle is determined by obtaining a protractor and drawing lines on these degrees: 110–70 degrees = 0; 111–140 (40–69) degrees = +1; and 141–180 (0–39) degrees = +2 (See Deflection Protractor, Figure 1) The modifiers listed next to the degrees will affect the round's ability to punch the armor. The firing player will place the protractor perpendicular to the tank's front, rear, or side, as shown in Figures 2 and 3. The stick shown is coming from the gun's barrel and not from the turret's center. If the shot is questionable as to the side or front, the attacking player will roll a 6-sided die to determine the placement of the round. A roll of a 1, 2, or 3 will result in a front shot. Also, when a stick or string is placed to the center of the target, it only matters where it enters the protractor to determine the modifier. Here the Sherman is looking at a side hull hit with a +2 (Figure 3) to the roll for a punch.

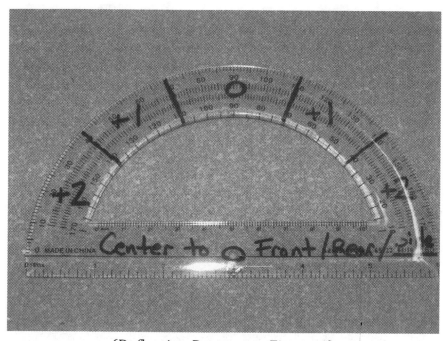

(Deflection Protractor, Figure. 1)

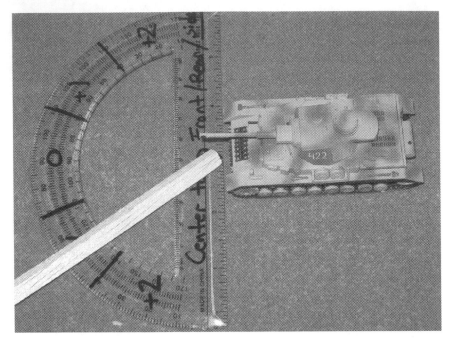

(Figure 2)

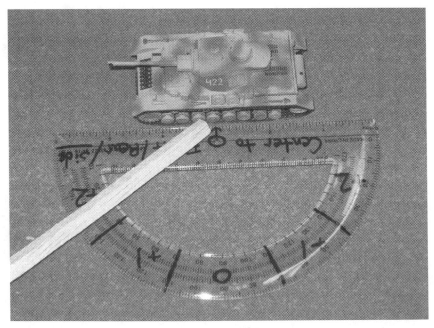

(Figure 3)

Tank Combat Chart Table 8.3

Armor in mm	Armor Class	2 .50 Cal	3 ATR	4 20mm AA	5 37mm AA	6 37mm	7 37mm ATG	8 40mm-47mm	9 50mm	10 50mm long to 57mm	11 75mm (a)	12 75mm (b)	13 76mm (a)	14 75/76mm long (b)	15 85mm-90mm	16 100mm	17 128mm or greater
250	AA	-	-	-	-	-	-	-	-	-	-	-	4	5	8	9	10
200	A	-	-	-	-	-	-	-	-	-	-	-	5	6	9	10	11
180	B	-	-	-	-	-	-	-	-	-	-	-	6	7	10	11	12
110	C	-	-	-	-	-	-	-	-	-	-	7	7	9	11	12	13
90	D	-	-	-	-	-	-	-	6	5	5	8	8	11	12	13	14
80	E	-	-	-	-	-	-	5	7	7	6	9	10	13	13	14	15
50	F	-	-	-	-	-	5	6	8	9	10	11	14	15	14	15	X
37	G	-	4	-	-	5	6	7	9	12	12	14	15	X	15	X	X
25	H	5	5	-	4	6	7	8	10	13	13	15	16	X	X	X	X
18	I	6	6	4	5	7	8	9	11	14	14	16	X	X	X	X	X
13	J	7	7	5	6	8	9	10	12	15	15	X	X	X	X	X	X
8	K	8	8	6	7	9	10	11	13	X	X	X	X	X	X	X	X

David W. Hall

Die Roll Modifiers:
−1 0–24 inches in range
+1 42–60 inches in range
+1 For AC*
−1 For AF*

Armor class modifiers:
All side shots decrease by one AC level.
Two AC levels for rear.
Three AC levels for top.

    Finally, the players will look into the Tank charts to check to see if the Sherman's AF has an asterisk next to the gun. If it did, it would indicate a −1 to the player's roll. The Sherman does not have an asterisk and its AF is a 12. The Panzer IVh has an AC of an E. By cross-referencing the 12 and E it is discovered that the player rolling for the Sherman needs a roll of a 9 or less on the roll of a 20-sided die. After a quick review of modifiers, there is nothing for range, +2 for the angle, and there was no asterisk next to the panzer's AC. Had there been one, there would have been a +1 added to the Sherman's roll. There is a change in Armor Class because this is a side shot, as shown above in the modifiers. It is reduced from an E to a F. Therefore, the player needs to roll an 11 or less with a +2 added for angle. The player rolls a 10 and it is declared a bounce. If the tank morale rules are in effect, mark the panzer accordingly.

Changes in Armor Classes

Another couple of points need to be made on the changes to Armor Classes. The tank charts are designed with the maximum armor listed as the AC for the front of the vehicle. Thus adjustments need to be made to the other sides of the AFV. Therefore, the side shot results in a reduction of one AC. Shots to the rear of an AFV result in a reduction of 2 and a shot on the top lowers it by 3. Top shots can occur with anti-tank fire from hills. When anti-tank fire scores a hit from a hill, a roll of a 1, 2, or 3 on a 6-sided die will make the hit a top shot. The angle of fire will automatically be a +2 to the roll on the Tank Combat Chart. Last, if the AC is reduced by more than the chart allows, the firing gun will get the missing number of Armor Classes as a minus modifier in penetration. For instance, an anti-tank rifle hits a Sdkfz. 222 in the rear. The AC for the armored car is a J. It should be reduced two levels, but the chart only drops one level. Therefore, the player rolling for penetration gets to take the missing level as a –1 to the die roll.

Armor Piercing and HE Rounds on Half-tracks, Trucks, and Other Troop Carriers

In the scope of the game, there are times when a round will hit a troop-carrying vehicle. Obviously, the hit location will have to be determined first for the Armor Piercing (AP) shell, which can immobilize the vehicle. In that case, there is no further effect on the crew or passengers. (Although HE rounds can destroy the carrier on any successful hit, the hit location is ignored. The player will refer to Tables 3.2 and 3.3.) If it has been determined that a troop carrier or truck takes a hit in the crew compartment by an AP round, the infantry will have to roll for the potential hits suffered from the round passing through the compartment. For AFs 8 to 13, hits are delivered on a 7 or less on a 10-sided die. If the AF is greater, the squad is wiped out and is removed from play. If the gun has an AF 7 or below, hits are delivered on a 4 or less on the 10-sided die. These rolls are done for each potential casualty. For example, a squad of (S)3 will roll three times. In this instance, the vehicle is considered not destroyed. However, jeeps or motorcycles that are hit are considered destroyed. Should it be determined that an AP round knocked out the vehicle, the passengers must be assessed for hits in the same way as if the round passed through the crew compartment.

Infantry Firing at Half-tracks, Universal Carrier or Truck with Passengers

The next chart may seem a little out of place. Nevertheless, it is included here because it logically falls after determining where an infantry unit fired at a half-track or other vehicle (see Table 8.2). Of course, the unit would first roll in the Infantry Firing table (Table 5.1) to check if it hit the vehicle. Once these two factors have been resolved, Table 8.4 below is used to check for damage. If an immobilized shot is rolled, the half-track will only have its movement reduced. The wheel column specifies a reduction in movement inches and does not require a further roll. The next column labeled Engine requires the roll of a 10-sided die to assess damage. For the MMG, it is assumed that the fire is capable of at least potentially immobilizing the AFV (a non-tank). For the passenger compartment, each type of unit inflicts one Strength Point hit. However, if an HMG blasts the passenger compartment, then the squad takes two hits. This is also used against a Bren Gun Carrier and for simplicity's sake it will be assumed that the wheel shot is actually having some effect on its mobility from bullets getting into gears or cutting its tracks. Also, for those troops hit in the passenger area, the troops get a saving throw of a 1 or 2 on a 6-sided die. This table can also be used for firing at a truck. If the truck is hit in the wheel or passenger compartment, the same rules apply. But the troops will get a −1 modifier to their saving throw. Finally, any hits to the engine will knock out the vehicle.

Infantry-Attacking Half-tracks and Trucks Table 8.4

Infantry Unit	Wheel	Engine	Passenger Compartment
Small Arms	−2 inches movement	No Effect	1 hit
LMG	−3 inches movement	No Effect	1 hit
MMG	−4 inches movement	3 or less immobilized	1 hit
HMG	−6 inches movement	5 or less immobilized	2 hits

Infantry Attacking an Armored Car

Continuing on the subject of infantry firing on AFVs, the next question is how do infantry units engage armored cars? Once the armored car has been hit by fire from an infantry unit, using the Infantry Firing table (Table 5.1), the player will roll a 10-sided die on the simple chart below to see if the AFV was immobilized. *Heavy machine guns will roll for their hit in the Infantry Firing Table, roll for location of the hit, and then proceed to the Tank Combat Chart to determine if the armored car is destroyed.* Should an infantry squad be within 2 inches of the armored car, the squad will get a −2 to its roll. It is assumed that the squad would be throwing hand grenades at this distance. The damaged is based on the player rolling the listed number or less.

Armored Car Immobilization Table 8.5

Small Arms	2 or less
LMG	3 or less
MMG	4 or less

Infantry Close-Assaulting a Tank or AFV

Occasionally during the game, infantry units my find themselves engaged in close assault situations with armored vehicles. Only infantry squads and special support elements can close-assault a tank. Regular support elements like a mortar team or LMG crew are prohibited from assaulting an AFV. They would not be equipped with satchel charges or other such devices unless they are "special purpose" teams. This tactic should really only be used in games that are for 1942 or after. It is assumed that after that time infantry units would be equipment with some sort of magnetic mine or other shape-charge device. This should be discussed prior to the game so that given the scenario both players understand the nature of the threat. For instance, playing a 1944 Eastern Front game with the Germans in defense against a tank assault, it would be logical for the German infantry to have magnetic anti-tank mines. However, a German armored assault against French infantry gamed with the invasion of France as the backdrop, may not have anything special to stop tanks.

The process to attack the vehicle is kept as simple as possible. To assault the tank, the squad must move to contact and have 2 inches of movement left to get away before blasting the tank. The only exceptions to this are Japanese squads. They did perform suicide attacks. If the Japanese squads are successful in either knocking out or immobilizing the tank or AFV, and remain within 2 inches, they are destroyed in the blast. For other nationalities, *the squad itself is not considered to be carrying out the actual attack*, rather a lone brave soul is. Also, this assault can take place in Opportunity Fire as well as the regular fire phase. In order to pull off the attack the team or squad must have at least 2 inches of escape left in its movement. If the tank or vehicle that is going to be the subject of the attack *is not* supported by infantry or other AFV machine guns, the attack is carried out on the chart below, Table 8.6. If the target *is supported* by one or more units capable of firing at the attacker, by means of line of sight, the attacker will have to roll to determine if it sends a man out to perform the assault. The roll is performed on a 6-sided die between the defender and the attacker. If the attacker rolls the high number, it sent its man out. The first unit capable of firing at the assault team triggers the roll. For each additional supporting unit the defender has, the player will get a +1 as a die roll modifier to his roll. If the player with the AFV wins, it is said that the assaulting unit was reluctant to carry out the mission. If a Japanese squad is assaulting, it gets a +1 for each Strength Point it has because it is assumed the entire squad is carrying out the attack. (Note to the Marines, support your tanks!!!)

The chart below will determine the success of the attack. The player will roll an 8-sided die and seek to roll that number or less. Without getting into rates of speeds for different vehicles and how infantry would deal with this, attacking them was left very basic. It is just a little harder to assault them.

Infantry vs. Tanks Table 8.6

	Destroyed	Immobilized
Moving AFV	3	4
Stationary	4	5

Other Conditions

This game is defined by 5 minutes per turn and the average game will last 12 turns. From this viewpoint, the game will potentially last "one hour" and some ventures will be of limited value to include, such as tank recovery. However, there are a few battlefield situations worth commenting on. But due to the 5 minute per turn rule, the "time" to do particular acts may be altered to achieve playability. The following section is dedicated to those other conditions such as: laying out a bridge, clearing a minefield, amphibious landings, and paratrooper assaults.

Bridging

It is one thing for engineers to lay out a bridge to cover a small ditch in a game using a Churchill Bridge Layer. It is something all-together different for a company of engineers to offload and construct a bridge with Bailey equipment. For simplicity, if a unit is going to lay out preassembled bridging equipment carried on one vehicle, it will take one turn to unload, one turn to lay it out, and one turn to get out of the way, for a total of 3 turns.

If players decide to design a scenario around combat engineers laying a pontoon bridge under fire or perhaps repairing a damaged civilian bridge, it will be important to consider the support elements along with replacements to pull it off. This guideline is recommended to handle the job: one squad, per turn, per inch to build or repair the bridge. For each squad lost, it will take an additional turn to complete the task. For example, there is a damaged bridge with 4 inches to be repaired so it is passable to tanks and AFVs. The defender is trying to prevent a river crossing. The attacker rushes his infantry across the bridge to secure the far side. He sends up his engineers to tackle the job. The column consists of 5 squads with 5 trucks. The task will take 4 turns and one replacement is in the ready. However, if he loses two squads, the job will take 5 turns to complete. It is important to note that the turn "clock" starts when the first squad dismounts and is at the bridge. The second squad must arrive immediately following the first in order to keep it going or there will be a 1-turn penalty. If the squads suffer casualties and maintain their morale, there is no reduction in time to repair the bridge. But if a squad is driven back, that will slow the work down. Thus, it is absolutely important to supply more units than the job requires to keep it going.

Minefields

If a minefield is to be employed, there are three issues that need to be resolved: how to cross it, its placement, and casualties. Crossing the field is a rather simple affair, in terms of the game. Remember, it is important to keep the game moving. Regular infantry squads can clear a path 2 inches by 2 inches per turn. Engineers can clear a path 3 inches by 3 inches. Units taking fire and taking hits do not slow down but are subject to regular morale rules. The placement of minefields fall into two categories: the visible and the nonvisible. The former may be laid out as part of a preinvasion beach defense. It may be marked for channeling the enemy into prepared crossfire zones or simply to keep friendly troops from wandering off for a nice stroll on the beach. The length and width of these fields should be given careful thought as to the size, scope, and scenario to be attempted. Individual minefields should not exceed 4 by 8 inches. The nonvisible are a bit trickier. The defender will have to sketch out a map of the battlefield and label exactly where the fields are located. Once an enemy unit enters the field the player will mark his map, while his opponent continues to move. After the player has finished his moving, the player with the minefield announces explosions in his Opportunity Fire. He will tell the player which units are subject to the minefield and he will mark the fields in question. The owning player will roll a 6-sided die to determine the fate of the units on Table 9.1, one roll per unit. When infantry units attempt to enter a known minefield, they are not assessed for hits. As it is a known obstacle, their penalty is the slow progress of movement through the minefield. Further, once a minefield is revealed, it reverts to a known minefield and the same rules apply.

Minefield Casualties to Infantry Table 9.1

Roll	Effect
1 or 2	Miss
3 or 4	1 hit
5	2 hits
6	3 hits

There are certain vehicles that are capable of slugging their way through the danger zone. These tanks used either specialized flails or heavy rollers attached to the front of the tank to explode the mines as the tank pushed through it. The primary tanks for this activity were the Sherman M4, Churchill, and Matilda II. When tanks enter the minefield, they can *only move 3 inches* regardless of movement modifiers and they clear a path 3 inches long by 2½ inches. If a vehicle wanders into an unknown minefield, the announcement of the minefield will be at the time of Opportunity Fire and the player will reveal the minefield. The player with the tank in the minefield will roll an 8-sided die to assess the damage. The following chart, Table 9.2, and modifiers will be used to check damage. All minefields in this game are assumed to be mixed with anti-tank mines.

Minefield Damage to Vehicles Table 9.2

Roll	Effect
1 or 2	No Effect
3, 4, 5	Immobilized
6, 7, 8	Knocked out

Modifiers:
−1 for Light or Medium Tanks
−2 for Heavy tanks

Amphibious Landings

For the purposes of this game, there are two classes of landing craft. There are those with landing ramps to the front and those with landing ramps to the rear. The former refers to the Higgins boat and the LCM (Landing Craft Mechanized). The Higgins boat can hold 2 squads and 2 support elements. The LCM can hold one tank or other AFV and 2 squads. If it is landing with no AFV or tank, it can hold 5 squads and 3 supports. For those rear ramp vehicles, there are the LVTs (Landing Vehicle Tracked). These can handle 2 squads or 1 squad and 2 support elements. When the crafts unload, there is no movement penalty for the infantry coming out. The penalty is associated with the craft. It will lose 3 inches of movement for the release of the ramp. (Landing craft movement is in the Tank Charts.)

Airborne Troops

In certain scenarios, airborne forces may be called upon to take a particular objective. Should they be used as regular ground infantry, no potential problems exist. What is of most concern here is how to set them up and get the game underway should the battle incorporate their actual landing. For each platoon or section landing on the field, the player will select his landing sites and the direction of the landing. Once the spots are marked, an 8-sided die is rolled to determine each "flight's" dispersion between squads. For instance, a 5 is rolled. Then each squad will be set out 5 inches apart in the direction of the flight path. The first squad will overshoot the mark by 5 inches. If some troops are forced off the board, it will take 2 turns for them to reenter from the spot they were forced off. Should that point be overrun by the enemy, the troops are cut off and removed from play.

Glider troops may also be called upon for action and they will follow a similar procedure. The player using gliders will have marked the proposed spots for each glider in the direction they are to land. In this case a 10-sided die is used to determine the number of inches from the marker. If the glider should overshoot the target and land off the board, the same 2-turn rule applies. The typical German glider for this game will hold 1 squad and the typical allied glider will hold 1 squad and 1 support element. Players who want to dig deeper into the exact glider load capacity are encouraged to do a little research on the subject. It is always important to keep the size, scope, and mission of the game in perspective, especially when developing a glider-based attack, particularly when most glider and airborne operations landed some distance from the target. Of course the German assaults on Eben Emael and Crete are the exceptions to that statement.

Further, all jumps and glider assaults are not without initial injuries, as Generaloberst Kurt Student could attest. To simulate this fact, the airborne player will roll a 10-sided die for each company landing or gliding into action. The number rolled will be the number of hits the company takes. The player will distribute the hits to his units as he sees fit to include any units that have "flown" off the board. These hits are exempt from any morale checks, but not a sergeant's casualty.

If the defender wants to have forces on the board, not all of them will be activated. Only 1 in 4 units can be in prepared positions. The remainder must be in a "bivouac" area, at least 1 move away. There is some assumption that the airborne assault comes as a surprise. To complicate matters more for the defender, he will roll a 6-sided die to determine the number of turns it takes to alert his forces to action. The alternative is to still roll the number of turns it takes before the defender rushes into the area but this is with all or most of the forces entering in via defined routes.

It is important to remember that most initial airborne assaults occurred in the early hours of the morning. If the attack occurs at dawn or earlier, the maximum shooting range will be 18 inches with a –2 for all firing. It will have to be declared at the start of the game at what turn the sun is fully up and these modifiers go away.

There is no doubt that *Blood and Guts* encompasses a broad scope of ideas and rules. The objective here has been to achieve a balanced game between all the competing units and weapon systems. I am sure there are some unique situations that I have not addressed. If players come across such an occurrence, I encourage them to create some simple method to resolve the issue. It is also worth reminding wargamers that should a dispute arise in the interpretation of a rule or a historical fact, they should let the roll of a 6-sided die decide the matter. It is my sincere hope that wargamers enjoy this system of rules and find it a useful and playable game. I have provided in the next chapter a summary of these rules to spare the reader from having to extract out the vast amount of detail to play the game.

CHAPTER 4

Summary of Rules

This next chapter is a rule summary of the details presented in the previous chapter. It is important that both chapters are read together to get a sense of cohesion. The objective is to present the summary in such a way that the players can use it as the basis for playing the game with the rules chapter to provide the needed explanation. At the end of the summary, there are the Tank Charts, which contain the needed information for battling tanks.

It is important that prior to playing the game the players have the appropriate equipment. These rules refer to various different dice being tossed about. The players will need to have a 6-, 8-, 10-, 12-, and a 20-sided die. This may seem a bit over the top. Nevertheless, using them for specific purposes helps change up the percentages in scoring the desired result. Also, a protractor will have to be obtained to account for the angles of impact of armor-piercing shells. In addition, some sort of color-coded beads or chits will be needed to mark units for morale and observation. Finally, a tape measure or long ruler will need to be obtained for measuring ranges. With these items in hand, a game can be played following the summary below.

Combat Order

1. Roll to see who moves first. (Player A) a. Morale checks b. General Movement c. Player B gets Opportunity Fire

2. Opponent moves second. (Player B) a. Morale checks b. General Movement c. Player A gets Opportunity Fire

3. Roll to see who fires first. (Player A) a. Aircraft b. Artillery/Mortars c. General Firing

4. Opponent fires second. (Player B) a. Aircraft b. Artillery/Mortars c. General Firing

Morale Checks

Basic Morale (M) number + the die roll on a 6-sided die.

Infantry Morale Check-Any unit that took a hit or was fired on. Table 1.1

Effects	Total Morale Points
No effect	6 or more points
Shaken and cannot move	4 to 5 points
Forced back 3 inches	2 to 3 points
Retreat 8 inches	1 or less points

Die Roll Modifiers
−1 for each hit in that turn
−1 for a sergeant's casualty hit
Any squad within 5 inches of its platoon commander gets a +1 to its roll.
Platoon and Company Commanders give themselves a +1 to their roll.

Sergeant's casualty

Once a hit is achieved, the owning player must roll for that unit. A 1 or 2 on a 12-sided die means the squad's NCO was killed. If this occurs, then the unit's morale level is reduced by 1 level.

<u>Any unit within 4 inches of a retreating unit takes a morale check</u>
−2 for any retreating unit that pass by
−1 for any unit that is forced back

<u>Overruns by tanks that approach within 5 inches of a unit</u>
5 or more the unit passes and moves up to 4 inches
4 or less the unit freezes

<u>Special note reminders:</u>
1. Shaken markers = yellow bead; must stay on until the next morale phase. The yellow marker indicates the troops are shaken and that affects their firing ability.
2. Mortar units that receive a shaken marker cannot fire while they have the marker. Also, crew-served weapons, such as medium machine guns cannot fire if they have had to retreat or were forced back.

<u>Optional Tank Morale</u>

Tank and AFV Morale Table 1.2

Effects	Total Morale Points
No effect	5 or more points
Stopped, shaken and cannot advance toward the enemy*	3 to 4 points
Back up one full move to the rear*	2 points
Back up two moves*	1 to 0 points
Retreat from board*	−1 or less

*Place a yellow marker until the next movement phase.
<u>Die Roll Modifier</u>
–1 for each tank destroyed in the platoon every time it is forced to take a morale check.

If immobilized by a hit: Table 1.3

Effects	Total Morale Points
No effect	5 or more points
Stopped and shaken	3 to 4 points
Crew bails out	2 points
Crew bails out and flees the field	1 or less points

Movement

AFV and Tank Movement Modifiers

–3 inches off road
–3 inches snow or mud
–2 inches per 45 degree turn
–5 inches for fording
–3 inches for designated rough ground to include lightly wooded areas
–2 inches for going uphill at each contour and/or light obstacles
½ movement lost for loading or unloading troops; limbering or unlimbering a gun; vehicles going in reverse

Infantry Movement

For purposes of Infantry Movement, the infantry are divided into two categories: those that carry crew served weapons and those that do not. Therefore, normal infantry move up to 8 inches and those manning crew served weapons move 6 inches. Crew-served weapons can move and fire in the same turn.

Infantry Movement Modifiers

–2 inches for wooded terrain, no movement penalty for light wood
–2 inches for snow or mud
–4 inches for rough terrain and streams
–3 inches for walls and obstacles
–2 inches for uphill at each contour
–4 inches for infantry loading (and unloading) into a vehicle or mounting/dismounting a tank

Firing: Aircraft, Artillery/Mortars, General Firing

Aircraft Strafing

Declare the target and endure anti-aircraft fire first.
In the first row, roll the number or less for a hit on a 20-sided die. Since not all hits equal a destroyed plane, roll for a kill on the second row using a 10-sided die, that number or less.

Anti-aircraft Fire Table 2.1

Small Arms	Machine Gun	Single	Double	Quad
2	3	3	4	5
2	3	4	6	8

If the aircraft is successful in getting through the fire, the player will roll for deviation.

Pilot deviation, roll on an 8-sided die. Table 2.2

1,2	3,4,5,6	7,8
3 inches to the left	On target	3 inches to the right

10-sided die to determine hit, that number or less Table 2.3

Rockets	ATGs
–3 per rocket	–4 per ATG, (Stuka)
AF 11	AF 7

Modifiers:
+1 for moving target

Aircraft Dropping Bombs

Dropping Bomb Chart: Roll an 8-sided die to determine results Table 2.4

1	Overshot the target by 12 inches
2	Undershot the target by 12 inches
3	Left of target; perpendicular to the plane's approach: 8 inches
4	Right of target; perpendicular to the plane's approach: 8 inches
5	Overshot the target by 6 inches
6	Undershot the target by 6 inches
7–8	Hit

Die Roll Modifiers
+1 for dive bombers
−1 for moving targets

Artillery and Mortar Plotting: Declare target and use a 10-sided die Table 3.1

1	Overshot the target by 12 inches
2	Undershot the target by 12 inches
3	Left of target; perpendicular to the unit's position: 8 inches
4	Right of target; perpendicular to the unit's position: 8 inches
5	Overshot the target by 6 inches
6	Undershot the target by 6 inches
7	Left of target; perpendicular to the unit's position: 3 inches
8	Right of target; perpendicular to the unit's position: 3 inches
9–10	Hit

For each successive turn firing at a stationary target the player gets a + 1 to his die roll.

Indirect and Direct HE Fire Blast Results Table 3.2

Gun	Burst Diameters	Hit Value	Saving Throws
Mortar 45/50mm**$$ 2.8cm, 37mm, 47mm, Grenade Launcher	¾ inch	(1 hit)	1 saving throw
Mortar 60mm, 75mm infantry gun, 57mm, 50mm	1 inch	(2 hits)	2 saving throws
Mortar 80mm or 75mm Howitzer, 76 mm	1¼ inches	(2 hits)	2 saving throws
85mm to 90mm	1½ inches	(3 hits)	2 saving throws
Mortar 120mm or 105 mm Howitzer	2 inches	(3 hits)	2 saving throws
120mm Howitzer	2½ inches	(3 hits)	2 saving throws
155mm Howitzer /250lbs. bomb	3 inches	(3 hits)	1 saving throws
500 lbs	4 inches	(3 hits)	no saving throws

Saving throw rolls are conducted on a 6-sided die with a 1 or 2 saving.

Die Roll Modifiers
−2 hard cover or bunker
−1 soft cover
−1 troops in a building

–1 Troops in an armored half-track, open top Self-Propelled Gun,
Universal Carrier
** Range 30 inches
$$ Japanese knee mortar and rifle grenade launcher; range 18
inches

For tank HE, pick the most logical equivalent from above.

HE Direct

Roll 12-sided die: Roll the number indicated or less to destroy the target. Table 3.3

	ATG and Howitzers	Tankette or Armored car, Half-Track	Light Tank	Med. Tank/ Or Earthen Bunker	Heavy Tank/ or Concrete Bunker
Mortar 45/50mm**$$ 2.8cm, 37mm, 47mm, Grenade Launcher	7	4	5	NA	NA
Mortar 60mm, 75mm infantry gun, 57mm, 50mm	8	5	6	3	NA
Mortar 80mm or 75mm Howitzer, 76 mm	X	7	8	5	2
85mm to 90mm	X	X	9	6	4
120mm Howitzer	X	X	10	7	5
Mortar 120mm or 105 mm Howitzer	X	X	11	8	6
155mm Howitzer /250lbs. bomb	X	X	X	X	8
500 lbs	X	X	X	X	X

Near Miss Chart Table 3.4

Within Kill Zone	45/50mm Mortar Grenade Launcher	60mm mortar	80mm mortar	120mm mortar	75mm	88mm to105mm	120mm	155mm	250lbs bomb	500lbs bomb
Soft Skin	Xx	X	X	X	X	X	X	X	X	X
ATG/Gun	-	-	-	X	X	X	X	X	X	X
Half-Track	-	IM	Xx*	X	Xx*	X	X	X	X	X
Tan-kette	-	-	IM	Xx	IM	Xx	X	X	X	X
Light Tank	-	-	-	IM	-	IM	Xx	X	X	X

Within Kill Zone	45/50mm Mortar Grenade Launcher	60mm mortar	80mm mortar	120mm mortar	75mm	88mm to105mm	120mm	155mm	250lbs bomb	500lbs bomb
Med. Tank Earthen Bunker	-	-	-	-	-	-	IM	IM	Xx	X
Heavy Tank Con-crete Bunker	-	-	-	-	-	-	-	IM	IM	X

(-)—no effect
M—Immobilized
X—Destroyed
Xx—Destroyed but crew is still alive
Xx*—roll for the effects of the passengers, the vehicle is immobilized, can be applied to universal carrier.

General Firing

Before beginning general firing, it is important for the players to determine what units can be seen. For explanations, the players should refer to "Notes on Terrain" in the previous chapter.

Observing Units

Sighting an enemy in a wood line or in a firing position in a building
Observing unit is a:_____? Table 4.1

Unit in woods/ building is a:	Recon	Infantry	Tank
Tank?	15	10	7
AFV or Artillery?	12	7	5
Infantry or ATG?	10	5	3

Sighting an enemy camouflaged or dug in
Observing unit is a: _____? Table 4.2

Unit dug in is a:	Recon	Infantry	Tank
Tank?	20	15	10
AFV or Artillery?	15	10	7
Infantry or ATG?	12	7	5

Units in the open can be observed moving. If the unit is stationary, but has not fired see the chart below. If the unit has fired, it is considered observed and thus can be fired upon.

Observing unit is a:_____? Table 4.3

Unit in open, but has not fired is a:	Recon	Infantry	Tank
Tank?	60	42	36
AFV or Artillery?	42	36	24
Infantry or ATG?	36	18	12

Infantry Firing

Infantry Firing 10-Sided (the number or less) Table 5.1

Weapon Type	Assault 0-6	Close 6 + to 12	Medium 12 + to 18	Long 18 + to 24	Extreme 24 + to 30	Machine Gun Extreme 30 + to 40
HMG	8	7	6	5	4	3
MMG	7	6	5	4	3	2
LMG	7	6	5	4	3	—
Small Arms	7	6	5	3	2	—

Die Roll Modifiers
+1 behind tank
+2 behind brick, sand bags, rubble/troops in a building
+1 behind brush
+2 behind hedgerow
+1 target on hill
−2 target fired on from hill to lower ground
+2 target dug-in

+2 target behind earthen cover
−2 target fired on by sniper
+1 target is a sniper
+1 for soft cover
+1 firer is shaken
+1 infantry unit moved
+2 darkness or predawn

Modifiers for Combat in Wood and Jungle with Visibility Factors

Light wood/ shrub bush	+1 if outside 6 inches	always observed
Medium wood and Light Jungle	+2 if outside 5 inches	Blocks beyond 10 inches
Heavy wood and Medium Jungle	+3 if outside 4 inches	Blocks beyond 8 inches
Heavy Jungle	+4 if outside 3 inches	Blocks beyond 6 inches

Flame Throwers

Flame Thrower vs. Tanks and AFVs Table 6.1

Tank/AFV	.5–1.0 inch	1.1–2.0 inches	2.1–3.0 inches
X	1or 2	1	—
X+1	3	2	1
X+2	4	3	2
N	5-10	4-10	3-10

Roll a 10-sided die: zero counts as 10.

X destroyed

X+1 destroyed in 1 turn

X+2 destroyed in 2 turns

N No Effect

<u>Die Roll Modifiers</u>

If the tank is moving it is a +1

If the target is an AFV or open top tank it is a –1

If the target is a soft skin it is a –2

Flame Thrower vs. Structure: Use a10-sided die Table 6.2

Bunker/ Structure	.5–1 inches	1.1–2 inches	2.1–3 inches
X	1–3	1–2	1
X+1	4–6	3–4	2–3
X+2	6–7	5–6	4–5
N	8–10	7–10	6–10

<u>Die Roll Modifiers</u>

–2 for earthen bunkers

–3 housing structures

If the structure is destroyed, the infantry unit takes one hit. If it is not, but it is damaged (X+1 or X+2), the player will proceed to the chart below to determine if the unit took a hit.

Flame Thrower vs. Infantry: Use a 10-sided die Table 6.3

Infantry	.5–1 inches	1.1–2 inches	2.1–3 inches
In Structure	6	5	4
Dug In	7	6	5
In woods	8	7	6
In the open	9	8	7

Bazooka/ATR

Bazooka/ATR Table 7.1

3–6	6.1–9	9.1–12	12.1–14	14.1–18
8	7	6	5	4

10-sided die, roll that number or less
(See firing modifiers under Table 5.1)

Anti-Tank Rifle: AF (3), range 18 inches
PIAT: AF (10), range 10 inches
U.S. Bazooka: AF (10), range 14 inches
Panzershreck 88mm: AF (13), range 10 inches
Panzerfaust: AF (14), range 6 inches

Tank Firing

Tank and Gun Firing Chart Table 8.1

0–6	6–12	12–18	18–24	24–30	30–36	36–42	42–48	48–54	54–60
–10	–9	–8	–7	–6	–5	–4	–3	–2	–1

Die Roll Modifiers
−1 The firing unit has an asterisk next to its AF
−2 Firing from a hill to a unit on lower ground
+2 The target is on a hill
+2 Mobile fire
+2 Firing at a dug in target
+2 Target is in the woods
+2 Target is behind earthen cover
+1 For a shaken marker on the firing unit
+1 Firing at a moving target
+2 Target is partially obscured
+2 Darkness or predawn

Special Notes: Single-man turrets can fire on the move, but on an every-other-turn basis. Also, all tank machine guns get an automatic (R) of 2. Next, when tanks or AFVs shoot HE at infantry, the burst radius and impact results for the millimeter used are listed in the Indirect and Direct HE Chart (Table 3.2).

Location Table:
Tanks and AFVs: Roll a 6-sided die Table 8.2

Tank Shot	AFV, Open Top SP, or Vehicle
1 immobilized	1 immobilized/wheel
2–4 hull	2–4 hull/engine*
5–6 turret/superstructure	5–6 passenger compartment*

*(If a troop carrier takes a hit in the passenger area by an AP round or the vehicle is determined to have been destroyed, the infantry will have to roll for the potential hits suffered for the round passing through the compartment. For AFs 8 to 13, hits are delivered on a 7 or less on a 10-sided die. If greater, the squad is killed. If the gun has an AF 7 or below, hits are delivered on a 4 or less on the 10-sided die. These rolls are done for each potential casualty. For example, a squad of (S)3 will roll three times.)

Tank Combat Chart: 20-sided die Table 8.3

Armor in mm	Armor Class	2 .50 Cal	3 ATR	4 20mm AA	5 37mm AA	6 37mm	7 37mm ATG	8 40mm–47mm	9 50mm	10 50mm long to 57mm	11 75mm (a)	12 75mm (b)	13 76mm (a)	14 75/76mm long (b)	15 85mm–90mm	16 100mm	17 128mm or greater
250	AA	-	-	-	-	-	-	-	-	-	-	-	4	5	8	9	10
200	A	-	-	-	-	-	-	-	-	-	-	-	5	6	9	10	11
180	B	-	-	-	-	-	-	-	-	-	-	-	6	7	10	11	12
110	C	-	-	-	-	-	-	-	-	-	-	7	7	9	11	12	13
90	D	-	-	-	-	-	-	5	6	5	5	8	8	11	12	13	14
80	E	-	-	-	-	-	5	6	7	7	6	9	10	13	13	14	15
50	F	-	-	-	-	-	5	6	8	9	10	11	14	15	14	15	X
37	G	-	4	-	-	5	6	7	9	12	12	14	15	X	15	X	X
25	H	5	5	-	4	6	7	8	10	13	13	15	16	X	X	X	X
18	I	6	6	4	5	7	8	9	11	14	14	16	X	X	X	X	X
13	J	7	7	5	6	8	9	10	12	15	15	X	X	X	X	X	X
8	K	8	8	6	7	9	10	11	13	X	X	X	X	X	X	X	X

Die Roll Modifiers:
-1 0–24 inches in range
+1 42–60 inches in range
+1 For AC*
-1 For AF*

Any missing AC levels will be a -1 or -2.

    Shots from an: extreme angle (141–180 or 0–39 degrees) +2
slight angle (111–140 or 40–69 degrees) +1
    (see Deflection Protractor)

Armor Class Modifiers:
All side shots decrease by one AC level.
Two AC levels for rear.
Three AC levels for top.

Infantry Attacking Half-tracks and Other AFVs Table 8.4

Infantry Unit	Wheel	Engine (10-sided die)	Passenger Compart-ment
Small Arms	-2 inches move-ment	No Effect	1 hit*
LMG	-3 inches move-ment	No Effect	1 hit*
MMG	-4 inches move-ment	3 or less im-mobilized	1 hit*
HMG	-6 inches move-ment	5 or less im-mobilized	2 hits*

    *Saving throw of a 1 or 2 on a 6-sided die; -1 for troops in a truck.

Infantry Attacking an Armored Car

Assuming a hit on the Infantry Firing chart (Table 5.1), the player will roll a 10-sided die on the simple chart below to see if the AFV was immobilized.

Armored Car Immobilization Table 8.5

Small Arms	2 or less
LMG	3 or less
MMG	4 or less

–2 for an infantry squad within two inches of the AFV.

Infantry Close-Assaulting a Tank or AFV

To assault the tank, the squad must move to contact and have 2 inches of movement left to get away before blasting the tank. The player will roll an 8-sided die and seek to roll that number or less. If the target is supported by one or more units capable of firing at the attacker, by means of line of sight, the attacker will have to roll to determine if it sends a man out to perform the assault. The roll is performed on a 6-sided die. If the attacker rolls the high number, it sent its man out. The first unit capable of firing at the assault team triggers the roll. However, for each additional supporting unit the defender has, the player will get a +1 to his roll, as a die-roll modifier. If the defender wins, it is said that the assaulting unit was reluctant to carry out the mission. If a Japanese squad is assaulting, it gets a +1 for each Strength Point it has because it is assumed the entire squad is carrying out the attack.

Infantry vs. Tanks Table 8.6

	Destroyed	Immobilized
Moving AFV	3	4
Stationary	4	5

Roll an 8-sided die for damage.

Tank Charts

The charts below contain the needed tank, gun, and AFV information for several tables in the game. The Class refers to the vehicle's classification as: light, medium, or heavy. These are used in Tables 3.3 and 3.4. It is used for the HE impacts against AFVs. The (AF) is the Assault Factor, (AC) is for Armor Class, and (MT) is for Movement. The Crew is used for crew bailouts and MPH is there for relative movement comparison between vehicles. In the AF column, there are instances of numbers followed by HE; this indicates the size of the gun and that it is used for high explosive shells only. Next, there are a few cases of AF classes with multiple numbers, such as the German 251. This simply means that the vehicle had different gun possibilities or was equipped with more than one gun, such as the American M3 Lee. Naturally, the chart is not all-inclusive. Players may want to add other AFVs in and can certainly do so. However, players should be careful to make the added vehicle relative to other ones in the chart. Last, anti-tank guns have facing and can shoot within a 45-degree angle of it. But it may become necessary to move them and if their MT denotes "Towed," this requires a vehicle to do the job. Nevertheless, the crew can change facing without a vehicle.

German Tank Chart

	Class	AF	AC	MT	Crew	MPH
Pz I	L	0	H	17	3	35
Pz 35T	L	6	G	11	4	21
Pz 38T	L	6	G	13	4	26
Pz II	L	3	H*	13	3	25
Luchs	L	3	H*	17	3	37
Pz IIIc	M	6	G	13	5	25
Pz IIIj	M	9	G*	13	5	25
Pz IIIn	M	12	F	13	5	25
Pz IVc	M	8	F	12	5	23
Pz IVh	M	14	E	12	5	23
Panther D	H	14	C	14	5	28
Panther G	H	14*	C*	14	5	28
Tiger I	H	15	C	12	5	23
Tiger II	H	15*	B*	13	5	26
Pz-jag I	L	9	H	13	3	25
Marder II	L	13	H*	13	3	25
MarderIII	L	14	H	13	4	26
Wespe	L	105HE	H	13	5	25
Grille	L	105HE	G	11	5	22
Nashorn	M	15*	G	13	4	26
Hummel	M	150HE	G	13	5	26
Stug D	M	8	F	13	4	25
Stug G	M	14	E	13	4	25

Pz-jag IV	M	14	E*	13	4	25
Hetzer	L	13	G*	13	4	26
Brummbar	M	150HE	C	14	5	28
JagPanther	H	15*	C*	14	5	28
Elefant	H	15	A	9	6	18
JagTiger	H	17	AA	12	6	23
232	-	3	H	17	4	43
222/3	-	3	J	25	3	50+
6 Rad	-	0	I	25	3	50+
Puma	-	14	H	25	3	50+
234/4	-	14	I	25	3	50+
250	-	0/7	J	17	6	37
251	-	0/7/14/75HE	J	17	10	37
88mm	-	15		Towed		0
75pak	-	14		Towed	1	0
50pak	-	10		Towed	2	0
37pak38	-	6		2	6	
37pak41	-	7		2	6	
2.8cm	-	7		4	4	

American Tank Chart

		AF	AC	MT	Crew	MPH
M3 Light	L	7	G*	17	4	37
M8	L	75HE	F	17	4	37
M24	L	13	H*	16	5	34
M3Lee	M	7/11	G	13	6	26
M4	M	12	F	12	5	24
M4A3E8	M	14	F*	14	5	29
M4A3E8	M	105HE	F*	14	5	29
M26	H	15	C	14	5	29
M10	M	14	G*	15	5	32
M36	M	15	F	14	5	29
M18	L	14	I	22	5	49
M12GMC	M	155HE	H	9	6	19
M7GMC	M	105HE	F	12	7	24
LVT	L	2	H*	12/(4 water)	4	24
M3 Scout	-	2	J	25	4	50+
M8/20 AC	-	2/7	J	25	3	50+
M3 HT	-	105HE/2	J*	17	4	37
M3 HT 75mm	-	11	J*	17	4	37
155mm	-	155HE	-	Towed	7	0
Tractor	-	2	J	22	4	48
37mm	-	8		4	4	0
57mm	-	10		2	6	
All Landing Craft	-	-	-	6		

British Tank Chart

		AF	AC	MT	Crew	MPH
MK VI Light	L	2/3	I	16	3	35
Cruiser MK IIa (A10)	L	8	G	8	5	16
Cruiser MK IV (A13)	L	8	I*	14	4	29
M3 Stuart	L	7	G*	17	4	37
Matilda	H	8	E	6	4	14
Valentine	H	8	F*	6	3	14
Crusader II/III	M	8/10	G/F	17/15	5	31/26
Grant	M	7/11	G	13	6	26
Cromwell	M	12	E	15	5	31
Churchill I/II	M	8/75HE	C	6	5	14
Churchill III	H	10	C	6	5	14
Churchill VII	H	12	B	5	4	12
Firefly	M	14*	E	14	5	29
Comet	H	14	C	14	5	29
Bishop	M	90HE	F	6	4	14
Archer	M	14*	F	6	4	14
Universal Carrier	-	0	J	14	3	29
Humber	-	3	H	25	3	50+

Daimler	-	8	H	25	3	50+
40mm	-	8		4	4	0
57mm	-	10		2	4	0
76mm	-	14*		Towed	4	0
Kangaroo	M	2	F	12	20	25

Soviet Tank Chart

		AF	AC	MT	Crew	MPH
T-26b/c	L	8	H	9	3	20
BT-7	L	9	I*	24	2	28
BA 6/10	-	8	K/J	25	4	50+
T-35	L	76HE/6	H	9	11	18
T-34/76	M	13	F*	16	4	34
T-34/85	M	15	D*	16	5	34
KV-1	H	13	C	10	5	22
IS-1	H	15	C	12	4	23
IS-2	H	17	C*	12	4	23
SU-76	L	14	H*	15	4	28
SU-85	M	14*	F*	15	4	29
SU-100	M	16*	F*	15	4	29
ISU-122	H	17/122HE	D*	8	6	16
ISU-152	H	152HE	D*	8	6	16
KV-2	H	152HE	C	8	6	16
57mm	-	10		2	4	0
76mm	-	14*		Towed	4	0
45mm	-	8		4		

French Tank Chart

		AF	AC	MT	Crew	MPH
FT-17	L	0/5	H	3	2	5
R-35	L	5	F	7	2	12
H-38	L	5	F	10	2	22
Somua-s35	M	8	F*	13	3	25
Char B1-BIS	M	8 / 75 HE	E	7	4	17
37mm	-	6	K	4	4	0

Italian Tank Chart

		AF	AC	MT	Crew	MPH
CV33	-	0	J	13	2	26
M11/39	L	6	H	10	3	20
M13/40	M	8	F	11	3	22
M40	M	11	H	10	3	21
SPA AB 41	L	3	I	17	3	37

Japanese Tank Chart

		AF	AC	MT	Crew	MPH
Type 95	L	6	J*	12	4	23
Ho-Ni	L	75HE	H	12	4	23
Type 97 Chi Ha	L	8/9	H	12	4	23
75mm	-	HE		Towed	4	0

CHAPTER 5

Basic Table of Organization and Equipment

The following section is made up of basic Tables of Organization and Equipment (TO&Es) for both mechanized and infantry formations from various nations. It is not intended to provide every change for every formation of every year of the war. Rather, its intent is to provide a framework for assembling reasonably accurate tank and troop units for wargaming. Also, where the word Standard is used, it denotes that the formation described underwent certain changes. These changes can be small and not worth noting, as they would have little effect on forming a wargame unit, such as a British infantry company. In some case, the units went through many changes as the war progressed. Thus, there are too many variations to note and it would be impractical for a wargamer to try and have each type of company formed up in a wargame army. An example of this is the many changes the panzer companies went through.

For those readers wanting to use the rules provided in this book, these TO&Es need to be assigned appropriate tactical values for their infantry units. As a rule of thumb, 1 Strength Point should be added for every 2 to 4 men in the squad, section, or team. When assigning Rates of Fire, belt-feed machine guns should get an (R) of 2, while clip machine guns like the Bren should get an (R) of 1. The typical infantry squad should get an

(R) of 2 or 3 depending on the type of weapons it contains. If the HQ component of a platoon or section has only 2 personnel, it should be given an (R) of 0 or 1. However, other support teams can be given a 1 or 2 depending on the types of weapons they contain. The reader is advised to refer back to the *Blood and Guts* chapter (Chapter 3) under infantry to get a better perspective on Rates of Fire. For those HQ command stands that have 1 or 2 men in them, they should still get an (S) of 1. These units act more or less as plain command stands with the regular morale effects on those units around them. The (M) is naturally up to the player and the scenario being played. The only thing to remember is not to stack the deck too heavily in favor of one side with too strong of a morale value.

The following formations are examples of how platoons from different nations might be configured for their respective (M), (S), and (R) values. Again, these are to be used as a guide. It is ultimately up to the player to determine the strength of his troops.

Polish Infantry Platoon:
    Each Squad: (M)1 (S)3 (R)2
    HQ Section:
        Command Stand: (M)2 (S)1 (R)1
        ATR Stand: (M)1 (S)1 (R)1

British Infantry Platoon:
    Each Squad: (M)2 (S)3 (R)2
    HQ Section:
        Command Stand: (M)2 (S)1 (R)1
        ATR Stand: (M)2 (S)1 (R)1
        2-inch Mortar Team Stand: (M)2 (S)1 (R)2

German Infantry Platoon:
    Each Squad: (M)2 (S)3 (R)3*
    HQ Section:
        Command Stand: (M)2 (S)1 (R)1
        ATR Stand: (M)2 (S)1 (R)1
        50mm Mortar Team Stand**: (M)2 (S)1 (R)2

* 1 point for the rifles and 2 points for the MG34
** This assumes the mortars were attached to each infantry platoon.

American Infantry Platoon:
     Each Squad: (M)2 (S)3 (R)3*
     HQ Section:
          Command Stand: (M)2 (S)2 (R)2
* 1 point is given to the BAR and 2 points for the M1 Grand rifles.

Soviet Infantry Platoon 1941:
     Each Squad: (M)1 (S)4 (R)2
     HQ Section:
          Command Stand: (M)2 (S)1 (R)0
          50mm Mortar Team Stand: (M)1 (S)1 (R)2

Polish Forces 1939:

Tank Company:
     3 Platoons of 3 to 5 AFVs
     Company CO section: 1 AFV

Regular Infantry Company:
     3 Platoons, 1 Mortar Platoon and a CO Section
          Platoon = 3 squads and HQ Section
          Squad = 1 LMG with 2 crew, 1 NCO, 8 Riflemen
          Platoon HQ = 1 CO, 2 NCOs, 1 anti-tank rifle with 2 crew
     Mortar Platoon = (3) 46mm mortars, 1 NCO, 9 crew, 6 Riflemen
     CO HQ Section = 2 Officers, 3 NCOs, 6 Riflemen

Battalion Machine Gun Platoon:
     3 Sections with 1 HQ section
          Section: 1 Medium Machine Gun, 1 NCO, 7 troops
          HQ Section: 1 Officer, 2 NCOs, 3 Riflemen

Battalion Mortar Platoon:
>> 2 Sections with 1 HQ section
>>> Section: (1) 81mm Mortar, 1 NCO, 7 troops
>>> HQ Section: 1 Officer, 1 NCO, 2 Riflemen

Regimental Anti-Tank Platoon:
>> 3 Sections with 1 HQ section
>>> Section: (1) Anti-tank gun, 1 NCO, 6 troops
>>> HQ Section: 1 Officer, 1 NCO

Regimental Gun Platoon:
>> 2 Sections with 1 HQ section
>>> Section: (1) 75mm gun, 1 NCO, 5 troops
>>> HQ Section: 1 Officer, 1 NCO

French Forces 1940:

Standard Tank Company:
>> 4 Platoons of 3 AFVs and 3 Motorcycles
>> 1 Company CO section: 1 AFV and 3 Motorcycles

FT-17 Company:
>> 3 Platoons of 5 tanks and 5 Motorcycles
>> 1 Company CO section: 1 AFV and 2 Motorcycles

Char B Tank Company:
>> 4 Platoons of 3 Char Bs and 3 Motorcycles
>> 1 Company CO section: 1 Char B and 2 Motorcycles

Regular Infantry Company:
>> 4 Platoons and a HQ Platoon
>>> Platoon = 3 squads and HQ Section
>>>> Squad = 1 LMG with 2 crew, 1 NCO, 8 Riflemen, 1 Grenade Launcher: for (12 men)
>>>> Platoon HQ = 1 CO, 1 NCO, 3 Riflemen
>>> Company HQ Platoon:
>>>> HQ Section: 1 CO, 4 NCOs, 10 Riflemen

Mortar Section: (1) 60mm Mortar, 4 Crew and 1 NCO
Support Section: 1 Truck, 12 Riflemen (5 bicycles)

Battalion Machine Gun Platoon:

2 Sections with 1 HQ Section
Section: 2 Medium Machine Guns, 1 NCO, 14 troops
(Should be broken into two teams)
HQ Section: 1 Officer, 1 NCO, 2 Riflemen

Battalion Mortar Platoon:

2 Sections with 1 HQ Section
Section: (2) 81mm Mortars, 1 NCO, 20 troops
HQ Section: 1 Officer, 1 NCO, 4 Riflemen

Regimental Anti-Tank Platoon: 25mm to 47mm

3 Sections with 1 HQ Section
Section: (1) Anti-tank gun, 1 NCO, 5 troops
HQ Section: 1 Officer, 1 NCO, 4 Riflemen

Motorized Infantry Company:

Platoon = 3 squads and HQ Section
Squad = 1 Truck, 1 LMG with 2 crew, 1 NCO, 6 Riflemen, 1
Grenade Launcher: for (11 men)
Platoon HQ Section = 1 Truck, 1 CO, 1 NCOs, 3 Riflemen
Weapons Platoon:
2 Light Machine Sections
Section: 1 Truck, 1 LMG with 2 crew, 1 NCO, 6 Riflemen,
1 Grenade Launcher: for (11 men)
Mortar Section: 1 Truck, (1) 60mm Mortar, 4 Crew, 1 NCO
HQ Section: 1 Truck, 1 NCOs, 3 Riflemen
HQ Platoon:
Support Section: 2 Trucks, 1 NCO, 11 troops (5 bicycles)

> HQ Command Section: 2 Motorcycles, 1, CO, 1 NCO, 2 troops

Motorized Battalion Weapons Platoon:
> Mortar Section: 2 Trucks, (2) 81mm Mortars, 1 NCO, 21 troops
> Anti-Tank Section: 2 Trucks, (2) 25mm Anti-tanks guns, 3 NCO, 14 troops
> (Should be broken into two teams)
> HQ Section: 1 Officer, 2 NCOs

British Forces:

Infantry Tank Squadron (Company) 1940–1945:
> 5 Troops of 3 Infantry Tanks
> 1 Company CO section: 1 Infantry Tank and 1 Close Support Tank

Cruiser Tank Squadron 1940–1945:
> 4 Troops of 3 Cruiser Tanks
> 1 Company CO section: 2 Cruiser Tanks, 2 Close Support Cruiser Tanks

Light Tank Squadron 1939–1941:
> 5 Troops of 3 Light Tanks (Mk VI)
> 1 Company CO section: 3 Light Tanks

Stuart Tank Squadron 1942:
> 4 Troops of 4 M3s
> 1 Company CO section: 4 M3s

M3 Grant Tank Squadron 1942:
> 3 Troops of 3 M3 Grants
> 1 Company CO section: 3 M3 Grants

M4 Sherman Tank Squadron 1942:
> 4 Troops of 3 M3 Grants
> 1 Company CO section: 4 M3 Grants

Armored Reconnaissance Squadron 1943–1945:
> 3 Troops of 3 M3/M5s
> 1 Company CO section: 2 M3/M5s

Armored Car Squadron 1940–1941:
> 3 Troops of 5 Morris ACs
> 1 Company CO section: 3 Daimlers

Standard Rifle Company 1939–1945*:
> 3 Platoons and a HQ Platoon
>> Platoon = 3 squads with 1 HQ section
>> Squad = 1 LMG with 2 crew, 1 NCO, 7 Riflemen
>> Platoon HQ = 1 CO, 1 NCOs, 1 Riflemen, 1 Anti-tank rifle or PIAT,
>>> (1) 2-inch mortar, 4 crew (7 men)
> HQ Section: 2 Officers, 3 NCOs, 8 Riflemen

This formation can also be used for an Airborne Company, except the ATR. The PIAT was used from 1943 onward.

Battalion Machine Gun Platoon 1939–1945:
>> 2 Sections with 1 HQ section
>>> Section: 2 Medium Machine Guns, 1 NCO, 10 troops
>>>> (Should be broken into two teams)
>>> HQ Section: 2 Officers, 2 NCOs, 2 Riflemen

Battalion Mortar Platoon 1939–1945:
>> 3 Sections and HQ Section
>>> Section: (2) 3 inch mortars, 2 trucks,1 NCO, 10 troops
>>> HQ Section: 1 Scout Car, 1 Officer, 1 NCO, 1 Rifleman

Anti-Tank Troop 1939–1945: 2pdr., 6 pdr., or 17 pdr.
>> 2 Sections with 1 HQ section
>>> Section: (2) trucks, (2) Anti-tank Guns, 1 NCO, 14 troops
>>>> (Should be broken into two teams)
>>> HQ Section: (1) truck, 1 Officer, 1 NCO, 2 Riflemen
>>>> *(Universal Carriers can be used in place of trucks.)*

Infantry Carrier Platoon 1939–1942:
>> 3 squads of 3 carriers with 1 HQ Section
>>> Squad = 3 Universal Carriers, 2 LMG with 4 crew, 1 anti-tank rifle with 2 crew,
>>>> 1 NCO, 2 Riflemen : for (9 men)
>>> Platoon HQ = 1 Universal Carriers, 1 LMG with 1 crew, 1 CO, 1 NCOs

Infantry Carrier Platoon 1943–1945:
>> 3 squads of 3 carriers with 1 HQ Section
>>> Squad = 4 Universal Carriers, 4 LMG with 8 crew, 2 PIAT with 4 crew, 1 NCO,
>>>> 1 Rifleman: for (14 men)

Platoon HQ = 1 Universal Carrier, 1 LMG with 1 crew, 1 CO, 1 NCOs

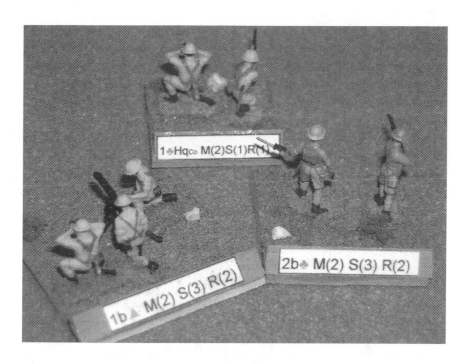

Motorized Rifle Company 1939–1943:
Summary:
      3 Motorized Platoons with HQ Section
      1 Carrier Platoon with HQ Section
      1 CO HQ Section
      Starting in 1942 a Weapons Platoon was added

      1 Motorized Platoon: 3 Squads with HQ Section
            Squad = 1 Truck, 1 LMG with 2 crew, 1 NCO, 8 Riflemen (11 men)
            HQ Section = 1 Truck, 1 CO, 2 NCOs, 1 Riflemen, 1 Anti-tank rifle or
                  PIAT 1943, (1) 2 inch mortar, 4 crew (8 men)

1 Carrier Platoon: 3 squads of 3 carriers with 1 HQ Command

> Squad = 3 Universal Carriers, 3 LMG with 6 crew, 1 anti-tank rifle with 2 crew or *PIAT 1943*, (1) 2 inch mortar, 1 NCO: for (9 men)

Platoon HQ = 1 Scout Car, 1 Universal Carrier, 1 LMG with 2 crew, 1 CO,

> 1 NCOs, 1 Rifleman.

Weapons Platoon 1942–1943,
> *2 Medium Machine Gun Sections*
>> *MMG Section: 1 Truck (2) .303 Vickers, 1 NCO, 10 Troops*
>>> *(Should be broken into two teams)*
> *3-Inch Mortar Section*
>> *(2) 3-inch mortars, 1 Truck, 1 NCO, 10 Troops*
>> *HQ Section*
>> *1 Officer, 2 NCO, 1 Rifleman*

Company CO Section
> 2 Trucks, 2 Officers, 3 NCOs, 8 Riflemen

Motorized Rifle Company 1944-1945:
Summary:
> 3 Motorized Platoons with HQ Section
> 1 Carrier Platoon with HQ Section
> 1 CO HQ Section

> 1 Motorized Platoon: 3 Squads with HQ Section
>> Squad = 1 Half-track, 1 LMG with 2 crew, 1 NCO, 8 Riflemen (11 men)
>> HQ Section = 1 Half-track, 1 CO, 2 NCOs, LMG with 2 crew, 1 PIAT with 2 crew,
>>> (1) 2 inch mortar, 2 crew (9 men)

> 1 Carrier Platoon: 4 squads of 3 carriers and 1 HQ Command
>> Squad = 3 Universal Carriers, 3 LMG with 6 crew, 1 PIAT with 2 crew,
> 1 NCO: for (9 men)

Platoon HQ = 1 Scout Car, 1 Universal Carrier, 1 LMG with 2 crew,
(1) 2-inch mortar with 2 crew, 1 CO, 1 NCOs, 1 Rifleman.

Company CO Section
(2) Half-tracks, 2 Scout Cars, (2) 3 inch mortars with 10 crew,
2 LMGs 4 with crew, 2 Officers, 3 NCOs: (19 men).

For the Commonwealth armies of Australia, New Zealand, and Canada, use the above formations. Their armies were modeled after the United Kingdom.

American Forces:

Standard Tank Company 1942–1945:
3 Platoons of 5 Tanks
1 Company CO section: 2 Tanks

U.S. Marine Tank Light Company 1942–1943:
3 Platoons of (5) M3 Light Tanks
1 Company CO section: (3) M3 Light Tanks

U.S. Marine Tank Company 1944–1945:
3 Platoons of (4) M4 Shermans or M5 Light Tanks
1 Company CO section: (3) M4 Shermans or M5 Light Tanks

M3 75mm Half-track Platoon 1942–1943*:
3 Squads and 1 HQ Section
Squad = 1 Half-track, 5 crew
HQ Section = M2 Half-track, 1 Officer, 1 NCO, 6 crew
*For U.S. Marines reduce the formation by 1 squad

HMC Gun Platoon 1944–1945:
3 Squads and 1 HQ Section

Squad = (1) 105mm Sherman or M8
HQ Section = M3 Half-track, 1 Officer, 1 NCO, 5 crew

Tank Destroyer Platoon 1943–1945:
2 Sections and 1 HQ Section
Section = (2) M10 or M36 or M18 tanks
HQ Section = 1 Jeep, 1 Officer, 1 NCO, 2 Riflemen

Half-track Mortar Platoon 1942–1945:
3 Squads and 1 HQ Section
Squad = 1 Half-track with mortar, 6 crew
HQ Section = M2 Half-track, 1 Officer, 1 NCO, 5 crew

Armored Rifle Company 1943–1945:
3 Platoons with HQ Sections, 1 Anti-Tank Gun Platoon, CO HQ Section
1 Platoon =
2 Half-tracks with 2 NCOs and 22 troops
1 Half-track with 60mm mortar and 1 NCO and 7 crew
1 Half-track with 2 MMG 1 NCO and 11 Troops
HQ = 1 Half-track, 1 Officer, 1 NCO, 10 Troops
Anti-Tank Platoon = 3 Squads + HQ Section
Squad = 1 Half-track, (1) 57mm* 1 NCO, 9 crew
HQ Section = 1 Jeep, 1 Officer, 1 NCO, 1 Rifleman
CO HQ Section = 1 Half-track, 1 Jeep, 1 Officer, 2 NCOs, 6 Troops
*For 1942 replace the 57mm for a 37mm.

Standard Rifle Company 1942–1945:
3 Platoons, 1 Weapons Platoon, and CO HQ Section
1 Platoon = 3 squads with HQ Section
Squad = 1 NCO, 1 BAR, 10 Riflemen
HQ Section = 1 Officer, 2 NCOs, 2 Riflemen

Weapons Platoon

> Mortar Section = (3) 60mm Mortars, 1 NCO, 16 Crew
>
> Medium Machine Section = 2 MMG, 1 NCO, 11 Crew*
>
>> (Should be broken into two teams)
>
> HQ Section = 1 Jeep, (1) .50cal HMG, 1 Officer, 1 NCO, 4 Riflemen
>
> CO HQ Section = 2 Officers, 4 NCOs, 17 Riflemen

Within the CO HQ, the company would have 5 to 6 Bazookas.
*Medium Machine Gun Platoon is two sections and is a battalion level unit. It would also have a small HQ Section of 1 Officer, 1 NCO, 4 Riflemen

Anti-Tank Platoon 1942–1943:

> 4 Squads and 1 HQ Section
>
> Squad = 1 Jeep, (1) 37mm, 1 NCO, 9 crew
>
> HQ Section = 1 Jeep, 1 Officer, 1 NCO, 1 Rifleman

Anti-Tank Platoon 1944–1945:

> 3 Squads and 1 HQ Section
>
> Squad = 1 Truck, (1) 57mm, 1 NCO, 9 crew
>
> HQ Section = 1 Jeep, 1 Officer, 1 NCO, 1 Rifleman

Mortar Platoon 1942–1945:

> 3 Sections and 1 HQ Section
>
> Squad = 1 Truck, (2) 81mm Mortars, 3 NCOs, 10 crew
>
> HQ Section = 1 Jeep, 1 Officer, 1 NCO, 4 Riflemen

U.S. Paratrooper Company 1942–1943:

> 2 Platoons with CO HQ section
>
> 1 Platoon: 2 Rifle Squads, (1) 60mm Mortar Squad + HQ Section
>
>> Squad = (1) .30cal, 1 NCO, 3 Crew, 8 Riflemen
>>
>> Mortar Squad = (1) 60mm Mortar, 1 NCO, 5 Crew

HQ Section: 1 Officer, 2 NCOs, 3 Riflemen
CO HQ: 2 Officers, 2 NCOs, 17 Riflemen
Within the CO HQ, the company would have 5 to 6 Bazookas.

U.S. Paratrooper Company 1944–1945:
  3 Platoons with CO HQ section
  1 Platoon: 2 Rifle Squads, (1) 60mm Mortar Squad + HQ
  Section
      Squad = (1) .30cal, 1 NCO, 3 Crew, 8 Riflemen
      Mortar Squad = (1) 60mm Mortar, 1 NCO, 5 Crew
  HQ Section: 1 Officer, 2 NCOs, 3 Riflemen
    CO HQ: 2 Officers, 2 NCOs, 17 Riflemen
Within the CO HQ, the company would have 5 to 6 Bazookas.

Marine Rifle Company 1942–1943:
  3 Platoons, 1 Weapons Platoon, and CO HQ Section
    1 Platoon = 3 squads, 1 BAR Squad, with HQ
    Section
        Squad = 1 NCO, 1 BAR, 8 Riflemen
        BAR Squad = 2 BARs, 1 NCO, 5 Crew
          (Should be broken into two teams)
        HQ Section = 1 Officer, 2 NCO, 4 Riflemen
    Weapons Platoon
        Mortar Section = (2) 60mm Mortars, 1
        NCO, 10 Crew
        Medium Machine Section = 2 MMG, 2 NCO,
        10 Crew
          (Should be broken into two teams)
        HQ Section = 1 Officer, 1 NCO, 2 Riflemen
    CO HQ Section = 1 Jeep, 2 Officers, 4 NCO, 9
    Riflemen
Within the CO HQ, the company would have 5 to 6 Bazookas.

Marine Rifle Company 1944–1945:
  3 Platoons, 1 Medium Machine Gun Platoon, 1 Mortar
  Platoon and CO HQ Section
    1 Platoon = 3 squads with HQ Section

> Squad = 4 NCO, 3 men armed with BARs, 6 Riflemen
>
> HQ Section = 1 Officer, 3 NCOs, 3 Riflemen

MMG Platoon = 3 Squads

> MMG Squad = (1) .30cal, 2 NCOs, 5 Crew
>
> HQ Section = 1 Officer, 2 NCOs, 6 Riflemen

Mortar Platoon

> (3) 60mm Mortars, 1 Officer, 4 NCOs, 6 crew
>
> CO HQ Section = 1 Jeep, 2 Officers, 4 NCOs, 10 Riflemen

Within the CO HQ, the company would have 5 to 6 Bazookas.

Soviet Forces:

<u>Standard Tank Company 1941</u>: BT5s, BT7s, and T26s

> 4 Platoons and 1 HQ Section
>
> 1 Platoon = 3 Tanks
>
> HQ Section = 2 Tanks

Standard Tank Company 1942–1945:
    3 Platoons and 1 HQ Section
    1 Platoon = 3 Tanks
    HQ Section = 1 Tank

Tank Destroyer Platoon 1943–1945:
5 Tanks: SU76 to the SU152. *The unit would be a homogeneous platoon.*

Early War Rifle Company up to 1942*:
    3 Platoons, 1 Medium Machine Gun Platoon, and CO HQ Section
        1 Platoon = 4 squads, (1) 50mm Mortar Squad, with HQ Section
            Squad = 1 LMG with 2 crew, 1 NCO, 9 Riflemen
            Mortar Squad = (1) 50mm, 1 NCO, 2 Crew
            HQ Section = 1 Officer
        Medium Machine Gun Platoon of 2 sections
            Medium Machine Section = 1 MMG, 1 NCO, 5 Crew
            HQ Section = 1 Officer, 1 NCO, 1 Riflemen
        CO HQ Section = 3 Officers, 3 NCOs, 2 Riflemen
In late 1942 an additional 50mm mortar section of 2 mortars and 7 men including an officer was added to the formation.

Rifle Company 1943–1945:
    3 Platoons, 1 Medium Machine Gun Platoon, and CO HQ Section
        1 Platoon = 4 squads with HQ Section
            Squad = 1 LMG with 2 crew, 1 NCO, 6 Riflemen
            HQ Section = 1 Officer, 1 Rifleman
        Medium Machine Gun Platoon of 3 sections
            Medium Machine Section = 1 MMG, 1 NCO, 5 Crew
            HQ Section = 1 Officer, 1 NCO
        CO HQ Section = 3 Officers, 3 NCOs, 2 Riflemen

<u>Submachine gun Company 1941–1945</u>: *All men were armed with Submachine guns*

> 3 Platoons and 1 CO HQ Section
>> 1 Platoon = 3 squads with HQ Section
>>> Squad = 1 NCO, 7 Troops*
>>> HQ Section = 1 Officer**
>> CO HQ Section = 3 Officers, 3 NCOs, 2 Troops

Recommend: R(3), S(2); **R(1)*; Firing range for the troops of this formation is 8 inches.

<u>Battalion Mortar Platoon 1939–1945</u>:

> 3 Sections and 1 HQ Section
>> Section: (1) 81mm Mortar, 1 NCO, 8 Crew
>> HQ Section: 1 Officer, 1 NCO

Battalion Anti-Tank Rifle Platoon 1939–1942:
    4 Squads and 1 HQ Section
    Squad: 2 Anti-tank rifles, 1 NCO, 7 Crew
        (Should be broken into two teams)
    HQ Section: 1 Officer, 1 NCO

Regimental Anti-Tank Platoon 1939–1945:
    2 Sections and 1 HQ Section
        Section: (1) Anti-tank gun*, 1 NCO, 7 Crew
        HQ Section: 1 Officer, 1 NCO
*Depending on the year, the guns could be 45mm, 57mm, 76.2mm or 85mm.

Italian Forces:

Standard Tank Company 1940–1943:
    3 Platoons and 1 HQ Section
        1 Platoon = 5 Tanks
        HQ Section = 1 Tank

Standard Light Tank* Company 1940–1943:
    3 Platoons and 1 HQ Section
        1 Platoon = 4 Tanks
        HQ Section = 1 Tank
This would include tankettes.

Armored Car Company 1940–1943:
    3 Platoons and 1 HQ Section
        1 Platoon = 4 Armored Cars
        HQ Section = 2 Armored Cars

Self Propelled Gun Battery (*Semovante*)1941–1943:
    3 Sections with 1 HQ Section
        Section: 2 Self Propelled Guns, i.e. 75/18 da M41
        HQ Section: Command Vehicle

Motorized Bersaglieri Rifle Company 1941–1943:
    1 Rifle Platoon, 1 Medium Machine Gun Platoon, and CO
    HQ Section
        1 Platoon = 2 squads, 1 anti-tank rifle squad, HQ
        Section,
            Squad = 2 LMG with 4 crew, 3 NCOs, 8
            Riflemen
            ATR Squad: 2 ATR's with crew, 3 NCOs, 8
            Riflemen
            HQ Section = 1 Officer, 1 Rifleman
        Medium Machine Gun Platoon of 3 sections
            Medium Machine Section = 1 MMG with 2
            crew, 2 NCOs,
            6 Riflemen
            HQ Section = 1 Officer, 1 NCO
        CO HQ Section = 1 Motorcycle with side car, 3
        Motorcycles, 2 Officers,
            1 NCO, 8 Riflemen

Bersaglieri Mortar Platoon 1941–1943:
> 3 Sections and 1 HQ Section
>> Section: (1) 81mm Mortar, 1 NCO, 7 Crew
>> HQ Section: 1 Officer, 3 Riflemen

Bersaglieri Anti-Tank Gun Platoon 1941–1943: 37mm or 47mm, or any infantry gun
> 4 Section and 1 HQ Section
>> Section: 1 Truck, 1 Anti-tank Gun, 1 NCO, 10 Crew
>> HQ Section: 1 Officer, 1 NCO

Bersaglieri Medium Machine Gun Platoon 1941–1943:
> 3 Sections and 1 HQ Section
>> Section: 1 MMG, 2 NCOs, 9 Crew
>> HQ Section: 1 Officer, 1 Riflemen

<u>Standard Infantry Company 1940–1943:</u>
 3 Platoons and 1 CO HQ Section
   1 Platoon = 2 squads, 2 LMG squads, HQ Section,
    Squad = 1 NCO, 10 Riflemen
    LMG Squad: 1 LMG with 2 crew, 1 NCO, 7
    Riflemen
    HQ Section = 1 Officer, 1 NCO, 4 Rifleman
   CO HQ Section = 1 Officers, 2 NCO, 12 Riflemen

<u>Medium Machine Gun Platoon 1940–1943:</u>
 2 Sections and 1 HQ Section
   Section: 2 MMG, 1 NCO, 10 Crew
    (Should be broken into two teams)
   HQ Section: 1 Officer, 1 Riflemen

<u>Regimental Mortar Platoon 1940–1943:</u>
 2 Sections and 1 HQ Section
   Section: (1) 81mm Mortar, 1 NCO, 8 Crew
   HQ Section: 1 Officer, 1 Riflemen

Japanese Forces:

<u>Standard Tank Company 1939–1945:</u>
 4 Platoons and 1 HQ Section
   1 Platoon = 4 Tanks
   HQ Section = 2 Tanks + 1 Light Tank

<u>Standard Rifle Company 1939–1945</u>: *For a Type A Company, add a MMG section of two guns and an anti-tank rifle section of two guns and 21 men and 1 NCO, to the Company formation.*
 3 Rifle Platoons and 1 CO HQ Section
   1 Platoon = 3 Squads, (1) 50mm Mortar Squad,
   HQ Section,
    Squad = 1 LMG with 2 crew, 1 NCO, 9
    Riflemen
    50mm Mortar Squad: (3) 50mm 'knee
    mortars' with 6 crew, 1 NCO,

6 Riflemen
HQ Section = 1 Officer, 1 NCO
CO HQ Section = 2 Officers, 3 NCOs, 14 Riflemen

Type 92 Machine Gun Platoon 1939–1945:
    2 Sections and 1 HQ Section
        Section: 2 MMG, 2 NCOs, 20 Crew
            (Should be broken into two teams)
        HQ Section: 1 Officer, 1 Riflemen

Battalion Mortar Platoon 1939–1945:
    2 Sections and 1 HQ Section
        Section: (2) 81mm Mortars, 1 NCO, 14 Crew
        HQ Section: 1 Officer, 1 NCO, 7 Riflemen

Battalion Anti-Tank Platoon 1939–1945: 37mm or 47mm
    2 Sections and 1 HQ Section
        Section: 1 Gun, 1 NCO, 7 Crew
        HQ Section: 1 Officer, 1 NCO, 7 Riflemen

Battalion Gun Platoon 1939–1945: Type 92 70mm
    2 Sections and 1 HQ Section
        Section: 2 Guns, 2 NCOs, 14 Crew
        (Should be broken into two teams)
        HQ Section: 1 Officer, 1 NCO

Within the image: `2☀ₐHq M(2)S(1)R(0)` and `2☀ₐ M(2)S(3)R(2)`

German Forces:

Standard Panzer Company 1939–1941:

    2 Light Tank Platoons, 2 Medium Tank Platoons, HQ Section

        Light Tank Platoon: 4 Panzer Is or IIs

        Medium Tank Platoon: 4 Panzer IIIs

        HQ Section: 2 Panzer IIIs

Heavy Panzer Company 1939–1941:

    1 Light Tank Platoons, 3 Heavy Tank Platoons, HQ Section

        Light Tank Platoon: 4 Panzer Is or IIs

        Heavy Tank Platoon: 4 Panzer IVs

        HQ Section: 2 Panzer IVs

Standard Panzer Company 1942–1943:
> 1 Light Tank Platoon, 3 Medium Tank Platoons, HQ Section
>> Light Tank Platoon: 4 Panzer IIs or Panzer IIIs
>> Medium Tank Platoon: 4 Panzer IIIs or Panzer IV's
>> HQ Section: 2 Panzer IIIs or Panzer IVs

Heavy Panzer Company 1942–1943:
> 4 Heavy Tank Platoons with HQ Section
>> Heavy Tank Platoon: 4 Panzer IVs
>> HQ Section: 1 Panzer IV

Standard Panzer Company 1944–1945:
> 3 Medium Tank Platoons, HQ Section
>> Medium Tank Platoon: 4 Panzer IVs or Panthers
>> HQ Section: 2 Panzer IVs or Panthers

Heavy Panzer Company 1944–1945:
> 1 Medium Tank Platoons, 2 Heavy Tank Platoons with HQ Section
>> Medium Tank Platoon: 4 Panzer IVs or Panthers
>> Heavy Tank Platoon: 4 Tiger Is or Tiger IIs
>> HQ Section: 2 Panthers, Tigers Is or Tiger IIs

Standard Assault Gun Company 1943–1945*:
> 3 StuG Platoons with 1 HQ Section
>> StuG Platoon: 3 StuG IIIs or StuG IVs
>> HQ Section: 2 StuG IIIs or StuG IVs

Same formation can be used for Jag-Panzer Tanks

Standard Rifle Company 1939–1942:
> 3 Rifle Platoons, 1 Weapons Platoon and 1 CO HQ Section
>> 1 Platoon = 3 Squads, HQ Section,
>> Squad = 1 LMG with 2 crew, 1 NCO, 6 Riflemen
>> HQ Section = 1 Kampfwagan, 1 Officer, 1 NCO, 1 LMG with 2

Crew, 1 ATR* with 2 Crew, 1 Riflemen
Weapons Platoon = MMG Section, 50mm Mortar
Section, HQ Section
MMG Section = 3 MMG, 12 Crew, 4 NCO
50mm Mortar Section** = (3) 50mm
Mortars, 1 NCO, 10 Crew
HQ Section = 1, Officer, 1 NCO, 2 Riflemen
CO HQ Section = 1 Kubelwagen, 1 Officer, 3 NCOs,
9 Riflemen

*By late 1941 the ATR was obsolete and can be left out of the TO&E.

** The mortars were typically detached one to each infantry platoon.

Standard Rifle Company 1943–1945:
3 Rifle Platoons, 1 MMG Section and 1 CO HQ Section
1 Platoon = 3 Squads, HQ Section*,
Squad = 1 LMG with 2 crew, 1 NCO, 6
Riflemen

HQ Section = 1 Kubelwagen, 1 Officer, 1 NCO, 1 LMG with 2 Crew, 1 Riflemen
MMG Section = 2 MMG, 12 Crew, 3 NCOs
(Should be broken into two teams)
CO HQ Section = 1 Kubelwagen, 1 Officer, 3 NCOs, 9 Riflemen

The infantry company by late 1943 was getting issued the Panzerfaust and these were more than likely issued to the Platoon HQ to be disseminated to the squads as needed. The amounts would vary depending on supply. However, for wargaming purposes, no more than 6 should be represented in the Company.

Battalion Mortar Platoon 1939–1945:
>   3 Sections and 1 HQ Section
>> Section: (2) 81mm Mortars, 3 NCOs, 12 Crew
>> HQ Section: 1 NCO, 2 Riflemen

Battalion Machine Gun Platoon 1939–1945:
>   3 Sections and 1 HQ Section
>> Section: 2 MMG, 3 NCOs, 12 Crew
>>> (Should be broken into two teams)
>> HQ Section: 1 Office, 1 NCO, 1 Riflemen

Standard Anti-Tank Platoon 1939–1945: 37mm to 88mm
>   2 Sections and 1 HQ Section
>> Section: 2 Trucks, 2 Guns, 2 NCOs, 14 Crew
>>> (Should be broken into two teams)
>> HQ Section: 1 Kubelwagen, 1 Officer, 1 NCO, 2 LMG with 4 Crew

Standard Howitzer Platoon 1939–1945*:
>   4 Sections and 1 HQ Section
>>   Section:1 Truck, (1) 75mm Gun, 1 NCO, 5 Crew
>>   HQ Section: 1 Kubelwagen, 1 Officer, 1 NCO, 1 LMG
>>   with 2 crew, 1 Rifleman

For late war, use two sections.

Standard Heavy Howitzer Platoon 1939–1945*:
>   2 Sections and 1 HQ Section
>>   Section: 2 Truck, (1) 150mm Gun, 1 NCO, 13
>>   Crew
>>   HQ Section: 1 Truck, 1 Officer, 3 NCO, 1 LMG with
>>   2 crew, 6 Rifleman

Panzer Grenadier Co. 1941–1942:
>   3 Platoons, 1 Weapons Platoon, 1 CO HQ Section
>>   Platoon: (3) 251/1s Squads + HQ Section
>>   251/1 Squad = 2 LMG with 4 crew, 1 NCO, 7
>>   Rifleman

HQ Section: (1) 251/10 with 37mm ATG, 1 Officer, 1 NCO, 5 Crew

Weapons Platoon:

(2)   251/1s, 2 LMG, 4 MMG, 2 NCO, 20 Crew

(2)   251/2s with 80mm Mortars, 2 NCO, 14 Crew

(1)   251/1, LMG with 2 crew, 1 Officer, 1 NCO, 1 Rifleman

CO HQ Section:

(1)   251/3 Radio Model with LMG and 2 Crew, 1 NCO, Officer, 1 Rifleman

(1)   251/1 with LMG and 2 Crew, 1 NCO, 1 Rifleman

Panzer Grenadier Co. 1943–1945:

3 Platoons, 1 Weapons Platoon, 1 CO HQ Section

Platoon: (3) 251/1s Squads + HQ Section

251/1 Squad = 2 LMG with 4 crew, 1 NCO, 5 Rifleman

HQ Section: (1) 251/10 with 37mm ATG, 1 Officer, 1 NCO, 4 Crew

Weapons Platoon:

(2)   251/9s with 7.5cm KwK 37 L/24, 2 NCO, 10 Crew

(2)   251/2s with 80mm Mortars, 2 NCO, 14 Crew

(3)   251/1s, 2 Motorcycles, 6 LMG, 1 Officer, 3 NCO, 12 Rifleman

CO HQ Section:

(1)   251/3 Radio Model with LMG and 2 Crew, 1 NCO, Officer, 1 Rifleman

(1)   251/1 with LMG and 2 Crew, 1 NCO, 1 Rifleman

(1)   251/1 with LMG and 2 Crew, 1 NCO, 4 Panzerfaust,

11 Crew

Standard Paratrooper Rifle Company1940–1945:
>3 Platoons with 1 HQ Section, 1 CO HQ Platoon
>>Platoon = 1 LMG with 2 Crew, 1 NCO, 7 Riflemen
>>HQ Section = 1Officer, 1 NCO, 5 Riflemen
>CO HQ Platoon
>>(3) 81mm Mortars, 3 NCOs, 15 Crew
>>3 Motorcycles with sidecars, 1 Officer, 1 NCO, 4 Riflemen

Battalion Machine Gun Platoon 1940–1945:
>2 Sections and 1 HQ Section
>>Section: 2 MMG, 3 NCOs, 12 Crew
>>>(Should be broken into two teams)
>>HQ Section: 1 Office, 1 NCO, 1 Riflemen

Airlanding Anti-Tank Platoon 1941:
>3 Sections and 1 HQ Section
>>Section: (1) 37mm, 2 Motorcycle with sidecar, 1 NCO, 5 Crew
>>HQ Section: 3 Motorcycle, 1 Motorcycle with sidecar, 1 Office, 2 NCO, 6 Riflemen

CHAPTER 6

Blood and Guts in Action

The following scenario is an example game between British and German forces set somewhere in North Africa, in late 1941. This is a fictitious scenario designed to illustrate the use of the rules in this book. The example is meant to be simple and easy to follow. Below each description of the German and British perspectives is a list of each side's forces. The game covers most of the fundamental aspects found in the rules and it should give the reader a good working grasp of how to use *Blood and Guts.*

In this battle, the German commander ordered a recon force to strike out and seize a small village nestled between two hills on the Afrika Korps' right flank. These hills were referred to as the North Hill and the South Hill. He suspected enemy forces lurking in the area because intelligence had reported activity was building in the southeast sector of the 90th Light Panzer Division. The commander reasoned that the British were probably hiding in the hills and town. Therefore, he instructed his men to concentrate and strike at the North Hill. He ordered the Jagd-Panzer I to take up a position on the road and cover the village. To that tank's right flank, the IG18 75mm howitzer set up and prepared smoke rounds for the first shells to be fired in support of the attack. The 232 and 222 armored cars led the way to the hill and they were trailed by the half-tracks and Opel Blitz trucks, as seen in Figure 4.

(Figure 4. Original positions taken by the German forces—author's collection and photo)

German Forces:

- (2) SdKfz. 251 half-tracks, with 2 squads of infantry
- (2) Opel Blitz trucks, with 1 squad and 1 light machine gun team
- (1) SdKfz. 250 half-track, with the HQ team for the infantry platoon
- (1) Jagd-Panzer I
- (1) SdKfz. 232, armored car *defined as recon*
- (1) SdKfz. 222, armored car *defined as recon*
- (1) 75mm Howitzer (7.5cm IG 18 gun) with supporting Opel Blitz.
- (1) Ju87 Stuka Dive Bomber (The Stuka was not to come in until after the enemy was located.)

The British Commander was indeed ordered to secure the village and hills in advance of greater forces to follow the next day. He deployed his troops to occupy the village and the hills to the immediate north and south of the village, as shown in Figure 5. On the South Hill, the British commander lined his MkVIc's and jeep behind the hill crest, with one squad manning a prepared position on the forward slope. In the town, the ATR team had set up behind some brush next to one of the buildings. In support of that team was another squad behind the second building. Covering both teams of troops was the Humber. On the North Hill were the medium machine gun and the two inch mortar teams. The HQ commander was behind the crest on the highest point of the hill. While there, they all waited for the Germans to come into range before opening fire and revealing their precious positions.

(Figure 5. Original positions taken by both forces—author's collection and photo)

British Forces:

(4) Bren Gun Carriers

The Bren Gun Carriers were transporting 2 infantry squads,
   1 anti-tank rifle (ATR) team,
            (1) two inch mortar team and the Platoon HQ.

(2) Mk.VIc

(1) Humber armored car

(1) recon jeep with a .50 caliber heavy machine gun (HMG)
   for anti-aircraft defense

(1) Truck with a one medium machine gun (MMG) team

The game had some very basic conditions for victory and the (M), (S), and (R) factors were also left simple for ease of understanding. The German player had 6 turns to secure his objective and declare victory. The British player just had to hold his position for the allotted time in order to declare his tactical win. The Morale, Rates of Fire, and Strength Points were all allocated at the start of the game and were as follows: All the units started with a basic morale of 2. The AFVs were not subject to general morale. They were, however, subjected if a unit suffered an immobilization shot. Thus, I modified the Tank Morale to fit the scenario. The Rates of Fire were 2s except the German infantry squads, which had a (R)3 and each player's platoon support teams had an (R)1. Rates of Fire of 2 were assigned to the German 7.5cm IG 18 gun and the British 2-inch mortar and MMG. The British and German infantry squads were given Strength Points of 3. The MMG was also given an (S)3. The platoon support element had an (S)1 and the German howitzer was given a 2.

Finally, before any game can start, the terrain needs to be explained if there is any doubt as to vegetation thickness or where a hill's crest line might be located. In this case, the hills were bisected with string to indicate the hills' crest line. The South Hill had a basic linear crest running north to south. The North Hill had a curved crest and it too ran north to south.

Turn 1:

The start of turn 1 was marked by the original opening positions of both forces and that constituted the opening movement. The next step was to roll a 6-sided die to determine which force would fire first. The British player rolled the higher number and he elected not to fire at the enemy, thus not revealing any units. The German player, having nothing to shoot at, held any firing. He could have chosen to fire his smoke rounds from the 7.5cm IG 18 gun, but he thought otherwise. Thus, turn 1 ended with no action.

Turn 2:

This turn started with a fresh roll to see which player would move first and who would move second. The British player won the initiative roll and with no morale checks to assess, he decided to stay in position and wait for further developments from the enemy. The German player moved next and, with no morale checks either, he consulted the armor charts to find out the specific movements for his units. He then checked for any modifiers that would reduce his maximum movements. The only modifier was for "off road," which was a 3-inch movement deduction. For example, the 232 armored car could travel 25 inches but was restricted to 22 inches for off road. After determining the movements for his units, he sent his forces toward the North Hill, while the Jagd-Pz.I held steady on the road waiting for any British units to appear. The 222 had reached its full movement and stopped short of being able to observe the British medium machine gun (MMG) team. The 222 needed to be within 12 inches of it to see the potential target, as shown in the picture below, Figure 6. (The armored car was classified for the game as a Recon unit and the machine gun team was classified as dug in. In the rules under *Observing Units*, the two units were cross referenced to find that 12 inches and under is the distance needed to observe.)

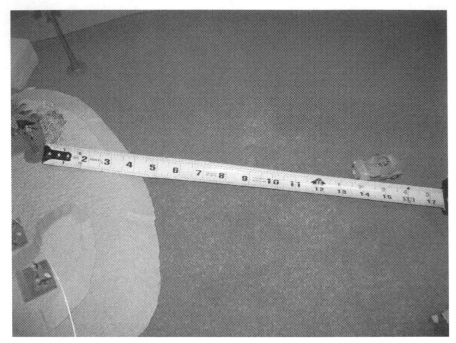

(Figure 6. The 222 is too far away to observe the British MMG team—author's collection and photo)

After all movements were completed, the initiative roll was performed to see which side would fire first. This time the Germans won. Because the player had not spotted any British units, his Stuka remained on call for this turn. So he decided to start firing smoke rounds. He selected a spot in the front of the North Hill as his target. He consulted the Mortars and Artillery Firing Chart (Table 3.1) and rolled a 4 on a 10-sided die. This placed the smoke rounds 8 inches to the right of his target. The 7.5cm IG 18 gun had a Rate of Fire of 2 rounds per turn. Thus, two puffs of cotton were placed on the board. However, they were blocking no unit's line of sight and this action concluded his firing.

The British, sensing it was now or never, decided to open fire. The first unit to fire per the Combat Order sequence was his 2-inch mortar. It took aim on the 222. He rolled a 2, which according to the Mortars and Artillery Firing Chart (Table 3.1), this put the rounds 12 inches short of the target. The resulting blasts landed 4 inches from the mortar's own position. (One could almost hear the little chaps screaming "Check Fire!") Next, the MMG, with an (R)2, blazed away at the 222. The range was 14 inches. The target moved, which added a +1 modifier, but the MMG was on the hill, which gave it a –2 to the die roll. The Infantry Firing Chart (Table 5.1) showed a 5 or less to hit at that range. The player rolled a 7 and a 9. The aggregate modifier of a –1 was too little to help the poor rolling. The MMG was then marked as revealed. At this point, the British concluded their firing, hoping for better luck next turn.

Turn 3:

The third turn began with the British getting to move first. With no morale checks to perform and having checked his units' movements and modifiers, the player lost no time in rushing his Mk.VIc's to the North Hill from their position on the South Hill. The Humber also scooted north to help block the oncoming Germans. The rest of the British forces stayed in position, ending his movement turn.

With British movement completed, the German player decided to declare an Opportunity Fire. (See Figure 7.) The lead Mk.VIc crossed the line of sight of the Jagd-Pz I when it descended the hill and dashed across the road behind a building in the village. The German player measured the range at 47 inches, which required a 3 or less on a 12-sided die on Table 8.1. The only modifier that applied was a +1 because the MkVIc was moving. This meant the player would have to roll a 1 or 2 to score a hit. It was a long-shot but certainly worth taking. He tossed the die and as luck would have it the magic 1 appeared and excitement filled the plastic souls of the Afrika Korps, not to mention that of the player. However, he was not done. He picked up a 6-sided die to roll for the hit location and a 4 came up indicating a hull hit. Next, he proceeded to check the Tank Charts for the Assault Factor (AF) of the Jagd-Pz I and Armor Class (AC) factor for the MkVIc. The Jagd-Pz I had an AF of 8*. The MkVIc had an AC of H* but because it was a side shot it was reduced to an I. He reviewed the Tank Combat Chart and modifiers. His modifiers were a +1 for the range, −1 for the asterisk next the AF value, and +1 for the asterisk next to the AC value. These netted out a +1 to his die roll. After cross-referencing the chart, he needed a 9 or less to punch. He rolled a 20-sided die and rolled a 6, plus his additional 1 gave him a punched and a burning tank.

(Figure 7. Jagd-Pz I fires an Opportunity shot—author's collection and photo)

Following that excitement, the Germans forces started their movement phase. With no morale checks to follow up on, the troops began moving. The 222 and the 232 headed around the North Hill to get into the rear of the British while the half-tracks and trucks moved closer to the hill. The Jagd-Pz I also got its motor in gear and headed up the road to the town.

With movement completed, the players rolled to determine which side would fire first. A 6-sided die was cast and the initiative went to the Germans. The commander realized it was time to bring in his aircraft, so he radioed his Stuka dive bomber to attack, as shown in Figure 8. It came in roaring and ready to drop its bombs of destruction. But first the plane had to endure the small arms fire and .50 caliber shots coming from the British jeep. The British player rolled the dice but failed to score a hit. The plane dropped its bombs but missed the intended MkVIc target. The German player rolled a 2 and got a +1 for the Dive Bomber Modifier on the Aircraft Dropping Bombs (Table 2.4), which resulted in the ordnance falling 8 inches to the left of the target. With that lackluster performance, the German player decided to order the 7.5cm IG 18 to fire high explosive (HE) shells on the MMG. The player consulted the Mortars and Artillery Firing (Table 3.1) and rolled a 3, which put the rounds in the middle of the town. (See Figure 9.)

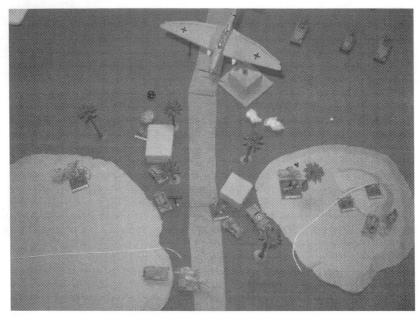

(Figure 8. Stuka attempts to bomb the second MkVIc.—author's collection and photo, Stuka by Daniel Erdman)

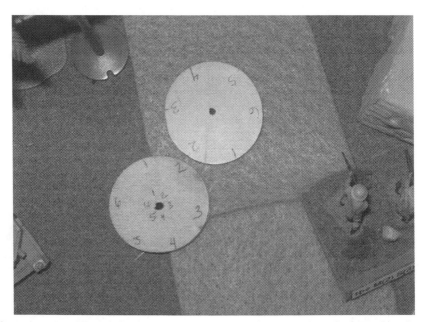

(Figure 9. HE in the center of town, upper round was the first shell—author's collection and photo)

Unfortunately, the shells produced no casualties. However, had he rolled a 6 or 1 on the placement of the second shell he might have hit the infantry squad sheltering next to the building. Next, the machine guns on the half-tracks got in on the act and began firing on the British machine gun nest. They were all within medium range, 12 to 18 inches, on the Infantry Firing chart (Table 5.1). The modifiers that affected their firing were a +1 for a target on a hill, +2 for firing at a dug-in unit, and a +1 for the machine gun (half-track) having moved. All this combined meant that the player had to roll a 1 on a 10-sided die. He had three machine guns with an (R)2, which gave him six die rolls. He gave it his best shot and all failed to produce a 1. Finally, the 222 and 232 tried to knock out the British Humber.

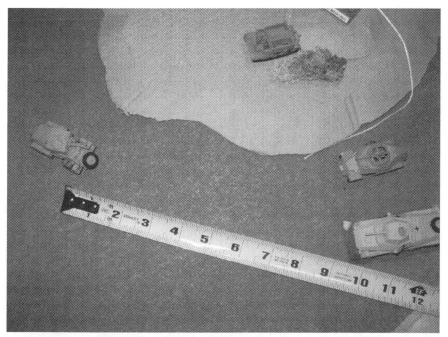

(Figure 10. The 222 and 232 fire at the Humber—author's collection and photo)

In Figure 10, both vehicles were 9 inches from their desired target. After checking the modifiers and Tank Firing table (Table 8.1), the player started with a 9 or less on a 12-sided die and had a +2 for his unit's mobile fire and a +1 for firing at a moving target. He rolled a 12 for the 222, which was a resounding miss. He rolled again and a 4 appeared that became a modified 7 for the 232. This was a solid hit. He rolled to see where the shot landed. The 6-sided die was bounced across the board and it turned up a 1. The Humber was immobilized and this concluded the firing for the German forces.

The British player, hoping for a bit of revenge, began sizing up his shots. The 2-inch mortar fired first. It took aim at the approaching 250 command half-track. With careful aim and a blow on the dice, the player rolled his luck. It was another 2! His mates started shouting "Send him back to gunnery school before he kills us!" The MMG took aim once more and tried to hit the 250 half-track. The range was now "close" per the Infantry Firing table (Table 5.1). He had a +1 for firing at a moving target, but he had a –2 for firing from a hill. The player rolled two 10-sided dice but they turned up an 8 and a 9-both missed. The last chance in this turn for a decisive hit on the Germans was a retaliatory strike by the Humber at the 232. With the range factors known, for they were the same as the German shot, the 12-sided die was rolled across the board. It rolled up a 2, for a hit. The 6-sided die was then cast and it gave up a 4. It was a hull shot. Quickly, he reviewed the charts to assess his odds. There was a +1 for the range and a –1 for the angle. Of course, these negated each other. The AC of the 232 was an H and the AF of the Humber was a 3. He needed a 5 or less on the 20-sided die, but he rolled an 8. The shot bounced to the relief of the German player. Unfortunately, this was all the British had to fire and turn 3 was concluded.

Turn 4:

Regardless of which player was going to win the movement initiative, each player was going to have to roll morale checks. As in turn 3, the British player rolled highest. He surveyed the battlefield and selected the MMG first for a morale check. Its (M) was a 2 and he was just out of range from his commander to get the +1. However, it was not needed. The player rolled a 4, which yielded a 6 for no effect. Next, the Humber had to check morale for having taken an immobilization shot. Its basic morale was also a 2 and the player rolled a 5, producing a 7 for no effect. At least the British could take solace that their morale was strong despite the failure of their gunnery.

With morale checks passed, the British player began his actual movement. Seeing his best option was to stay put and, as long as possible, to take advantage of firing from a stationary position. He chose to move just a few units. The jeep on the far side of the South Hill was moved north, while the squad on the forward slope of the hill moved 5 inches to the rear of the village. The lone MkVIc continued moving north off the hill in support of the Humber battling the German armored cars and this ended his movement.

Again, as in turn 3, the German player declared an Opportunity Fire. The Jagd-Pz I fired at the second MkVIc crossing the road in nearly the same spot as the last tank. The range was 38 inches and the modifiers were a –1 for the asterisk on the Jagd-Pz I's AF, a +2 for mobile fire, and a +1 for firing at a moving target. These modifiers combined netted out a +2 on the player's die roll. According to the Tank Firing Chart (Table 8.1), he needed a 4 or less to hit; this meant he needed to roll a 1 or 2 on a 12-sided die. He gave the die a roll and hoped for a repeat hit of his last action. Sadly, it was not to be. He rolled an 11 and with a +2 this produced a 13 for a clear miss.

The German player began his movement phase with only one morale check to perform. The command team in the 250 half-track had received fire from the British MMG. It had an (M)2 and it got a +1 for being a command stand. The player rolled a 5, which meant the machine gun bullets had no effect on the resolve of the commander. With morale unfettered, he started moving his units. The 222 continued by passing the 232 and Humber to get into the rear of the British forces. The 232 halted to give a second blast to the Humber. The Jagd-Pz I advanced closer to the town, while the half-tracks came to the edge of the North Hill. The Opel Blitzes were ordered to the north of the hill for possible dismounting of their infantry in the next turn.

With the movement phase completed, each player anxiously rolled his 6-sided die to see who would get to fire first. To the relief of the British player, he won. He immediately shifted his mortar fire from the advancing half-tracks to his front to the Jagd-Pz I approaching the town. Though the mortar team fared better in firing, it still missed. The player rolled a 7, putting the rounds 3 inches to the left of the tank and out of range of a near miss. The MkVIc swung its turret around to fire at the passing 222. Being right at 6 inches, the little tank needed a 10 or less to hit. But it still had the movement modifiers of its mobile fire (+2) and firing at a moving target (+1). The player rolled a 6, giving it a modified 9 for a hit. The player gleefully rolled his 6-sided die to determine where the shot landed. He rolled a 6 for a turret shot. He checked the Tank Charts to see an AF 3 for the MkVIc and AC J for the 222. Because it was a side shot (see Figure 11), the 222's AC was reduced by one class. The angle of the shot gave no additional modifier. It was nearly perpendicular to the MkVIc. Therefore, the player needed an 8 or less on the 20-sided die. He rolled with anticipation, but was disappointed with a 19. Next, the Humber exchanged shots with the 232. The range was still at 9 inches and because neither vehicle moved it was a simple 9 or less on the Tank Firing table (Table 8.1). The player rolled a 4 and quickly rolled for the location of the impact. He rolled the 6-sided die and it came up a 4 for a hull hit. The angle gave it a +1 modifier and the shot had a −1 for the closeness of impact. The 232 had an H for its AC and the Humber had a 3 for its AF. These factors cross referenced on the Tank Combat Chart (Table 8.3) meant the player needed a 5 or less on the 20-sided die. He rolled a frustrating 12. On the other side of the board, the anti-tank rifle team fired off a shot on the advancing Jagd-Pz 1. The range was 11 inches. Checking the Bazooka/ATR table, it showed a 6 or less was needed to hit. It was not the day for the Brits. The player rolled another miss. Last, the MMG rattled off a blast at the 251 half-track. The range was 6 inches. Its modifiers were a −2 for firing from a hill and a +1 for firing at a moving target. That, of course, left him with an aggregate of a −1. He needed a 5 or less on the Infantry Firing table (Table 5.1). He rolled two dice for his MMG and produced two hits, with a 1 and a 4. Now, because the

MMG was firing bullets at a half-track it is not entirely assumed that the bullets hit the troops inside. The player reviewed the Location Table: Tanks and AFVs (Table 8.2) and rolled a single 6-sided die two times for the two hits. He rolled a 5 and a 1, resulting in a wheel and a passenger compartment hit. Next, he went to the Infantry Attacking a Half-Track table (Table 8.4) to see his damages. The 251 was hit in the wheels, producing a slight reduction in its movement (–4 inches). Also, one hit went into the passenger compartment, which gave the troops inside one hit. The German player failed to make the saving throw of a 1 or 2 on a 6-sided die. He subsequently had to roll the sergeant's roll, which was a miss. With that, the British player rested his firing dice and conceded the firing phase to his opponent.

(Figure 11. MkVIc fires at 222—author's collection and photo)

The German player was only too happy to pick up the dice and test his luck at firing his forces. Following the Order of Combat, the Stuka came back (Figure 12) with its machine guns blazing. The player then positioned his plane for attack and awaited the results of the British general anti-aircraft fire, which came up short of hitting the JU-87 Stuka. The German player measured the distance between the wing machine guns. They were 3 inches apart and he laid out his string accordingly. On one side of the strafing path were the MMG team, the 2-inch mortar crew and the platoon commander. On the other side, the Bren Gun Carrier and light truck for the MMG were hit by the machine gun fire. But the German player had to see if it deviated from its flight path. Fortunately, it did not. Instantly, the soft-skin truck was destroyed. The Stuka AF factor was a 2. The Carriers AC was a J, but since it was a top hit it suffered a reduction of 3 ACs. However, this was not possible because the Tank Combat Chart stops at K. The player was granted a –2 to his die roll. He needed an 8 or less on the chart and rolled a 9. But with the modification, it brought his roll to a scoring 7 for a destroyed vehicle. Next, the infantry units were assessed. The infantry stands took an automatic hit but were given a saving throw of a 1 or 2 on a 6-sided die. The Platoon Commander was saved by a saving throw of a 2. The mortar team was not so lucky; it was eliminated from the game. Finally, the MMG also suffered 1 casualty hit but still had 2 more Strength Points, preventing it from being eliminated. The British player still had to roll for a sergeant's casualty, which fortunately came up a miss. Next, the crew of the 222 decided to return fire on the MkVIc. The German Player rolled a hit with a 5 on the 12-sided die. The range was 6 inches for a 10 or less, but the same movement modifiers were added in from the MkVIc's shot. The player needed a 7 or less on a 12-sided die. The shot location was rolled on a 6-sided die and a 4 was rolled, which indicated a hull hit. Next, the German player cross-referenced the AC H* and the AF 3. The side shot had no angle modifier, but the side shot did reduce the MkVIc's AC to an I. Nevertheless, the player still received a +1 for the asterisk on the AC. This effectively meant that a 5 or less would have to be rolled on the 20-sided die and, as luck would have it, he rolled a 3. The little tank was destroyed. The 232 also took a second shot at the Humber. It recorded a hit but it bounced off the hull. The half-tracks repeated their fire at the British medium machine gun, but the three of them were only able to inflict an additional hit, but also scored a sergeant's casualty.

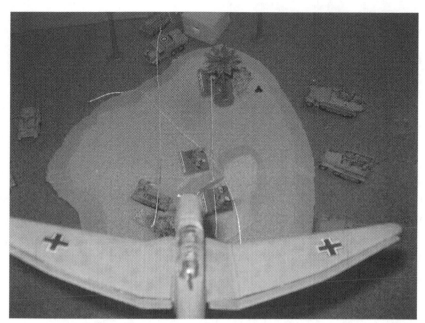

(Figure 12. Stuka blasts the British—author's collection and photo, Stuka by Daniel Erdman)

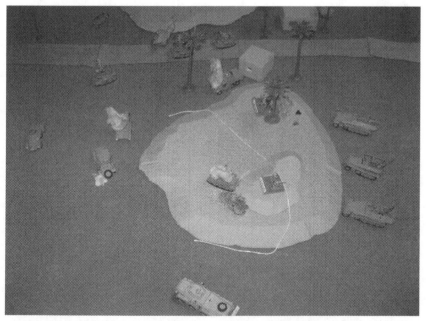

(Figure 13. British Retreat—author's collection and photo)

Aftermath:

Clearly, the battle had not gone well for the British player. He had lost two tanks, a truck, and some infantry, and his armored car was immobilized. He sensed certain defeat and decided to call the game to a halt and conceded the day to the German forces. He did carry out a last move (Figure 13) to see how far he could theoretically get in an attempt to escape further destruction. But turn 5 was not played and the game ended. This was a real game carried out and, as some games go, it was not pretty for one player. The dice being what they are can produce some very unpredictable results, as in this case. It seemed that the mood of frustration experienced by the British player manifested itself in the poor rolling of his dice. It was a fun game to observe and it lasted about 2½ hours.

CHAPTER 7

Solo Wargaming

Solo wargaming is another wonderful aspect to miniature gaming that can yield an abundance of entertainment. I have always marveled at the near stigma or apathy toward solo wargaming that many experienced gamers exude. There is much to be said for filling a few free hours with toy soldiers advancing on a position with the simulated sounds of gun fire and shell bursts filling the air with only the lone player to hear. For some unknown reason, I have come across several gamers that have wonderful armies for different periods but they hardly get to engage them in plastic or metal figure combat. It seems like such a waste not to set up a solo skirmish and let a few dice hit the board. I suppose, given their lifestyle, they may feel a little silly as grown men playing with toys in the garage. It may seem much easier to go over to another buddy's house and think of it as "guy time." I am here to declare that that does not have to be the case. There are great reasons to remove the fruit bowl from the center of the dining room table or kick open a few folding tables in the garage and lay out whatever terrain may be on hand. The terrain can be as simple as laying out a green blanket over a few books for hills or breaking out the deluxe stuff reserved for the wargame gang. Moreover, setting up a game to battle against oneself does not have to be a complex affair. There are several books that discuss intricate methods for solo wargaming and techniques to enhance the element of surprise, though they do not have to be employed to have a rewarding experience. The hope of this chapter is to inspire and motivate gamers to gather up their forces for a fun and enjoyable contest that will expand their satisfaction in the hobby.

At this point, it is worth tackling the skeptic's view of how to play against oneself. The goal for the player should be as an impartial participant with the objective to observe how the game unfolds. Further, he should spend more time on the intellectual pursuit of the scenario and not necessarily the outcome. Some players may get stuck in the trap of trying to think too critically about the next several turns down the road for each force. This will put a player's brain in a twist and can spoil the affair. When playing, the wargamer should play each turn one at a time and play it as best it can be played for both forces, without dwelling on the what ifs or favoring one side. If these ideals can be achieved, the solo experience can be a fulfilling and satisfying activity.

One of the best reasons to solo wargame is to develop a working knowledge of a set of rules. Play testing them allows the player to gain valuable experience in the games' charts and methods of play before going head to head with another player. Therefore, solo wargaming can be thought of as wargame exercises for wargamers. Often times this is the most important aspect. On many occasions, I have tested rules to see how certain tanks can battle other tanks of the same period. To illustrate, imagine a troop of M3 Stuarts forming a reconnaissance mission on the plains of the Libyan Desert only to encounter two Panzer III Ausf Js lying in wait on a small rise. This small game can yield important information such as how the ranges work, how speed and maneuver influence the outcome of the game, and how complicated it is to work out a combat sequence. Obviously, the more familiar a player is with the rules the more competitive he becomes as a player.

Battle-testing tactics is another great advantage to playing a solo game. World War Two games present some fabulous tactics to try out, especially in the area of combined arms exercises. Players can test how artillery or mortars support infantry advances using both HE and smoke. Knowing this allows the player to develop screening tactics while his infantry attack another enemy location. The HE and smoke rounds block out other enemy troops that might otherwise present a problem. Fire and maneuver tactics can also be worked out. The more familiar a wargamer is with this tactic the more likely he is to use it against an opponent. There are two easy ways to play-test this approach. One is to advance an infantry company supported by a medium machine gun platoon and a mortar section against a dug-in enemy. The second is to attack with a mixed tank task force. In both cases, it is critical to remember the three main elements: the reserve, the main attack element, and the maneuver element. The infantry company will have one platoon in reserve, while one platoon lays down a base of fire with the support of the mortar section and machine gun platoon. At the same time, the maneuver platoon should move to attack a weak spot in the enemy's defenses. With a tank force, this is very similar. Suppose two platoons of Sherman tanks supported by two M10 Jacksons are attacking a German held crossroad manned by a few anti-tank guns. The M10s can be the base of fire with one Sherman platoon maneuvering on the flank while the other slowly moves in across a broad front as the reserve. Both examples will give a gamer a feel for fire and maneuver, which he can then employ against an opponent at his next game meeting.

Another great cause for solo wargaming is testing something creative that no other player would be interested in playing because the battle might be too one-sided and there would be no chance to win. Case in point, as mentioned early, I play-tested a solo game of a World War Two Japanese battalion performing a Banzai charge. This made an ideal solo battle. Very few players are willing to take a perfectly good battalion and send them on a suicide mission. They are bound to deviate from it and engage in a typical Western-style slug fest. In addition, if the rules work properly and imitate history, the Japanese should be wiped out. This is just one example of testing and seeking out a new adventure. There are countless opportunities to investigate. Imagine setting up an Italian valley with a reinforced platoon of Germans holding a farmhouse. However, they are actually the support force for a dug in 88mm anti-tank gun hidden in a clump of trees. Coming around the bend is a British armored column made up of a few tanks. I am not sure how that game would end, but I would not necessarily bet against the Germans. Another fun example is to set up a German anti-tank gun screen and have a Soviet tank force try to penetrate it. A solo gamer could place three German 75mm guns spaced out at about 200 yards (20 inches in my rules) supported by a medium machine gun platoon. These troops could try to stand firm against two platoons of T34/85s. The tanks could even have mounted troops on them to spice it up. Ultimately, the gamer can think of solo gaming as an adventure and a departure from the typical wargame battle.

For those diehard wargamers needing something to add an element of surprise, I offer up a few suggestions. After determining the scenario to be played, the gamer can use a few note cards to develop a few different forces to encounter. To illustrate this, envision a company of G.I.s and a platoon of Sherman tanks advancing across a green field with a few farmhouses scattered about the pasture. There is a road running the length of the board on the American's right flank. Parallel to the length of the road, on the far side, is a short wall. It is intermittently broken up by clumps of trees and shrubs. Resting at the rear of the battlefield is a lonely hill. The gamer can take 8 index cards and write down different forces to be encountered on each, but he should leave 3 cards blank. It is highly recommended that there be at least one nasty surprise to run up against. In this case, a pair of camouflaged Tigers Is will do nicely. He can then shuffle them facedown and set 3 aside, which are not to be used. Of course, this now creates a degree of uncertainty. Are those Tigers there to be encountered and will they create havoc with the Americans? There are two ways to see what is written on the cards and they can be used together. One is to write down the turn in which the card will be flipped over. The next way is to have the solo player get a unit within 12 inches of the card and automatically reveal it, in that turn. The player places his 5 cards on the table: 1 on the hill, another by a farmhouse, with a third by the other farm and 2 in the woods. With everything set out, the battle can begin and the player can test his skills.

Breaking for a moment from World War Two, I would be remiss if I did not briefly mention solo gaming for a different historical period. I find playing the late British Colonial period, in particular the Zulu War, a wonderful exercise. Again, not too many players are going to want to play the side that during the war lost nearly every battlefield engagement. For this period, I have two regiments of British, about 20 figures each, one regiment of British cavalry of 15 mounted troops and one battery of artillery, which consists of one gun and two figures. Of course I have the usual limber and supply wagons. The Zulu natives consist of 140 painted men with a few of them armed with rifles. This alone is not enough to recreate the hordes of brave Zulu warriors that swept toward the Red Coats. Therefore, I have numerous black wooden squares labeled Zulu in white paint. As the trays of figures get blasted off the board, the black squares take their place. Recreating a few battles in this period allows me the opportunity to reach out into military history and get a glimpse into the warfare of the time that books just cannot deliver. To be sure, solo wargaming can become more of an avenue of discovery than a simple game with toy soldiers.

Hopefully, I have made the point that solo wargaming does not have to be a play of last resort and that it can yield splendid intellectual results from testing tactics or ideas to exploring the mechanics of a set of rules or exploring one-sided contests. The gamer should always look to the solo venture as his chance to run a wargame exercise before the next big game. If that is a rare event, then it is a chance to play with what he has spent so much time creating. So for those gamers that have been reluctant to game by themselves, think of some great ideas to put on the battlefield and let those dice fly!

(Zulu braves try to overrun British Redcoats)

CHAPTER 8

Scenarios for Wargaming World War Two

World War Two contained some of the largest battles known to man and was fought over some of the most difficult terrain imaginable. To replicate the large battles in 15mm or 1/72 scale would be outside the reach of my rules. Therefore, I have selected the following scenarios because they offer some unique opportunities from a wargaming perspective. They are not intended to be large, epic struggles between adversaries. To the contrary, they are designed to be smaller in size and offer the players some real challenges that were faced by genuine people fighting for their lives. (This point should never be overlooked or minimized. I am firmly convinced that as wargamers we are more aware of the brutal natural of conflict because most of us are students of history and many of us have served in the armed forces.) The selected battles are inspired by actual events. Of course, some things have had to be scaled back to match the perimeters of a wargame board. Furthermore, getting detailed information down to the company level is not always straightforward, nor is the material written on the subject written in such a way that a wargamer can easily extrapolate the needed facts to recreate the action on a wargame table. For instance, ascertaining the time, sequence of events, spatial relationships between units, friend or foe, and the exact equipment used are difficult, just to name a few items. Subsequently, I have had to make judgments in creating the scenarios that best capture the drama of the event. These judgments have ranged from weapons to the deployment of units and vehicles. At the end of each scenario, I have provided a list of forces to be used in the game. Ultimately, I hope these battles present some real insights into modern warfare and what the participants were actually called to do. At the end of this chapter, I have included a historical fiction scenario and thoughts on how to recreate some aspects of World War Two. Some of the combat action is similar to what is discussed in the chapter on solo wargaming. But it is more directed toward portraying a battle between two players. Also in the Basic Table of Organization and Equipment chapter (Chapter 5), there are listings that define the unit formations which can be used to construct the units in these scenarios.

Scenario 1: French Cavalry to the Rescue?

With the close of the Phony War in Western Europe, the Germans invaded France and the Low Countries on May 10, 1941, which marked the reemergence of open conflict. The German use of the Blitzkrieg caught the Allies flat-footed, and they were unable to cope with German Panzer divisions flooding into the frontier. Within a few weeks, Wehrmacht units were within 50 miles of the English Channel and threatening to cut off the French and British Expeditionary Forces in northern France. As German units continued to push ever westward, British General Harold Franklyn reacted on orders to clear the area in and around the south of Arras. His mission was to break communications between lead enemy forces and their positions in eastern France. However, with the interference of other British and French generals, the mission evolved into an all-out Allied offensive. This attack is often referred to as the Counter-Attack at Arras. Its purpose was to disrupt the German advance into the west and close the gap with their forces in the north. The attack started on May 21 and was reasonably successful at first. So much so that Allied High Command realized the ground gained could not be held with the troops on hand and with increased pressure being applied by the German forces in the area, the troops started to withdraw by that evening. To the west of Arras, some French infantry units in the town of Warlus found themselves cut off and surrounded. The Germans held the Walrus-Duisans road a few miles north of Walrus. The trapped infantry units managed to escape with the help of six French tanks and two armored personnel carriers, which arrived from a nearby sector. Together they broke free of the enemy's grip on the road and linked up with friendly forces in the north.

I picked this account because it offers a nice challenge in a limited context, which works well for wargaming. Unfortunately, I could not find references to the types of French tanks nor the exact units used for the French and German infantry. Moreover, an assumption is made that the armored carriers were Bren Gun Carriers of the 9th Durham Light Infantry. They were also active in the area of this action. So some "artistic license" has been applied here to recreate the event.

The French forces will start the game at the edge of town ready to advance "north." The German units will be scattered across the road on the northern section of the board. The action will take place under cover of darkness, which adds a +2 to the *to hit* roll. But should the units fire at each other within 12 inches this modifier goes away. The darkness also reduces vehicle movement by 3 inches. The French player will have 12 turns to fight his way out. If more than one-half of his force is able to escape in the time allotted, he wins. If not, the Germans are declared the winner.

SCENARIO 1: FRENCH CALVARY TO THE RESCUE?

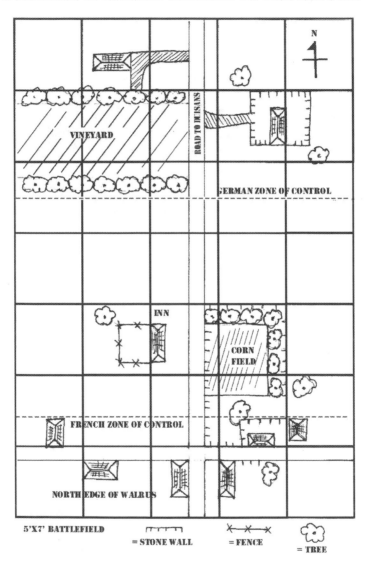

VINEYARD

ROAD TO DUISANS

GERMAN ZONE OF CONTROL

INN

CORN FIELD

FRENCH ZONE OF CONTROL

NORTH EDGE OF WALRUS

5'X7' BATTLEFIELD

= STONE WALL

= FENCE

= TREE

French Forces

3 Somua S 35

3 H38s

2 Bren Gun Carriers (British) loaded with 1 ATR rifle team, 1 LMG Team

1 Infantry Company—Morale used should be a mixture of 1s and 2s

German Forces

2 Panzer IIf

1 Panzer IIIc

3 Opel-blitz trucks

3 Motorized infantry squads—Morale 2

1 Kubelwagen with HQ team

Scenario 2: Failure at Tavronitis Bridge

With the pending invasion of Russia quickly advancing on Hitler's timeline for conquest, events in the Balkans frustrated his plans. The Italians had botched their efforts in Albania and the Greeks held up their advance. Also, dealings with the government in Yugoslavia did not go according to Hitler's political demands. These events caused him to divert his attention from the task at hand, and he decided to turn south and invade Yugoslavia. The British, seeing that Greece would eventually fall prey to the Wehrmacht armies, decided to reinforce the country. The Germans indeed invaded Greece on April 6, 1941, and despite heroic resistance, the Greek and British troops fell back, forcing many to either surrender or flee. Many did manage to evacuate and dig in on the Island of Crete.

German intelligence believed that the island was not well defended and that the troops there were in no condition to put up strong resistance should the island be invaded. The Germans also believed that the sites selected for airborne forces would be satisfactory to permit gliders and paratroopers to land with minimal damage to their combat strength. Moreover, German intelligence suspected that the civilian population would be passive to a German attack. They were absolutely wrong on all counts. The British, Greek, and New Zealand forces were digging in and preparing for invasion. Their morale was high but admittedly their leadership was less than expected from professional military men. The ground was littered with olive groves and low stone walls, and broken and hilly terrain was in abundance. Finally, the civilians were not only hostile to the invaders but engaged in what the Germans claimed were atrocities. There were reported instances of the civilians killing injured and wounded paratroopers. This led to several villages being the site of German firing squads.

On the morning of May 20, following a spectacular pre-invasion air bombardment, the Ju52s started filling the sky, towing gliders or carrying paratroopers. One of the objectives of the first wave was the airfield at Maleme. It was situated on the west end of the island, and it nearly sat on the beach. The glider troops went in first and some 15 to 20 minutes later the paratroopers started dropping. The first landings were slightly west of the Tavronitis River and the airstrip. From the beginning, the battle did not go well for the Germans. The 22nd New Zealand Battalion was stationed around the airfield: Company C covered the airstrip, D Company sat on the western slope of Hill 107, while A Co. straddled the hill itself and B Co. occupied the east slope. The New Zealanders let loose with machine gun and anti-aircraft fire, killing and wounding many Germans. The paratroopers, while contending with bullets flying about them, had to deal with the terrain ripping them to shreds on impact. To make matters worse, the paratroopers landed with only side arms and hand grenades. Airborne tactics and methods had not caught up to the realities of modern warfare. The troopers had to make heroic dashes to their weapon canisters before starting their attack. While doing so, many were killed.

Due to *esprit de corps* and rare courage, the Germans managed to overcome the initial shock of landing under such severe circumstances and mounted their attacks on the airfield and the Tavronitis Bridge. Major Franz Braun, leading the Germans, secured the west bank of the dry riverbed while other units battled for the airfield. The bridge was key, not only to flanking the airstrip, but it paved the way east to link up with other German units on the island.

Colonel Andrew, commander of the 22nd Battalion, found himself being attacked across his entire front but unable to communicate with his companies to get a clear picture of events, which was a major problem for British forces throughout the island. He gathered the best information he could and he requested help several times but was denied by his superior. With the enemy pushing and threatening to take the bridge, he authorized Company C to counterattack with its two tanks. Platoons 15 and 13 held the field while platoon 14 went forward to the bridge to push the Germans back. Unfortunately, one tank became immobilized by running off an embankment and the other tank, upon seeing this, claimed mechanical problems and withdrew. This naturally left the infantry unsupported. The attack was soon driven back and the Germans captured the bridge. With communication still presenting problems, the New Zealanders found themselves in a confused state and withdrew from Hill 107 the following morning. The withdrawal from the hill had a drastic effect on the western defense of the island, as it allowed the Germans to capture the airfield and pour in reinforcements from the west for the continued effort to subdue the island.

This scenario is based on the effort to push the Germans back and take command of the bridge. There is some historical confusion about what kind of tanks were at the battle. Some accounts indicate they were Matildas and some claim they were Vickers Mk.VIs. I have chosen the Vickers tanks for this game because I believe Matildas would unfairly weight the game in favor of the New Zealand forces. For starting positions, the map outlines the unit start areas and the positions for the tanks. It is important to note that this wargame simulates a battle within a battle. The 13th and 15th platoons had already been engaged with the Germans for several hours, but platoon 14 had been held in reserve. The New Zealand player will roll an 8-sided die to determine the number of hits to spread out to platoons 13 and 15 and the covering platoon from D Company before the game begins. The German player will roll a 12-sided die and do the same thing to his forces. Also, his forces will be a collection from different units. Thus, the 16 squads listed are not of the same company. The game should last 10 turns with a victory going to the New Zealand player if he can get control of the "west" end of the bridge for two consecutive turns.

One last note should be made for the units themselves before a game begins. The German and New Zealander *squad* stands' Strength Points (S) should start at 3 before any pre-battle casualties are assessed. Once that has been done, the Rates of Fire can be adjusted. (See Other Conditions, Airborne Troops in the rules chapter.)

New Zealander Force (See: Standard British Rifle Company)
1 Company
1 Platoon for D Company
2 MkVIb Vickers

German Forces
16 various squads
1 Company command stand
2 Platoon commander stands
1 Motorcycle
1 28mm, ATG Rate of Fire 2
1 80mm mortar, Rate of Fire 2
1 MMG Section.

SCENARIO 2: FAILURE AT TAVRONITIS BRIDGE

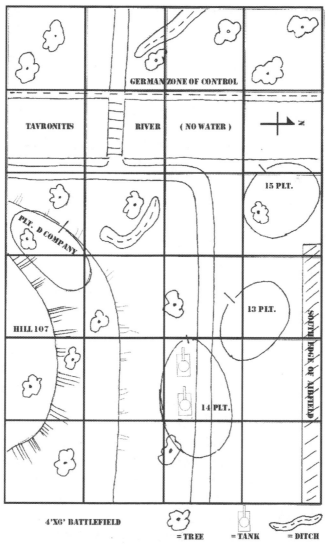

GERMAN ZONE OF CONTROL

TAVRONITIS   RIVER   (NO WATER)

N

15 PLT.

PLT. D COMPANY

HILL 107

13 PLT.

SOUTH EDGE OF AIRFIELD

14 PLT.

4'X6' BATTLEFIELD   = TREE   = TANK   = DITCH

(BATTLEFIELD IS FILLED WITH OLIVE TREES AND ROCK OUTCROPPINGS)

Scenario 3: First Armored Clash

Operation Torch began on November 8, 1942, with the objective to hit Erwin Rommel, commander of the German Afrika Korps, from the west. The Allies would push through French held territories in Morocco and smash him in Tunisia with the help of the British. Within a few weeks, following the collapse of the French resistance, the Americans were making strong headway in the rugged terrain of Tunisia and closing in on Tunis. As the Americans were forming their offensive, they began probing the areas near Medjez el Bab, a German strong hold. The 1st Battalion of the 1st U.S. Armored Regiment under the command of Colonel John Water set out to reconnoiter the Chouigui Pass and the bridges east from El Bathan to Djedeidi. On November 25th, elements of Lt. Colonel Water's command skirmished with German and Italian units heading south toward the Chouigui Pass. The enemy was repulsed and took up positions in a walled French farm, later known as Coxen's Farm. On the following day, tanks from the 190th Panzer Battalion headed south again from Coxen's Farm. The tank column consisted of 6 Panzer IV Gs and 4 Panzer III Ls. The Americans launched their assault from covered positions to the rear and east of the Germans. The attack started with the 1st Battalion's M3 75mm half-track platoon opening fire first. Major Carl Tuck's Company A, consisting of M3 Light tanks, rose over a low ridge and blasted the rear of the column from close range while Major William Siglin's Company B, also M3 Light tanks, revealed itself from another ridge and began blasting at the column's flank. The exchange did not last long. When the dust settled, the Panzer IVs and one of the Panzer IIIs were burning and scattered about the road. The remains of the armored column fled to the farm. The Americans lost six of their M3s and the life of Major Siglin.

This brief and violent clash was the first American and German armored battle of World War Two. As a game, it will last until one of the players is depleted of armor or is forced to retire from the field. The game will start with the Americans firing first after the initial set up. Armor morale will be used for this scenario. The attached map will show the starting points for the units and the points of concealment for the Americans. Because this scenario evolves a large number of tanks, it will be best to have a large table. The recommended size is 6ft. by 8ft.

American Force*
A Co.   2 M3 Light Tanks—*Set up on Ridgeline 1*
B Co.   12 M3 Light Tanks—*Set up on Ridgeline 2*
        Assault Platoon: 3 M3 Half-tracks with 75mm guns and
        1 M2 scout car
        —*Set up on Ridgeline 3*
*The American tank companies are not full strength.

German Force
The German force will set up in any order between points A and B on the road.
6 Panzer VI G's
4 Panzer III Ls

SCENARIO 3: FIRST ARMORED CLASH

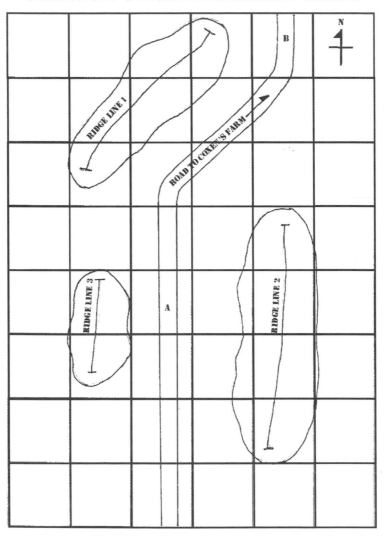

6'X8'   BATTLEFIELD IS NONDESCRIPT DESERT TERRAIN

Scenario 4: Gavin Stops the Tigers!

The invasion of Sicily began in the early morning hours of July 10, 1943, with Allied airborne troops making their run over the southeastern tip of Sicily. However, strong winds broke up their formations causing many to land miles from their intended drop zones. Some were forced to turn around and return to North Africa and others inadvertently ditched in the sea. This was hardly the way to begin the assault on the soft underbelly of Fortress Europe. The unintended dispersion of the airborne forces did have one positive effect on the enemy. The Germans and Italians believed the forces used in the drop were much larger than they were and caused much confusion in the ranks. The landings thankfully went much smoother later that morning. The U.S. 2nd Corps made landings at Licata, Gela, and Scoglitti. The British struck east of the Americans with 30 and 13 Corps hitting the beaches from Pachino to Avola.

The Axis response at first was lacking nearly in every way. General Alfredo Guzzoni, of the Italian forces, had dismissed reports that the British had taken Syracuse. He thought these reports to be a mistake. Early in the day, he had lost all communications with his forward positions and was relying on curriers for information. It was not until General Fridolin von Senger reported to him on the morning of July 11 did he understand what was happening. Field Marshal Albert Kesselring, at his headquarters in Rome, was also learning of the unfolding disaster on the inland. Being unable to communicate with General Guzzoni and believing that the Italians were not putting up an effective and organized resistance to the invasion, he ordered the Hermann Goering Division into action against the Americans in the Gela port area. The order was passed down to General Conrath who quickly organized his attack columns. To his west, he instructed the Italian Livorno Division to push southeast toward Gela, while his division would swing wide and down Highway 117 to cross at Highway 115, the coastal road. The objective was to drive the Americans back into the sea before they could establish a strong beachhead. One of those columns was a heavy infantry force that was to move out from the vicinity of Biscari and proceed to Highway 115 and move northwest across the Acate River.

It is here that Colonel James Gavin enters the picture. He had been moving up the 115 from Biscari Station, collecting scattered paratrooper units as he advanced. After having driven back German units near the Biazzo ridge, he continued west to seize Ponte Dirillo and secure the crossing at the Acate River. A mile or so past the ridge his attack ground to a halt. It was 1000 hours and his men had run into 4 Tiger Is tanks supported by infantry. Armed with bazookas, the paratroops did the best they could, but they could not score any knockout blows to the Tigers. Just behind Biazzo ridge two airborne howitzers, presumably M8 75mm Pack Howitzers, gave support and pounded the German infantry. By noon, one of the guns was in position on the ridge, exchanging direct fire shots with one of the Tigers. Miraculously, the airborne crew knocked it out. As this was unfolding, two half-tracks towing 57mm anti-tank guns arrived and began blasting the German tanks. This signaled that reinforcements were on their way, one of which was a naval gunfire support party. They were all too happy to call in the big guns sitting off the coast. By 1500 hours the Germans pulled out and Gavin went back on the offensive.

This particular battle is quite a stunning tail of American paratroopers grappling with some of the most powerful tanks of the war. Frankly, when I read the account, I was amazed the Tigers did not win the day. I can only surmise that the German infantry were reluctant to advance under fierce small arms fire and the tank commander was not going to run headlong into infantry without his own infantry support.

The obvious change in the scenario from what is described above is the time difference. The actual event lasted some 5 hours, which in game time would be 60 turns! This would be enough to exhaust the most avid gamer and would be a ridiculous number of turns to try to replicate any battle, let alone such a small action. I selected 10 turns as a reasonable amount of time to drive the Tigers forward and still give the paratroopers a tough challenge to meet. The game will last a total of 10 turns. By the 10th turn, the German infantry must be on the ridge and the Americans must be completely driven off for it to be declared a German tactical victory. The American player, of course, must do the opposite and hold the ridge. If the paratroopers have control by turn 10, the Germans are considered defeated and begin retreating due to increased indirect fire from the arrival of the naval gun party.

The map below displays the beginning points for the players' troops. The German forces will start the game at the "West" end of the board and will receive no reinforcements or indirect fire support. Their mission is to drive the American troops back and secure the ridge with infantry. The initial force of U.S. paratroopers will start the game deployed forward of the ridge with the two jeeps and pack howitzers on the reverse slope. The reinforcements will arrive on turn 7 on the road entering from the "East" side of the board. For this game, all the engaged forces "West" of the ridge are considered revealed due to the arid nature of the terrain and because both force were moving toward Ponte Dirillo.

German Forces
4 Tigers—*see tank placement on the map*
1 Company of infantry—*can be placed anywhere in the German zone of control*
1 Medium machine gun section—*can be place anywhere in the German zone of control*

Initial American Force
2 Companies of paratroopers—*see map for initial deployment*
2 Medium Machine Gun sections—*can be placed anywhere between the ridge and American zone of control*
8 Bazooka teams—*one attached to each platoon*
(2) 75mm Pack Howitzers, Rate of Fire (3)
2 Jeeps

American Reinforcement
2 Half-tracks
(2) 57mm anti-tank guns, Rate of Fire (2)
1 Jeep with liaison party—any American command stand
2 Platoons of paratroopers

SCENARIO 4: GAVIN STOPS THE TIGERS

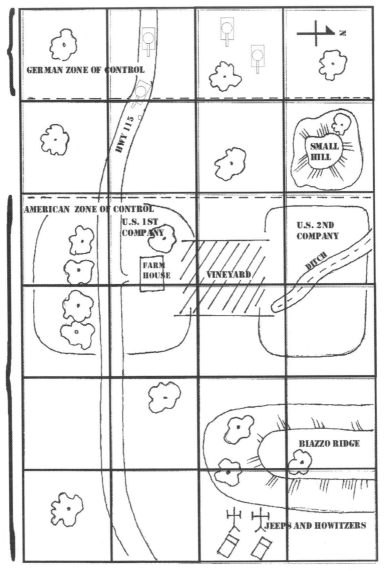

4'X6' BATTLEFIELD: TERRAIN IS FILLED WITH BRUSH AND SCATTERED TREES

Scenario 5: The Buna Hell

By late 1942, the combined efforts of the American and Australian forces had stopped the advance of Imperial Japan on New Guinea. Japanese forces had come within reach of taking Port Moresby. But exhausted and ground down, they halted in the Owen Stanley Mountains surrounding the city. The Allies, led by the efforts of the Australians, pushed them up and over the Kokoda trail into the Buna area on the northeast side of the inland. Thus began the long struggle to drive the Japanese troops from the Buna Mission. General Douglas MacArthur ordered the start of the campaign on October 1, 1942. Through rain, disease, sweltering heat, and tenacious fighting by the enemy, the Allies secured victory by early January 1943.

In the final push to drive the Japanese out of Buna, elements of the 128th and 127th Infantry Regiments launched an attack to envelope the Buna Mission on the morning of January 1. Company F of the 128th, under the command of Captain Jefferson Cronk, moved in conjunction with E Company of the 127th to attack up the village spit and secure the north end of a narrow wooden plank bridge that led into the village and Mission. If successful, companies H and G of regiments 127 and 128, respectively, would cross and take the Mission. Unfortunately, this was not to be the case. As E and F companies moved out, crossing a shallow waterway to the spit, some noise was made and the attack was detected. Flares and machine gun fire erupted on the American troops. Company E, already suffering low morale, broke and ran, while F Company, under the cool leadership of Captain Cronk, worked its way to the bridge. Regrettably, fire from numerous bunkers blocked their attempts to secure the bridge. They were forced to fall back on the spit and await orders to renew the offensive. During the night, it became evident that Japanese were collapsing. The Americans observed some enemy troops abandoning their positions and running into the sea to swim away. Nevertheless, the men of Company F laid down a fierce machine gun fire to halt the escape. The next morning the attack reopened with a hail of artillery and mortars. Cronk rallied his men to make another attempt at securing the bridge. After a tough fight, the bunkers were overcome and the remaining Japanese retreated into the ruins of the Mission.

This scenario is the first attempt to capture the bridge after E Company left the scene. The Americans will have 8 turns to meet their objective, which is to wipe out all the bunkers. The Japanese will be in 5 bunkers. Two will cover the spit and three will overlook the bridge. (See the map for placement of bunkers and other units.) Each bunker is considered an earthen one and will be manned by a Japanese squad with a Rate of Fire of 2, Morale 2, and Strength of 2 points. Each of these squads is armed with rifles and a light machine gun. Fire from the bunkers can be in the three positions; i.e., the front and flanks but not the rear. Should the Japanese remain in one bunker by turn 8, that player will win the game.

American Force
(1) U.S. Standard Rifle Company
(complete with mortars and medium machine guns)
        2 Flame thrower stands

Japanese Force
5 Infantry Squads in bunkers, no command stands
(1) 50mm "knee" mortar squad, Rate of Fire per gun 2

SCENARIO 5: THE BUNA HELL

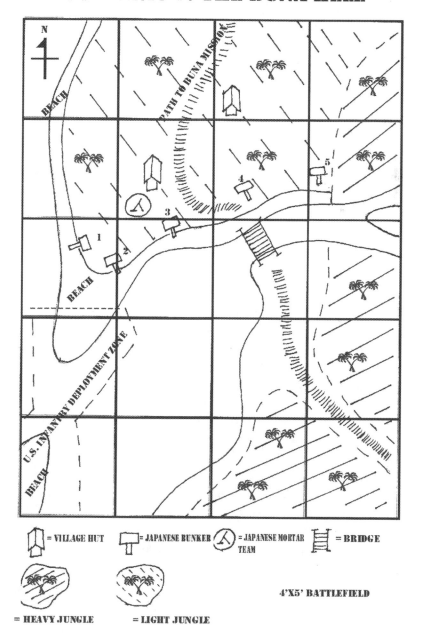

= VILLAGE HUT   = JAPANESE BUNKER   = JAPANESE MORTAR TEAM   = BRIDGE

= HEAVY JUNGLE   = LIGHT JUNGLE

4'X5' BATTLEFIELD

Scenario 6: Night Assault

The Marianas Campaign commenced on June 15, 1944, with the amphibious landings on Saipan. The fight was a bloody and difficult struggle. Nevertheless, the island was secured by the end of July. As the struggle for the island was coming to a close, preparations were being made for the invasion of Tinian, which lay only a few miles to the south. With landing sites on the island severely limited, the Marine and Naval command decided on a feint toward the well-defended port city of Tinian. However, the Marines actually landed on two very narrow beaches: White Beach 1 and White Beach 2. These beaches were located on the northern portion of the island. Unfortunately, they were so narrow that the U.S. Marines had to land in columns of companies, instead of the usual company abreast formation. White Beach 1 was only 60 yards wide and White Beach 2 was slightly bigger at 160 yards.

The landings started at approximately 0700 hours on the morning of July 24, following the customary pounding from air and naval ordnance in the days prior to the invasion. Also, from their position on Saipan, a battery of 155mm "Long Tom" guns fired smoke shells on Tinian's command post on Mount Lasso. This laid down a screen of smoke to protect the Marines at their most vulnerable moment. The preparatory bombardment smashed the shores defenses. The most important effect was that it crippled Japanese internal communications. This hampered Colonel Ogata's ability to lead and coordinate a successful night counterattack. The attacks ended up being clumsy and without proper timing for maximum effect. The Japanese response to the Marine landings was weak. They did not consider this sector open to assault because of the limited beaches. Therefore, the Marines made quick and relatively easy work of the few defenders and pillboxes. By nightfall, the troops of the 24th and 25th Marines had their beachhead secured. Its span was 3000 yards north to south with a penetration of 1500 yards into the island. They settled in by digging defensive positions and getting ready for the standard Japanese Banzai night attack.

One of the forward companies that took a direct hit from the Japanese attack was K Company of the 24th Marines. They set up their line in front of a gully, which later became the launch point for the defenders. Just after midnight on July 25, the enemy struck with a vengeance. With screaming and fixed bayonets, they came running into the defensive line. Many were cut down within seconds by the .30 caliber machine guns in the forward areas. Despite great valor, those posts were overrun. As repeated flares were shot into the sky to illuminate the battle, the Marines fought on and sometimes hand to hand. They also employed 37mm anti-tank guns loaded with buckshot to blast holes in the ranks of the Japanese. Some enemy troops managed to get into the rear of the defensive area and got within a few hundred yards of the beaches. Just before dawn, the attack collapsed and hundreds of dead Japanese lay about the defensive area.

In another part of the perimeter, the Marines faced an attack of a different sort. Coming up from the direction of Tinian Town at about 0330 hours were six Japanese tanks. They were supported by limited infantry when they roared into the Marine line. The Marines fought back with everything they had at their disposal. More bazooka teams came up from the rear, and they began blasting the tanks. With the only light coming from illumination rounds of the enemy, the Japanese tank drivers were having great difficulty maneuvering and fighting through the defenses. Eventually, the Leathernecks knocked out five of the six tanks. The sixth reportedly was driven off by an infuriated Marine in a jeep. However, there are some disputes as to whether there was a sixth tank.

The attacks that night were the largest launched by the Japanese defending Tinian. It is clear that the strategic failure of the Banzai charge seriously undermined the defense forces. There were to be other assaults and more bloody days before securing the island in August. But the Japanese could only manage small isolated attacks. The following morning 1,241 Japanese dead littered the ground. In addition, untold numbers of wounded were carried off by their comrades. On the other hand, the Marines suffered approximately 100 casualties.

I have purposely selected these battles for wargaming and have broken them up into two games. The first selection epitomizes the Japanese tactic of night assault. The other highlights the use of Japanese tanks. Most people generally do not think of the Japanese as having used their tanks in the South Pacific. There were a few, albeit minor, instances of their use in trying to repulse the American invaders. The action will take place under cover of darkness, which adds a +2 to the *to hit* roll and reduces vehicle movement by 3 inches. Each game will last 12 turns with the Japanese objective of breaking through the Marine defenses as laid out in the respective maps below. Breaking through is defined as getting behind the Marines and escaping into the rear. The Japanese player wins in *Infantry Night Assault* by getting 40% of his forces into the rear of the Marine player and off the board. Also, the Marine player can pick two secret prearranged artillery target points and it adds a +2 to the HE die roll. For the *Tank Night Assault*, 3 Japanese tanks must exit the board. Of course, the American player wins by preventing these events.

Infantry Night Assault

US Marines
1 Company (complete with mortars and medium machine guns)
1 (2) gun battery of 105mm Howitzers—(off board, Rate of Fire 4)

Japanese
3 Companies (without mortar or medium machine gun support)

SCENARIO 6: INFANTRY NIGHT ASSAULT

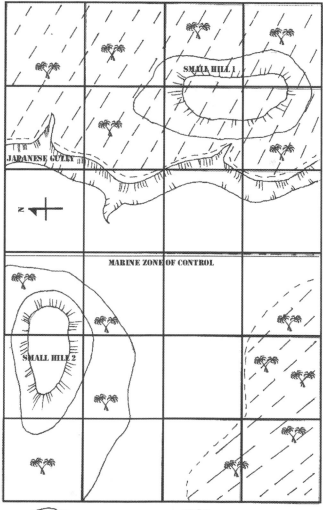

SMALL HILL 1

JAPANESE GULLY

N

MARINE ZONE OF CONTROL

SMALL HILL 2

4'X6'
BATTLEFIELD   = HEAVY JUNGLE   = MEDIUM JUNGLE

(NOT SHADED AREAS ARE CONSIDERED LIGHT WOOD OR SHRUB)
JAPANESE DEPLOY IN GULLY AND EAST OF IT.

Tank Night Assault

Marines

(1) –1944 Company (complete with mortars and medium machine guns and six bazooka teams). One infantry platoon will occupy Hill 2, while the other platoon takes up positions

"West" of the road in the heavy jungle. The remaining platoon and support units can be set up anywhere in the Marine's zone of control.

(1) 37mm anti-tank gun, Rate of Fire 2

Japanese

6 Type 97 Chi Ha tanks

2 Platoons of infantry with command stands and 1 Co. HQ stand (without mortar or medium machine gun support)

SCENARIO 6: TANK NIGHT ASSAULT

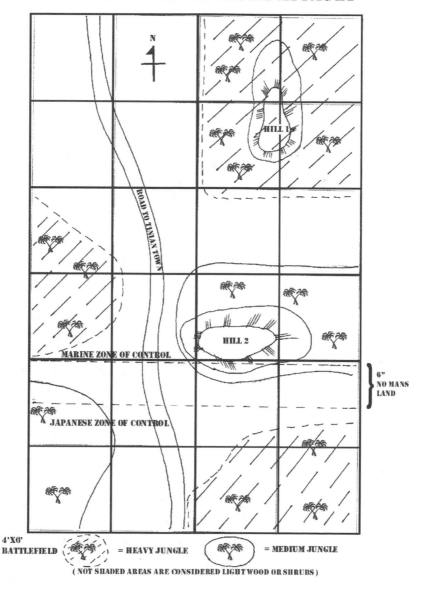

N

HILL 1

ROAD TO TINIAN TOWN

HILL 2

MARINE ZONE OF CONTROL

6"
NO MANS
LAND

JAPANESE ZONE OF CONTROL

4'X6'
BATTLEFIELD = HEAVY JUNGLE = MEDIUM JUNGLE

(NOT SHADED AREAS ARE CONSIDERED LIGHT WOOD OR SHRUBS)

Scenario 7: Hill of a Battle

As the British were fighting for national survival at the start of World War Two, the CBI Theater (China, Burma, and India) took a back seat to the events in Europe. The main interest to the British was keeping India from falling into the hands of the Japanese. The Americans, though uneasy about supporting Britain's colonial interests, needed the partnership to keep China in the war, via the airlifts from India. Despite China's lack of mechanized strength to resist Japanese armies, she had troops that could tie up tens of thousands of Japanese forces that would otherwise be sent to the Pacific. Japan turned her attention to Burma in March 1942 to capture much needed raw materials. The nation's collapse was just one more domino in a series of Imperial Japanese victories. With Burma in Japanese hands, this closed the famed Burma Road, the last land route to re-supply China.

The Allies had few available troops to cover such a vast area of terrain, let alone drive out the enemy. The commander of the CBI Theater was American General Joseph Stilwell. He did manage, by mid-war, to develop and employ some irregular forces to raid and harass the Japanese holding Burma. Among these were the local Kachins, British Chindits, Gurkhas, Chinese, and the American 5307th Composite Unit. It was not until early January 1944 that the Allies launched a grand offensive aimed at striking deep into Burma, with one of its main goals being to take the airfield at Myitkyina, which would take pressure off the American supply flights up and over the Himalayas to China. Merrill's Marauders, the nickname given to the 5307th after General Frank Merrill, led the way over some of the most treacherous jungle in the world. Standing in his way was Japanese General Shinichi Tanaka leading the 18th Japanese Division. The Second Battalion of the 5307th was ordered to occupy Nhpum Ga, a small hill on a rocky ridge south of the Hsamshingyang airstrip. The Battalion's mission was to shield the airstrip and prevent Japanese movements west of the Tanai River. Getting there was not easy. The Japanese detected their movements and stated pursing the Marauders as they made it to their objective,

Nhpum Ga. Although exhausted, the men dug prepared positions and waited for an attack. At 1400 hours, on the afternoon of March 28, 1944, the shelling started, followed by a Japanese infantry assault. This would be the first of many to be repulsed. It was on March 31 that conditions took a turn for the worse. The Japanese surrounded the hill and launched a multidirectional attack. This stretched the defenders ever thinner. On the north end of the hill, two platoons had the responsibility of holding the hills' only access to water. Unfortunately, they could not hold out and the water source was lost against overwhelming numbers and mortar fire. The Marauders held their position for 11 days before 3rd Battalion, 5307 relieved them. They had seen the "gates of hell," but resting was not an option. The mission to take Myitkyina was paramount and General Merrill ordered them to move on. It was not until that August that they claimed their objective.

The map below shows the start positions for each side in the scenario. The time set for the Japanese to take the water hole is 6 turns. The defenders simply must hold the Japanese off for the prescribed time.

Japanese Force—use Type A without ATR teams
2 Infantry companies with their 2 inch mortars

Merrill's Marauders—see U.S. Standard Rifle Company
2 Infantry platoons
2 Medium machine gun teams
(1) 60 mm mortar, Rate of Fire 3

SCENARIO 7: HILL OF BATTLE

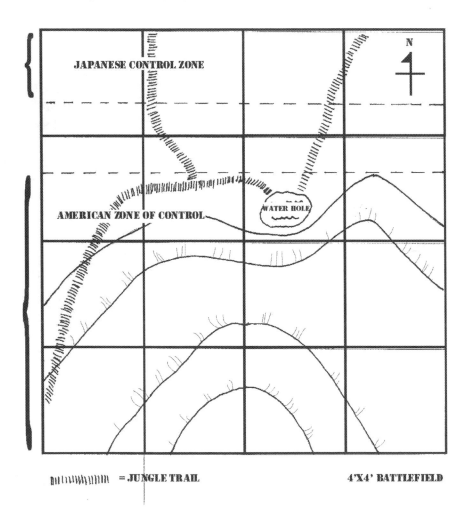

JAPANESE CONTROL ZONE

N

AMERICAN ZONE OF CONTROL

WATER HOLE

|||||||||||||||| = JUNGLE TRAIL

4'X4' BATTLEFIELD

ALL TERRAIN IS CLASSIFIED AS LIGHT JUNGLE

Scenario 8: Rescue at Korsun

Following the disasters at Stalingrad and Kursk, the Germans founds themselves struggling to preserve a defensive line against the Soviets. It was during the Russian winter offensive of 1943–1944 that the German defenses collapsed on the middle Dnepr River. One group that did manage to hang on was part of the German 8th Army. This consisted of the 57th, 88th, and 389th Infantry Divisions and the 5th SS Panzer Division, along with other severely weakened units. This created a salient in the Russian line on the western bank of the river. These units were far from full strength and their continued resistance was only a matter of time. But they were led by a very capable commander, General Wihelm Stemmerman, who would later be killed in this action. His superior, Field Marshal Erich Von Manstein, had made repeated requests to Hitler to withdraw the troops to another defense line. Hitler refused any such action. Instead, he believed that he could use the salient to spring a trap on the Russians. Thus, he ordered the troops to hold. The Russians, seeing the German bulge in their lines, sensed an opportunity to trap and destroy a large number of enemy soldiers. Generals Ivan Konev and Nikolai Vatutin, commanders of the 1st and 2nd Ukrianian Front forces, respectively, attacked the pocket from the north and south in an attempt to close the gap. On January 28, 1944, they achieved their objective and the two forces linked up at Zvenigorodka. They trapped some 57,000 troops in what became known as the Korsun Pocket.

Not wanting to repeat another horrific event like Stalingrad, the Germans launched a counteroffensive on February 4. The goal was to open a path to their trapped comrades and allow them enough time to escape. Several infantry and panzer divisions struck out east to probe the Russian line for weakness. Unfortunately, an early spring thaw had disrupted their efforts in making good progress because the roads turned to mud. But, the 16th and 17th Panzer Divisions were able to push the Russians across the Gniloy Tikich River, on the west side of the besieged group. By February 12, the relieving force was within a dozen miles of the pocket. Nevertheless, the 16th Panzer Division came to a halt on the road toward Medvin; this essentially marked the high-water mark for the counterattack.

Seeing his situation worsen, General Stemmerman ordered the pocket pulled back to the southwest and he made plans for his own breakout. Regrettably to his troops, he was killed on February 15. His command passed to General Theobald Lieb, who organized the remaining aspects of the breakout. Hill 239 became critical for the escape, as a rally point and a place to provide cover for the withdrawing forces. Thinking it was in friendly hands, the trapped troops were ordered by Manstein to make an early morning assault toward the hill to force a linkup. Upon learning that Russian T34 tanks defended the position, Major Kaestner made a fateful decision to carry out the attack and make a break for it. The Germans succeeded and by the end of February 16, they had successfully breached the Russian line and were able to extract nearly 35,000 men from the grip of the enemy.

Though there are some very interesting ideas to base a game on from this story, I decided to create a scenario based on the 16th Panzer Division trying to break through near Medvin. The map below lays out the Russian and German positions. The terrain will be snow-covered and the road will be mired in mud. The snow/mud movement modifier for infantry is a deduction of 2 inches and vehicles will suffer a 3-inch reduction. The objective for the Germans is to annihilate the Russians before they can withdraw toward the town, which is the far end of the board. The Russians must hold their ground for 8 turns before attempting to withdraw. If they can defeat the Germans without a withdrawal it will be a decisive victory. The withdrawal means a tactical victory. If the Germans can smash the Russians prior to turn 8, they open a channel to the pocket and the German player will win the game.

Russian Force
(2) 76mm anti-tank guns, Rate of Fire 1
1 Truck
1 Company of infantry
3 T34/85s
1 Battalion Mortar Section, Rate of Fire 4

German Force
3 Panther Gs
2 Tiger Is
(5) 251 Half-tracks
(1) 250 Command Half-track
(5) Infantry squads, (1) Platoon Leader Stand, (2) Anti-tank teams

SCENARIO 8: RESCUE AT KORSUN

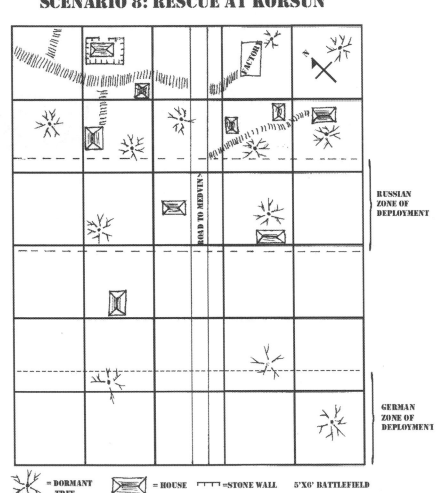

RUSSIAN
ZONE OF
DEPLOYMENT

GERMAN
ZONE OF
DEPLOYMENT

= DORMANT
TREE
= HOUSE
=STONE WALL
5'X6' BATTLEFIELD

Scenario 9: In Defense of Bailey

After breaking out of the Normandy beaches, the Allies succeeded in driving back the Germans. By August, however, it became apparent that the supply situation was a problem, complicating further advancement against the enemy. In addition, Generals George Patton and Bernard Montgomery were competing for top billing to lead the next great campaign. General Dwight Eisenhower had studied each commander's plan, but he also found himself under political pressure to use his vast airborne forces under his command. Appealing to this, Montgomery revised his proposal. He offered to seize the bridges north through Holland and over the Rhine with Allied airborne troops. He would then send ground forces to link up with the paratroopers with the goal of outflanking the Germans and crossing into Germany from the north over the Rhine River. Eisenhower accepted the plan both for its audacity and the prospect to render Antwerp as a badly needed supply point for the continued war effort.

Montgomery's plan, Operation Market Garden, called for delivering 30,000 paratroopers, the largest airborne drop in history. The American 101st would take the bridges at Eindhoven and Veghel. The 82nd would capture the bridges at Grave and Nijmegen. The British 1st Airborne would seize the prized bridge at Arnhem. The ground troops were to blaze a path connecting these bridges with the soldiers of the British 2nd Army, which was spearheaded by 30 Corps. It was thought by Allied High Command, because of the weaken state of the German army in the area, that the operation could be pulled off in four days. Alas, the Germans were not as beaten and demoralized as anticipated. General Gerd von Rundstedt had stopped the retreat of the 15th Army and begun preparing them for battle by September. Unbeknownst to the Allies, the Germans expected Patton to lead the strike against them in southern France. Thus, the 9th and 10th SS Panzer Divisions opposing Patton were transferred to Arnhem for rest and retrofit to gain strength to meet that predicted challenge.

The offensive started on Sunday, September 17, with airborne forces landing in daylight to reduce the risk of undue dispersion. Most of the initial landings went well. The 101st captured the small bridge at Veghel, but the one at Eindhoven was blown up by the local German commander on the scene. The 82nd quickly nabbed the bridge at Grave, but the unit was involved in a tough fight for the bridge at Nijmegen. The British 1st landed successfully on the far side of the Arnhem Bridge, thus placing the Rhine River between them and 30 Corps, with the Germans holding the South bank. The armored ground attack met strong initial resistance from dug-in anti-tank guns, costing them valuable time and numerous tanks. They continued to advance north to link up with the 101st. With the bridge at Eindhoven lying in ruins, the Royal Engineers were called up to build a Bailey bridge, again costing more time. While this was happening, the Germans were gathering strength and starting to strike at the allied paratroopers in all their landing areas. Most perilous were the attacks against the British 1st Airborne. Their communications were in shambles and the Germans were leading assaults across the Arnhem Bridge, while other German units were moving in to surround them from the North. Already 36 hours behind schedule, 30 Corps began crossing the Bailey bridge to unite with the 82nd and capture the bridge at Nijmegen. But the Germans held the north end and the 82nd had to wait for boats to cross the river. Delaying their arrival was a traffic jam on the lone route to the river. With more time slipping away and German attacks increasing throughout the allied captured areas, the 82nd made a daylight crossing. Twenty-six boats filled with brave men crossed the river with the armor of 30 Corps providing cover fire. They captured the bridge on day 4 of the operation. As the Allies tried to push forward, continued attacks in their rear halted their advance just north of Nijmegen. The trailing British infantry had to secure the route's flanks in order to permit a continued push. On day 6, the Germans were able to cut the route between Veghel and Grave. This sealed the fate of the British in Arnhem and British Command decided to go over to the defensive and extract out the trapped paratroopers. By day 9, the offensive was over. Of the 10,000 troops dropped at Arnhem, only 2000 escaped. The objective failed.

In one of the rear attacks, a small force of German infantry and Panther tanks emerged and began shelling the Bailey bridge at Eindhoven. This caught the American paratroopers completely by surprise. They were able to successfully defend their position because several anti-tank guns had recently arrived and had been deployed. It was attacks like this that halted the advance to Arnhem, which is the basis of this scenario. The objective of the German force is to score 8 hits on the bridge to destroy it. This will result in a German victory. The Americans must prevent this by knocking out the Panthers. The recommended model bridge is one of the sections from the Airfix Assault Bridge set. The game will last 10 turns. The Germans will advance starting from point A on the map. The other initial starting points are denoted on the map below.

American Force
1 Paratrooper company 1944 (each mortar squad will have a Rate of Fire of 2)
1 Medium machine gun section
3 British 76mm (17 pdrs.) anti-tank guns, Rate of Fire 1
1 Sherman Firefly

German Force
4 Panther Gs
3 251s
3 German infantry squads
1 Panzerfaust team
1 HQ Team, kubelwagon

SCENARIO 9: IN DEFENSE OF BAILEY

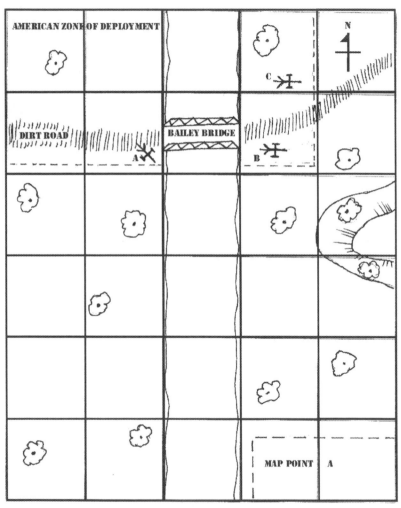

MAP POINT (A) GERMANS ENTER ON THIS SECTION OF THE BOARD

 = TREE   A, B, C, = ANTITANK PLACEMENT   5'X6' BATTLEFIELD

Scenario 10: General Scenario Creation

Whether it is due to lack of time to research a scenario or simply just wanting to put something together for a friendly wargame, it is important to have a few key factors in mind when creating your own game. Time period, terrain, and length of game are all crucial to forming a well-planned event. It is certainly universal that all gamers enjoy a good tabletop fight to discuss for years to come.

The most critical aspect is the time period. In the case of World War Two, players must decide on whether the game will be early, mid, or late war. This may seem obvious, but it is important to have a grasp on when certain equipment was used and phased out. In addition, most armies changed their tactical unit organizations in terms of infantry and armor formations. For instance, the U.S. Marine Corps changed its unit organization in late 1942 and incorporated more firepower as a result of the Tarawa experience. Also, it might be tempting to include a unit of German Wespe self-propelled guns in a North Africa battle. However, these guns were never issued to the troops in that theater of conflict, despite the good box art on the Matchbox tank model. A quick Internet search might reveal a few facts to assist in the planning of a game.

The next area to ponder is the plausible terrain to be encountered between combatants and its affect on the scenario. The general rule is that including more terrain will lengthen the game. It simply takes longer to negotiate hills and wooded areas than the open expanses of the "Libyan Desert," for a game featuring the famed 8th Army. If the intention of the game is going to be a contest fought in a dense forest or built-up town centers, the players should also think about the size of the board and the placement of the units. For example, a jungle scenario, with Gurkhas and Japanese slugging it out in the forests of Burma, could potentially limit movement by 50%. If the game board is six feet long, it could take nine turns just to reach the center of the battlefield. It may make sense to have the units well advanced on the board to get to combat within two to four turns. Conversely, if the scenario allows for good visibility, it is a good idea to give the units as much room as possible to maneuver. Once, while testing some wargame ideas, I created a small scenario and violated this basic idea. I wanted to see how a platoon of 5 Sherman tanks with some armored and unarmored infantry support would fare against a German 75mm anti-tank gun and a Panzer IVh. These German units were supported by a reinforced infantry platoon. It was a disaster for the Americans. The board was 3 ft. by 3 ft. and my opponent had nearly no room to maneuver. The mistake was thinking we would have a small game because we had limited time to play. We deployed our forces on a small table and gave it a try. The scenario was not matched to the needed terrain and frankly became a "near" waste of time. (Honestly, gaming with miniatures and getting a break from the general tasks of life can never be a waste of time!) The point here is to think in terms of the space, time, and scenario relationship beforehand so as to maximize the game experience.

Continuing on the subject of terrain, it is important to carefully review or take mental notes while reading about events of the Second World War. Many authors will describe a particular battle with good detail about the landscape and fighting conditions. Painting a mental picture of the battle and its topographical components is a great way to assemble the terrain and possibly the mood of the combatants. The same can also be gleamed from watching documentaries. Again, such things may seem natural to a wargamer, but it is easy to overlook simple things like stone walls, hedgerows, sparse vegetation, or small ravines. Practicing this method of observation will speed up the game setup and help create a level of realism.

Something that can be very helpful in the day or two prior to the game is to draw up a quick map of the proposed battlefield. The player should think of the scenario and ask himself a few generic questions. Where and when will this fight take place? Is it summer, winter, or sometime in between? Will there be roads or trails? Is there to be an urban area or is it to be fought on farmland? How much vegetation should there be? Asking these questions allows for a little forethought and makes the game far more interesting. It helps to keep games different each time they are put together and the players will have a much more enjoyable time.

The creation of terrain for a game can take a couple of different forms. There are numerous terrain features that can be purchased from a local hobby store or found online from Internet retailers. Fortunately, there are some things that are easy and inexpensive to make. A friend of mine has made several board coverings from locally purchased canvas, and he has painted them in desert tan and medium green. Both are painted with different colored blotches to break up the overall color. He has done the same thing to sheets of Styrofoam to form hills after he has cut away the right angles. Another friend has created his trees using large nails driven up through nicely cut and colored pieces of thick poster board with a chunk of lichen placed on them to create the canopy of the tree. Naturally, the ongoing joke is never lean over too far on his game board or you risk becoming impaled on the trees! Roads, rivers, and firing positions can be cut from sheets of felt purchased from arts and crafts shops. These are just a few ideas to think about when developing terrain pieces inexpensively when on a tight budget.

Turning to the actual game itself and the scenario, it will always be important to think about the desired battle. Similar to the design of the battlefield layout, asking a few questions is always useful. Will the game be a meeting engagement of two forces? Will the units be mobile or immobile? Is the game going to be a tactical exercise or is it going to test an idea or method of attack? These few questions can help the players think through the battle to enhance the quality of the game itself. Nothing is more frustrating than just lining up two forces to oppose each other with no thought as to what the battle is suppose to represent. One great resource for getting ideas is to review back issues of old wargame magazines, such as *Wargamer's Digest*. There are several websites that sell used copies. In them the authors usually put together wonderful historical fiction scenarios that revolve around tactical problems. After reading over a few of these, a player can use them to create similar games. These scenarios can be great fun because the mixture of weapon systems is usually proportionate for the game being played and allows the players to use their critical thinking skills to achieve a victory. The ideas I put forth in the Solo Wargaming chapter (Chapter 7) can be used here as well. As I mentioned, idea testing is a great way to build up experience with rules or sharpen the mind for larger games at conventions or local club games. It is definitely worthwhile to game modern tactics in these ad hoc small scenarios for a quick Saturday evening battle.

Next, many times after a game has been set up the players often find themselves without a "game master" or referee. That person can assist in acknowledging where certain forces might be hidden, so the two sides are equally unsure of the exact forces each other face in the game. One way to overcome this is to have some variability in what those forces can be. The players can number six separate forces with missions designed for a battle group. In secret, they roll a 6-sided die. The number rolled, matched with the force number, becomes the battle group used. This way there is some mystery as to what each other will face once the battle starts. Another easy way to hide forces is to have the defending side place index cards face down with information about what is on the table at that spot or leave them blank. It is the job of the aggressor to probe the defenses. Either way, the goal is to provide a level of uncertainty that a real battle would entail.

In addition to all these elements of game design, it is always important to plan out the number of turns it will take to finish a game with the given scenario. Remember, the more terrain features and units used the longer the game will take. The best way to analyze it is to think about the number of turns it takes the infantry or AFVs to reach combat with enemy units and how many firefight exchanges could be reasonably expected. These two factors should give a player a good idea of how long a game should last. Then think about the type of mission involved. This may add or deduct turns from play. For example, if one of the players is going to be probing an unknown enemy force, then it is sensible that he may move somewhat cautiously. Therefore, a few more turns added may be acceptable. However, adding too many turns may produce a sluggish approach that is not realistic and put the defending player at a disadvantage. The point here is to achieve a time-balanced game.

I hope these historical game scenarios and the discussion on creating a historical fiction game will spur some exciting wargames. My intention was to provide a broad scope of games to play, which cover most of the interesting theaters of war. Certainly, there are countless scenarios that can be played and many wargaming books have been published on just World War Two simulated battles. I encourage wargamers to read different subjects on the war to expand their breadth of knowledge. I have always enjoyed selecting a topic and spending several months digging into the details. Also, I recommend having a notebook handy to write out a few thoughts for some interesting battles. Of course, this helps in creating reasonably accurate scenarios for a later time. Last, if some players decide to alter the forces in the first nine scenarios, I would advise keeping the above topics in number 10: General Scenario Creation in mind. Those games were designed with a particular balance between objectives and game time duration.

CHAPTER 9

Tactics and Theaters of World War Two

This chapter will deal with different tactics used in the course of the war for both tanks and infantry. For the most part, the explanations are general in nature, but this should not limit the impact it can have on a seasoned wargamer. It would be beyond the scope of this book to get into great detail about the tactical deployment and formations used prior to the combat phase. What I am concerned with here is presenting a wargamer's tactical view as he starts his "combat" at the edge of the game table. I will attempt to explain some basic tactical doctrines used by the belligerents and make the players familiar enough with them to incorporate these tactics into their games. Also, following each tactical discussion, I will offer up recommendations in what I term *Wargame Implications* to aid a player in formulating his own historical, but simulated, battles and help the gamer visualize using these methods on the board.

Blitzkrieg

The most likely place to start with tactics in the war is with the tank. At the beginning of the war, many of the leading national army commanders were stuck in the experience of World War One. At that time, the tank was seen as an infantry support weapon. The main battle tactics for employing tanks in that war were two-fold. The first wave of armor would advance without infantry to flatten barbed wire and fill ditches with fascines, which was a bundle of wood tied to the top of a tank. The second wave would follow up with infantry to breach the enemy's fortifications. The attacks were shallow in nature with few instances of deeper penetration. The limiting factors for the First World War generation were poor mechanics and communications. The first tanks were plagued with breakdowns due to tough terrain, battle conditions, and a limited national industrial capacity to produce superior components. Also, tactics of the day were constrained by a lack of radios and the general inability to communicate between other tanks and support elements. It was not until late in the war that any thought was given to deep penetration tactics. With the advent of lighter tanks with better speed like the French FT-17, the idea of sending them forward on the flanks to get into the enemy's communication zone while heavier tanks and infantry assaulted the front were only just being considered in what was known as Plan 1919 created by British Colonel J.F.C. Fuller. However, the war came to an end and the idea died.

After the war, the British and French continued tank development, but the pace was slow. With the idea still prevalent about tanks supporting infantry, the British focused on armor protection and less on firepower and to a similar extent so too did the French. This is not to say the British did not influence the progress of armored warfare. It is quite the contrary. Basil Liddell-Hart wrote extensively on the subject and to a degree persuaded some international military professionals on the new age of mobile warfare. Regrettably, many of his ideas fell on deaf ears, especially in Britain and France. The Russians and Germans began thinking in terms of tanks fighting tanks and thought of firepower and mobility as paramount to armored warfare. But it was the Germans under the leadership and foresight of Heinz Guderian that brought forth the best ideas to capitalize on the tank's mobility. He was particularly keen on the thoughts of Liddell-Hart. Guderian created the Panzertruppe, which later became the Panzer Division. These divisions would contain not only tanks but motorized infantry, artillery, engineers, and administrative units. They were also linked by radios. This alone made a dramatic difference when the war began. Communication was easily spread to the rear about enemy movements and strong points. It also enhanced tank-to-tank fighting abilities. Tank commanders could easily pass vital information about enemy actions. This was something that was lacking in the other nations at the time the war started.

Guderian's Blitzkrieg model emphasized two tactical points. First, once the Panzer Divisions could break through the enemy line, they would cause mass confusion by destroying supply and communication lines. This would keep the enemy off balance and force him to retreat and to reestablish his frontline. At the point of attack, massed tank formations would punch a hole in the enemy's defenses and continue into the enemy's rear while mechanized infantry units fought to secure the hole until regular ground forces relieved them to catch up with their Panzer units. He also understood that while deep in the enemy's territory it would be difficult for the enemy to concentrate against the Panzer Divisions. This would cause the enemy to fight in piecemeal operations, which would be easier to destroy. Second, when an enemy tank force had to be engaged, reconnaissance units would seek and locate weak spots that would permit an armored strike in the enemy's rear. Once the force was in the enemy's rear, an anti-tank gun screen would be set up in the enemy's path, resulting in a devastating blow to the enemy's armor. These tactics were carried out from the top down; i.e., from the division to the company level.

The Blitzkrieg success was not solely the domain of the ground forces. Many times the ground forces would outpace their artillery unit's ability to stop and deploy their guns. Therefore, the role of support fell to the dive bomber. The Stuka JU87 could deliver accurate ordnance to the needed spot to eliminate enemy obstacles or positions. This ability also ties back to the Panzer Division's excellent communication networks to request such assistance. The other help from the sky came in the form of paratroopers. Learning from other nations, the Germans led the way in the creation of an airborne troop force and they were the first to incorporate them into attack plans. Their role was to capture and seize key positions well in advance of the panzer formations. The best known example of this is the Battle of Eben Emael. The Germans sent glider troops to capture the fortress and pave the way for advancing German columns to strike the Low Countries and France.

It is interesting to note that not all the initial offensive actions by the German were as the propaganda portrayed. The Polish campaign was indeed short, but it did have some difficult fighting. The Germans invaded with 2200 tanks against the Polish 660, which were spread out to cover their vast frontier. They learned some valuable lessons in the Polish invasion. In the struggle to subdue Warsaw, there were several incidents in which the Germans took heavy casualties. The 4th Panzer Division lost half of its 120 tanks fighting in the suburbs. In one instance, a line of Polish anti-tank guns and a few 7TP tanks knocked out or immobilized 40 panzers. These combat actions struck home the idea that using tanks in cities was a terrible venture. It channeled and restricted the tank's ability to maneuver and outflank the enemy. Moreover, infantry were called for to neutralize anti-tank gun positions and other obstacles. Tanks fighting anti-tank guns proved to be more difficult than first thought. Tank commanders riding in a buttoned up turret had difficulty identifying the anti-tank gun's location. Hence, more troops were needed to provide a screen to the leading elements of the Panzer Division; this led to increases of motorized infantry. Very little of this information was disseminated past the German High Command, for there were few foreign observers in positions to influence the Allies.

As the war progressed and the Allied Nations did recover from their initial defeats, they began applying the lessons inflicted upon them by the Germans. By the latter half of 1942, the Russians and the British had gained substantial victories at Stalingrad and El Alamein, marking the high tide of the German Third Reich. Within a year of those battles, air superiority had virtually passed to the Allies and placed them squarely in control of using Blitzkrieg tactics against their tormentors, though without the same effect. The Germans subsequently revealed that they were also masters of defense and not so easily beaten. It was only sheer numbers and fighting enemies on two fronts that doomed Germany's effort to achieve final victory.

Wargame Implications

When making up a battle scenario involving a Blitzkrieg, it is important to provide the German forces with a solid balance between armor, infantry, reconnaissance, artillery, and potential air support. It is unlikely that any player would create a full-scale battle in the style of the Blitzkrieg. But small, company-sized actions present attractive battles to have on the war board. Thus, when drawing up a battle for a company and a few platoons of tanks, it is essential to attach to the Panzergruppe some motorized infantry. This can be on a ratio of (2) 251 half-tracks with grenadiers to 3 or 4 tanks. Also, some element of reconnaissance must be involved. This can be as simple as adding a 222 armored car or a few motorcycle troops. Finally, the group will need to have indirect fire support. It can take the form of off-board artillery, mortars, or a Stuka dive bomber. Nevertheless, whatever is decided upon, the Rate of Fire should be robust, for indirect fire support was always critical to the success of the Blitzkrieg.

The enemy units in the early period of the war should not be given the same considerations. Polish and French armored units should, for the most part, act alone or be in direct support of an infantry line. It would be reasonable in a wargame to have two or three tanks supporting an infantry company but without any fire support such as artillery. In addition, motorized infantry should act without tank support. The same can be said for the British and the Russians during their first experiences of the conflict. The British would, however, by 1941, in the Desert War, start to immolate their adversary. The Russians would have to wait until late 1942 to start adopting changes. It is absolutely critical to remember that in the early days of the war the Allies had few radios to go around and getting fire support and reinforcements would be a challenge to say the least. Last, Allied tank assaults should enter the game in staggered turns. This will help simulate the piecemeal approach to how tanks were used.

Advance and Breach

Staying within the scope of wargaming and what can be depicted on a game board, there are two tactical tank attacks to review. The first is the general armored advance past the Start Line, where enemy resistance is expected but not fully known. The other is the breach of a known enemy position, where resistance is expected to be difficult.

Once the strike force has crossed the start line, preparatory artillery was typically called in. The purpose of the artillery barrage was to hit suspected enemy anti-tank gun positions or logical infantry positions across the line of initial advance. It was also usual for the enemy to return fire to try and disrupt the attack before it could gather strength and hit the defenses. The strike force would generally have armored reconnaissance troops or light tanks out in front, followed by medium tanks advancing in depth. To the rear and acting in direct support would be other tanks capable of firing high explosive shells at targets of opportunity that either revealed themselves by firing or were observed by recon elements; these were known as the overwatch team. The Russians and Germans were known to use self-propelled guns for this role. If the targets became elusive or the mission called for it, smoke rounds would be fired to confuse the enemy and provide cover for the attackers. It should be noted that once the attack started to receive direct fire, the tank commanders would drop down in their turrets. This would greatly reduce their vision and give further credence to the overwatch tanks covering from the flank or rear. Hence their reliance on the radio networks became absolutely necessary, and it is amazing in hindsight that not all tanks in all nations contained radio equipment as a must at the start of the war.

If the defender was reasonably prepared, he would stagger his forces in mutually supporting positions and place them in layers of defense. Anti-tank guns would be concealed and withhold fire as long as possible to score a kill. Defensive tanks or self-propelled guns would move from position to position as much as possible to deceive the enemy into thinking a greater presence of resistance existed. Sometimes the defending force had a reserve of tanks and infantry to either plug a gap or swing to a flank to destabilize the attacker's momentum and hopefully precipitate a withdrawal.

From 1943 on, the Germans many times found themselves on the defensive and could only hope to cause a delay in the advance of their opponent. By using tanks and/or self-propelled guns to put up some opposition and perhaps knock out an enemy unit or tank, the German crew would pull out quickly and advance to the next position. They obviously wanted to be gone before a sortie of fighter bombers swooped down and made them a part of the permanent landscape. This tactic would cause great delays in the Allied advances and spread caution among junior tank commanders. Once the obstacle was fully recognized, the tanks and armored infantry travelling in depth would maneuver to the flank of the enemy. Still operating from a position of support, the rear tanks and artillery would then lay down a base of fire for the maneuvering troops and tanks. The infantry typically would dismount in order to probe ahead looking for enemy infantry, anti-tank teams, or anti-tank guns concealed in the terrain. Once something was uncovered or suspected, the armored units would blast away. This was usually enough to dislodge the defender and get him to retreat. However, this is where defense in depth played an important role. The fleeing unit was typically playing leapfrog with another friendly unit. The other unit would provide supporting fire for his withdrawing comrade, causing the attacker to repeat the process. This type of action could grind down the assault and cause a considerable delay in the enemy's overall advance.

Sometimes these delaying tactics were a part of a greater defensive plan or they were simply the remains of a retreating army trying to escape with their lives. If the latter was the case, the attacker sooner or later scored his breakthrough and would pursue his foe until an established defensive line was erected. In the former, the attacker just might hit that defensive line sooner.

In either case, he was going to have to breach a barrier. Those lines could be manmade, like the Siegfried Line, or divinely created, like the Rhine River. Thankfully, most of them were not so daunting. The usual line was established across a small river, a set of ridges, or a lengthy hedgerow. The manmade obstacles might be a minefield or system of trenches. Of course the breach of a defensive line does not have to come on the heels of a routed enemy; it might be the start to a grand campaign.

Smashing a defensive line was not usually done in haste. Some deliberate planning was an absolute necessity. Recon forces would be sent forward to probe the line to look for weak spots and register targets for artillery or fighter bomber aircraft. The planners would compile that information and present it to local field officers. Infantry, artillery, armored, and aircraft commanders would share notes and work out timelines and unit movements until the last minute when the battlefield erupted into a fiery of punishing violence.

After the opening volleys, the attacking units would step off the demarcation line. The infantry, with the support of some tanks, would begin the drive forward. The job of the infantry was to create holes in the defenses of the enemy, while the supporting tanks laid down direct covering fire. The hole could be created by sapper units cutting wire or blasting gaps in a minefield. Occasionally, tanks fitted with flails or heavy rollers were dispatched to open channels in a minefield. As this work was being done, smoke rounds would be used to create a smokescreen to cover the breaching infantry. Also, working to the flanks would be armored infantry and tanks hoping to pierce a weak spot indentified by the reconnaissance teams. Assuming the main attack force breached and secured a gap, tanks and armored infantry followed in depth and attempted to get to the rear of the enemy and begin to disrupt the enemy's lines of retreat. On occasion, the effort of the breach would be a feint to distract the enemy, while the real attack was being perpetrated on a flank. They too would have to breach a line in the same way as a feint or, if the enemy failed to recognize the threat, they were able to advance up the flank and throw the enemy off balance and force a retreat.

As in the case of the advance attack, the enemy was not likely sitting back ready to take one on the chin without putting up a fight. The idea of defense in depth still applied. The defending commander would have worked out his mutually supporting fields of fire, different covering positions to fall back to, and the best concealment the terrain could provide. His troops, tanks, and anti-tanks guns would be dug in and their positions prepared as much as possible to defy the blasts of artillery and mortar shells. He would lay out obstacles that would channel enemy infantry into machine gun kill zones. Finally, the commander would determine which units were available for a counterattack. Unfortunately, all these defensive measures took time. The less time at his disposal, the weaker his defense would be. This is why his knowledge of the terrain was critical to his success; the more he knew the faster he could deploy his men. He had to be able to select the best terrain that offered a good defensible position with routes of escape that could not easily be overtaken, should the enemy punch through his line. Also keenly important to the commander was his ability to keep a cool head and keep his subordinates calm under fire. If he showed a lack of confidence, his men would doubt his skills and be more likely to retreat without orders. Next, the frontline commander had to be able to predict his opponent's moves and place himself in the mind of his adversary and ask himself: "If I were to attack my position, how would I hit it?" If events appeared desperate, he would have to know when to withdraw. If he saw an opportunity, he would have to know when to issue the order to counterattack with his reserve. All these matters taken together, the defensive commander could create a formidable challenge to his opponent.

Wargame Implications

When wanting to wargame an advance type of attack, it is important to remember size, scope, and mission. The average wargame board can only hold so many units before it becomes an artillerist's dream. The usual wargame setup gives the attacker maybe 18 to 24 inches at one edge of the board to deploy his forces and perhaps 48 to 60 inches across. He will be lucky if he gets a length of 78 inches to penetrate from one end to the other. This is hardly enough room to launch an offensive in 15mm let alone 1/72 scale and still enjoy the dynamics of maneuver. In addition, the poor defender can hardly place his forces in any kind of good defensive depth. Therefore, I recommend for the advance type of attack to seek out a larger area to wargame on, such as a living room floor. The hope is to allow the attacker and defender ample room to move and challenge each other.

Assuming an adequate space has been found, let us suppose a hypothetical scenario. A force of British armored units has been ordered to clear the area of Germans outside the Normandy beaches. The British would need several components. First, a reconnaissance unit made up of a few jeeps or armored cars. Their objective would be to get out and reveal the enemy anti-tank guns. An overwatch team would be required to provide direct fire support from a commanding position that oversees the forward units. The mechanized or armored infantry would be needed to rapidly engage the discovered enemy's infantry positions. These troops may also need their own tank support. In addition to all these units, a maneuver element would be needed to exploit any hole opened by the infantry. They would also need to get into the flank of the enemy to force a withdrawal. Finally, the British would need some sort of indirect firepower either coming from off-board artillery, mortars, or air support. At a minimum, this force should consist of 12 tanks, 5 to 8 infantry half-tracks, and a couple of recon units, plus any other additional support units. This may seem small, but given the scope and mission of having to maneuver and possibly flank the enemy, the last thing needed is a traffic jam.

The player taking on the role of defender will need to think of defense in depth, as discussed above. This means taking advantage of all possible terrain features. The Germans might have 3 to 4 anti-tank guns with potentially one being an 88mm. All the guns would need to have their own tractor or truck for quick escape. The infantry element might only be a reduced company with a few support machine guns and a mortar team.

For their escape, the infantry could have a couple of Opel Blitz trucks. If the mission allows for a possible counterattack, then three Panther tanks would do nicely. The players will have to determine a mutually acceptable way for allowing the defensive player to hide his anti-tank guns. This would allow the attacker to use his recon teams properly and prevent the anti-tank guns from becoming artillery targets at the start of the first turn.

Last, from a tactical standpoint, the British player will have to remember to concentrate his fire at particular points and utilize smoke to screen his attack. This will help his infantry close the gap to the enemy with the objective to put as much machine gun fire on the anti-tank gun crews as possible. As they are knocked out, the accompanying tanks should advance deeper into enemy territory, performing leapfrog actions to cover each other's progress. This cannot be overstated. This action in wargaming allows the firing unit a better firing roll vs. moving and firing.

On the other hand, the German player will have to use concealment as a weapon. If properly sited, the infantry squads should be able to give cover fire for each anti-tank gun crew. When the enemy begins closing in, the troops should have covered escape routes to the rear. If all goes well, as they withdraw, the German player's forces should leave burning British tanks on the field. Further, if the Germans have indirect fire, smoke rounds will make excellent cover for the retreat.

The breach assault for wargaming is somewhat easier to play and it can take up less room than the advance. The attacker has pretty much the same equipment at his disposal. Additional equipment may be needed if the defender has placed mines in front or is situated behind a river. The main tactical point here is to get the attacking infantry to the enemy's position under direct tank support, to breach a hole in the line, and to allow the mechanized forces to punch through the hole to the enemy's rear.

In this case, let us assume the Russians are mounting a large offensive. As part of it, a Russian company with the support of a reinforced tank platoon lends its weight to the attack. For this type of attack, recon elements can be dispensed with. The opening phase should start with as much indirect HE and smoke shelling as possible to cover the initial wave of attack. The players will again have to work out the best way to conceal the defensive positions so that the attacker does not have an easy advantage. From a wargaming perspective, the attacker will have a very shallow front to start. It will be necessary to bring the infantry and tanks with engineers, if they are to be needed in the first turn of the game. The infantry and tanks will provide the fire support to cover the engineer's work. If there is room to have tanks or self-propelled guns in a position to cover the attack, then they should be in the overwatch role. If not, it may be wise to increase the initial tank strength to provide direct HE support. Here again, as the tanks and other units move forward, leapfrog firing becomes needed to increase the likelihood of scoring hits on the enemy. Once the breach is made, the attacker should start to roll the flanks of the hole to widen the gap. While that is occurring, the tanks will need to push into the rear, hopefully with the support of mechanized infantry. It will be very likely that the defender will have dispersed out his anti-tanks guns in depth to weaken any penetration. This is why the armored infantry play such a critical role. They must be close enough to the action to tackle anti-tank guns or infantry possessing anti-tank capabilities. If the breach is not a physical barrier, it will be important to pick a point of concentration for the attackers to capture. From that point, once secured, the attacking player will have to rush his mechanized forces through the hole. The point here is not to treat this type of action as an infantry attack with the support of a few tanks and set off on a broad front thus thinning out the attacking troops. Doing so will only weaken the attack and give the defender the advantage of selecting the best targets to slow down the assault.

As in the advance attack, the defender will need a plan that incorporates depth. This can mean placing units in a staggered formation on the field of play. However, for wargaming it is necessary to have enough firepower forward to slow the opponent's ability to claim a foothold on the board. Also, the mobile reserve should not be placed too far back. It should be within two or three movement turns of getting into action. These simple steps can help ensure the defender does not get overwhelmed at the start of the game and can have a fighting chance at winning.

Infantry Attack Basics

Unlike the differing strategic thoughts on armored warfare, the major nations that entered the war held similar ideas about infantry combat tactics, at least at the company and squad level. They also shared similar ideas on mechanized infantry. This is not to say fire and maneuver were the same, but the makeup of fire and support were similar enough to classify them in one section for wargaming.

World War Two infantry tactics stressed boldness, skill, and quick action. The troops on the line worked closely with their supporting arms, similar to that of their armored comrades. Reconnaissance teams, artillery, air support, and mortars all had a role to play in the success of an infantry attack. The recon teams helped the infantry commanders locate weaknesses and avenues of approach, which could conceal the infantry's movement to its jump off point. In that instance, the infantry needed to be brought up as close as possible to the enemy without being spotted before leaving their transports behind. Oftentimes, starting points were within the enemy's line. Penetrating enemy positions before the assault began was done to create confusion in the enemy's rear and generate the illusion that the attacking force was larger than it was. Further, at the company level this is where the support weapons started to get into position. The battalion or company-level mortars might start to deploy along with the medium machine gun sections. Much depended on the mission and the proximity to the enemy. It was not unheard of for heavy weapons platoons to have to march some distance up to their starting points, especially if that point was within enemy lines.

As the troops gathered in their pre-assault positions, the attack started to take form. It often commenced with indirect fire from artillery and mortars. Sometimes their fire was used to deceive the enemy into thinking an attack was immediately forthcoming in that sector while the attacking troops launched an attack in a different sector of the line. Other times the artillery was used to draw out the enemy's artillery to engage it with counter battery fire before the assault. In addition, artillery fire was used in the area to be attacked not only to soften up the enemy but to provide shell holes for cover. Once the troops stepped off their line of departure, it was important not only to have indirect cover fire but to have the heavy and medium machine gun fire hitting suspected targets. It was common to have two companies forward and one in reserve for battalion attacks and two platoons forward and one platoon in reserve for company assaults. The reserve unit was there to exploit gaps that might open. While advancing, the units would leapfrog past each other to provide covering fire to the rushing units. Smoke shells and light machine guns would watch the flanks to guard against enemy incursions. If the objective could be seized, the reserve unit might take possession of it, while the attacking units began working the flanks to widen the hole. If the attack was a particular obstacle, a specialized task force might be assembled for the mission. Depending on the job, the team could be as large as a platoon. In it, troops could be armed with Bangalore torpedoes, satchel charges, flame throwers, extra grenades, and any other type of weapon to bring down an enemy strong point. After the gap was opened or a wedge was created in the enemy line, the infantry's support units would pile in and set up fire lanes to prepare for a counterattack or get ready to support the next infantry move.

The Germans at times used their self-propelled (SP) guns to lend a hand in the infantry assault. In the early years of the war, the Stug III with its short 75mm was the primary SP used. This weapon was seen as a complement to artillery and could be used right up to the objective. Just as in the case of a mechanized penetration or breakthrough, the ability to have direct high explosive support was vital to the success of the mission. The main tactical use was to gather several together to knock out enemy infantry support weapons and positions. Over open sights these gunners could destroy machine gun nests, put smoke on bunkers, or neutralize counterattacks. The SPs would not lead the attack but would remain in or just slightly to the rear of the infantry or tanks. When the mission was accomplished, the SPs would reverse to the rear to await further orders. The Allies would, of course, use tanks for this role as the infantry mission required. Russia was the only other nation to develop the SP gun in the likeness of the Germans and they used the weapon similarly. The emphasis here again was on getting accurate HE direct support while tackling the objective.

World War Two witnessed the mobilization of small infantry units in what has become known as mechanized or armored infantry. The Germans were the first to really pioneer the use of infantry in this way. Having done so, they created combat groups for specific missions. The Panzergrenadier Battalion was supported by two tank platoons, an anti-tank company, an engineer platoon, and an anti-aircraft platoon. Each Panzergrenadier platoon was comprised of four 251 Hanomag half-tracks, three with medium machine guns and one with an anti-tank gun. The Americans developed armored infantry tactics similar to the Germans, but each platoon had five M3 half-tracks with one towing a 37mm anti-tank gun, which was later exchanged for a 57mm gun. The British and Canadians were not as keen to develop armored infantry until later in the war, when they adopted American M3 half-tracks, Kangaroos (the Kangaroo was a M7 Priest/Sexton without its gun and had a modified front and side shields), and Ram Kangaroos, which were essentially turretless M4 Shermans. They did have a Bren Carrier infantry platoon attached to an infantry battalion. It consisted of 62 men in 13 carriers. There were three sections of four carriers each and one carrier as the HQ. The sections were armed with Bren guns, 2-inch mortars, and Boys anti-tank rifles, which were later replaced by the PIAT (Projector Infantry Anti-Tank). Their platoon was not as aggressive as the American and German mechanized infantry. It played a purely supportive function to the battalion, acting as a reconnaissance group. The Russians also developed mechanized infantry using American half-tracks, though it was rarely publicized due to Stalin not wanting to give credit to the assistance provided by Lend-Lease. The Soviets were primarily known for having entire specialized units armed with submachine guns riding tanks into combat. They were basically fulfilling the role of shock action armored troops.

For all intents and purposes, the attack plan for mechanized units was to penetrate or break through enemy positions just like their fellow foot infantry. They usually rode into action and dismounted much closer to the enemy or rode on through the enemy if resistance was light. Generally speaking, the assault force would attack in depth, with the first wave hitting and seeking out enemy anti-tank guns and machine gun positions. The second wave would then assault the remaining infantry while the third wave acted as the reserve to strike tough spots or exploit gaps. They would also outflank the last remaining enemy holdouts.

Wargame Implications

As was the case with the armored attack, the gamer is typically only given a small piece of the battlefield to deploy his units. When the game is an infantry battle, it can present some challenges to the attacker. The most obvious one is where to set up support elements like a medium machine gun section or an 80mm mortar team or platoon. The latter is the easiest, for it can be an off-board unit. This is not the case with a machine gun team. It must be on the board to fire. If there is a suitable terrain feature, such as a ridge, it can become a nice place to set up the weapon because it can provide a great field of view for firing. Another difficultly is how to tactically deploy the platoons. If at all possible, linear tactics should be avoided. This also goes for the defender. Depth is always essential. In modern warfare speed and fire power dominate. Players setting up squads on line present easy targets at consistent ranges for enemy machine guns to destroy. The best method to enter the board is in the oblique order; that is, squads and platoons staggered in a diagonal fashion with enemy fire expected on the inside flank. This presents the enemy with targets at unequal ranges and allows support machine guns placed at the base of the platoon a greater field of fire. Anti-tank guns, small 2-inch mortars, grenade launchers, and additional light machine gun teams should be within a reasonable distance to the rear of their platoon. They need to be able to get into a firing position within one movement turn. If tanks are a part of the advance providing cover fire, the tanks should also advance in a similar manner with some infantry out in front to spot anti-tank guns and enemy infantry positions. The remainder of the attacking infantry should be slightly behind the tanks. Again, the attacking units should always be using the leapfrog method to advance to their objective.

While on the subject of advancing, and having discussed tanks and infantry, there is a basic tactical method of fire and maneuver that should always be pondered when preparing to game a battle. It applies to both infantry and armored forces. First, a player should analyze his forces to be used and the scenario to be gamed. It is important to know what element will be used as the main base of fire. These units allow the other ones to become more mobile and pose a greater threat to the enemy. The next thing to determine is which force will become the maneuver element. This will force the enemy to make decisions and react to opposing troops. This assists the attacker in maintaining momentum. The last choice to make is which units make the best reserve to exploit opportunities left open by the opponent. Naturally, a defender can go through the same line of thinking as he formulates his counterattack, though his base of fire may be proportionally larger and the maneuver element may consist of most of the reserve. At first glance these ideas may seem simplistic and hardly worth a comment. Nevertheless, I have been involved in numerous games in which the players just show up and started rolling dice. Sure, there was a "council of war" among the sides to discuss strategy. But rarely is the subject of tactics discussed in any detail.

The Pacific War

The Chinese and, to a lesser extent, the Russians had been engaged in a conflict against Japan, and it largely followed the European style of modern combat because the terrain was principally similar in the Manchuria region of Asian. The Pacific War, as an element of World War Two, did not kick off until

December 7, 1941, with the bombing of Pearl Harbor and the Japanese sweep that began gobbling up Western Colonies from Guam to the Philippines and from Malaya to Burma. These initial victories were a result of Western prejudices about the quality of fighting soldiers found in the ranks of the Imperial Armies of Japan and Japan's ability to wage a modern war. Furthermore, the Allies held the belief that jungles imposed such a limitation on warfare—by restricting movement via mechanized forces, the constraints forced upon fields of fire, problems of disease, and the restrictions placed on logics for supporting troops—that the jungle itself was viewed as impenetrable. Therefore, jungle warfare training was nearly nonexistent in the British, British Commonwealth, and American armies, though the Americans at least had some experience in jungle conditions due to its military actions in Central America in the 1930s. These views combined created an extremely vulnerable Allied position in the Pacific.

The Japanese, on the other hand, had been developing plans for invading these territories to support the mainland's economy and quest for dominance over Asia. The Imperial High Command had set up a training center on the Island of Formosa in 1940 to study the problems the jungle imposed on combat. It was from this research that the Japanese were able to move so quickly in the jungles. It was not that the Japanese were better warriors favorably suited for jungle fighting. It was that their commanders who had already preplanned for dealing with certain problems and coping with the logistical issues that gave the Japanese the initial advantage at the outbreak of the Pacific War. Their jungle training itself, however, was very inadequate, much like that of their enemies. However, what gave them the edge was that many of the Imperial soldiers already had combat experience from fighting in China. The Allied armies deployed in the region had next to no combat exposure save a few commanders and the quality of the soldiers was questionable, particularly those from India.

Tactics

Due to the harshness of the terrain in South East Asia and the Pacific Islands, tactics to combat an enemy within the jungle were very different than those used in the European and Mediterranean theaters. In those arenas, the tank was the key to victory. Success in the jungle was dependent on the ground-pounding soldier rooting out and destroying the enemy.

In general terms, the infantry was the basis for offensive and defensive plans, with all other weapon systems playing a support role. (This is not to diminish the role played by the Navy, but their contribution is beyond the scope of this work.) Most tactics used on both sides deep within the jungle were small unit formations. Radio equipment was often of poor quality and it was difficult to maintain communication with adjacent units. The companies and platoons had to set themselves up in small "islands" by covering their own perimeter defense. As best as possible, these units would try to be set up in mutual support of each other. When on the march to seek contact with the enemy, they could not spread out on line because visibility was severally restricted. They had to advance in columns while their lead elements hacked through the dense undergrowth. Once the infantry made contact, the columns could then move to envelop the enemy. The heavier support weapons were limited by road access. Artillery units could be deployed near a beach landing zone or within clearings with traversable roads. Larger caliber mortars also faced similar challenges, though they could be more readily manhandled into position; however, road access was still a priority to maintain adequate resupply. The most preferred weapons were 2-inch mortars, light machine guns, and submachine guns because they could easily be brought into the jungle and still provide a decent level of fire power.

Japanese

The Japanese were the first to implement specific infantry tactics to overcome an enemy in the jungle. The most famous of these, from which the Allies gained valuable lessons, was the Scorpion. The leading units would maneuver down a trail or road until contact was made. While fighting was taking place, the foot mobile element would be darting through the jungle on the flank to deliver the sting by a flank attack. Some forces would move across roads and cut off the enemy's escape route. In the beginning of the war, the Western Forces had believed the jungles were impenetrable and were burdened with heavier equipment that was bound by roads. This caused great defeats of the Allies. Perhaps the greatest were the defeats of the British in Malaya and Singapore.

The Japanese also practiced quick rushes to keep the enemy off balance. For instance, at the battalion level, companies 1 and 2 would rush two to three hundred yards abreast of each other in small trailing columns and secure the first objective. Companies 3 and 4 would rush through companies 1 and 2 to the next objective 500 to 1000 yards ahead. This movement was across a 400-to 500-yard width of space. If the attack was performed by a company for a specific objective, it was typically confined to a width of 200 yards. The medium machine gun teams would also run in support of the advanced units. It should be noted that these teams were large by Western standards. One section or team was comprised of 10 men. The reason for this was that the Model 92 machine gun was very heavy and the Japanese rushed with it into combat and carried it ready for action on long running poles.

The rush tactic was at times interpreted to be a Banzai charge, which was not necessarily the case. Whether it was or not made little difference to the soldiers fending off the attack. The classic Banzai charge was usually delivered as the last great offensive maneuver left by a local commander. It was often seen in the island campaigns as the big assault to drive out the invaders. Communications and command structures were often broken because of fierce naval bombardments from the U.S. Navy. The

Japanese officers were trained on individual aggressive action and because of this they would often call for a charge, even if not directed from higher up the chain of command. This had a tendency to result in attacks coming in piecemeal, making them easier to neutralize. From the Japanese perspective, at least in the latter years of the war, it was fully understood what the Banzai charge meant. It was an order to die for the glory of the Emperor. The charge itself could be carried out at nearly every level, from a few companies to whole regiments. Although it may seem contrary to the Hollywood version of a Japanese charge, frontal assaults were discouraged. They did prize infiltration and night assaults. They would send in small groups of soldiers to probe enemy defenses to locate weak spots. These groups would also attempt to cut holes in the defenses not only by cutting down wire and other entanglements but also by quietly killing sleepy-eyed sentries. Once they established an opening, a charge or rush attack would start.

One of the preferred methods of a Japanese attack was to hit an enemy while his units were in motion. The Meeting Engagement, as it was known, had four simple principles. First, the local commander would seize and maintain the initiative. Second, the subordinate leaders were to make bold and independent decisions to take advantage of moments of opportunity. Third, the attacking forces would rush to capture and occupy the important terrain features to deny them to the enemy. Finally, it was expected that all officers would exhibit vigorous leadership during combat to inspire their men and live up to the Bushido Code, which was a very large component of Japanese military doctrine. Officers and soldiers were taught that they were far superior to their enemies in spirit and that their fighting spirit would transcend material deficiencies and lead them to victories. Unfortunately, Japan's early victories reinforced this notion and caused their leadership to repeat actions that the Allies had learned from and were prepared to meet and destroy.

Japan, in its experience with fighting the Chinese and Russians prior to the formal start of World War Two, at least in the East, did use its tank forces. Their use of mechanized forces was similar to Western methods. But beyond that theater of action, their use of tanks was limited. They did use a few armored units to fight the British, Australians, and Americans, but the numbers were small and usually the Allies made quick work of the outdated machines. When the Japanese took on a defensive posture, the use of tanks became a matter for a local commander. They would often attempt to use them to smash holes in the defenses of their enemies and neutralize machine gun positions with or without infantry support.

When the Imperial Navy was put on the defensive in the South Pacific, so too was the Army. The Japanese on the islands many times found themselves digging in and waiting to be attacked. While on the defensive, they deployed some creative tactics. The first line of defense was a thin line of snipers or small machine gun teams. These soldiers would fire on the approaching enemy. This method served two objectives. First, when the gunshots were heard, it provided an early warning to the troops in the rear that the enemy was approaching in their direction. Second, it slowed the enemy's advance along the way. The enemy would be required to bypass the opposition and leave some troops to destroy the Japanese soldiers. This would cause the enemy to slowly weaken his attacking force as he progressed. Alternatively, he could keep his line intact while he engaged these isolated Japanese troops. This would delay and disrupt the timetable for the offensive. At the main line, they would construct pillboxes or bunkers in depth and in mutually supportive positions. Depending on the denseness of the jungle, the bunkers could be within 30 yards of each other. They would often be constructed of palm tree logs, dirt-filled oil drums, concrete, and other scraps found in the area. They would be well camouflaged, making them difficult to see until the enemy stumbled upon them. Knowing the growing firepower of her enemies, the Japanese troops would withhold fire until their foe was within 50 yards or closer. It was common practice for Japanese to get as close as possible or allow the enemy to get within close range to deny him the use of his heavy support weapons such as artillery and ground strike aircraft.

The Japanese use of artillery was somewhat limited as the war went on, especially when compared to the struggle in the

West. Many times infantry units were far from road access. This limited the artillery's ability to provide support. Also, what artillery support they did have was typically knocked out by Allied aircraft. Last, when the islands were attacked, U.S. Naval gunfire would nearly wipe out all their prepared positions. Those not completely destroyed could not communicate with the forward troops because the communication network was obliterated.

When confronted with Allied tanks, the Imperial Army used some anti-tank guns and organized some successful tactics to combat the tanks one on one. They were not known for having large caliber guns like the Germans. Their anti-tank guns were primarily limited to 37mm and 47mm calibers, and they were not used in great numbers like that of the European Theater. They did utilize an anti-tank rifle, but its ability to punch beyond 30 millimeters of armor was questionable. The "idiot stick" was used to some effect. This device was an explosive attached to the end of a 5-to 6-foot bamboo pole. It required a brave Japanese soldier to run up to a tank and thrust the bomb at the vehicle. When it exploded, that soldier was killed. Of course the Japanese made great use of the satchel charge, in much the same way as the "idiot stick." Last, it was not unusual for an entire squad to rush a tank and attempt to assault it with hand-grenades with the hope of getting one down a hatch.

Allies

After the initial Japanese victories, the Allied nations began a slow recovery, first to secure the lifeline to Australia and then to take the offensive against Japan. In doing so, the jungle slowly became less and less of an obstacle to victory as they learned tactics from the Japanese and employed them against the Imperial Forces. Small unit infiltrations, circular defense perimeters, less reliance on mechanized forces, and smaller more portable weapons became the norm. Also, to the benefit of the Allied ground troops, they slowly gained air superiority, which gave them the needed firepower to keep the Japanese troops under duress and limit their means to get re-supplied.

Specific tactics were designed by the Allies to counter the Japanese. The British devised the tactic of counter penetrations by having small mobile reserves move into flank positions to hit the enemy. The Australians developed combat drills for their troops to have an instant response to encountering opposition.

If a company was advancing and ran into Japanese troops, the first platoon would halt while the second would rush to the right and the third platoon would rush to the left. Once in position, an envelopment of the enemy would begin. If one of the flank platoons rushed high ground, the opposite platoon would start the flanking maneuver to fire on the enemy's side or rear. These tactics were shared with other Allied nations to capitalize on successes. The Americans were known for their innovative skills and procedures in amphibious landings, which will be covered below. The American army was noted for its heavy use of all available firepower. They wanted to hit the area of attack with all possible munitions before a soldier set off on his mission. This is not to say that they lacked the nerve to engage the enemy on equal footing. All one has to do is read the accounts of Buna in New Guinea to see the spirit of the U.S. soldier.

It could be stated that the Americans led the way in deploying tanks wherever and whenever possible to defeat the Japanese, and the British and Australians naturally followed suit. Tanks that were deemed obsolete in the West remained in service longer in the Far East, such as the M3 Stuart and British Matilda. It was in the Pacific Theater that tanks were used as true support weapons. They would move in direct support of an infantry advance to lend firepower in dealing with bunkers and other hardened Japanese positions. The tanks would lay down high explosive and machine gun fire while infantry moved in with flame throwers, bazookas, and satchel charges. Usually, if tanks were assigned to an infantry assault, there was one tank platoon per infantry battalion. The tanks would rarely lead the way, for that role was left to the foot troops. They would stay close to the tanks to protect them from the various anti-tank tactics of the enemy.

American Amphibious Assaults

As war broke out between Japan and the western nations, the South Pacific islands became a slugging match between the Imperial Forces and the United States. It was there the U.S.

Marine Corps gained its fierce reputation as an elite fighting force, although it should be noted that the U.S. Army played just as important a role as the Marines did in the Pacific, especially in Guadalcanal, New Guinea, and the Philippines.

General Douglas MacArthur and Admiral Chester Nimitz were at odds over the strategic direction to defeat Japan. MacArthur believed the best plan was to return to the Philippines because it offered more land mass for maneuvering and better forward bases for operations against Formosa and the main islands of Japan. Nimitz felt that the islands in the Pacific would allow him greater flexibility in dealing with Japan's navy and would keep the enemy off balance while he speculated which islands under his control would be the next target. Moreover, the islands would present stepping stones with active naval bases for logistical support and airstrips for greater and greater naval air cover and more importantly bomber bases to strike deeper into Japan's industrial heartland. Admiral Ernest King was able to work out a compromise between both men and each man pursued his objective, albeit in a limited manner.

At the start of World War Two, amphibious landings were a historical fact from Caesar's invasion of Ancient Britton to George Washington's crossing of the Delaware. The history of warfare is filled with such examples. What made the Pacific War unique was that specialized boats and crafts were designed to deliver not only men and their personal weapons but large equipment from tanks to trucks. For the purposes of this book, the discussion will be limited to those craft that specifically affect wargaming. Some craft were far too large to be relevant in terms of setting up a wargame that depicts a beach landing.

The most familiar landing craft used in the war was the Higgins boat. It had a forward-dropping ramp that allowed the troops to exit directly onto the beach. Though there were several in its class, the Landing Craft Vehicle Personnel (LCVP) was one of the more common during invasions and it could hold up to 36 combat troops. The Landing Craft, Mechanized, 3rd version (LCM 3) was another widely used boat. It could deliver up to 60 troops or one medium tank. Due to its size, it was typically reserved for later waves in the invasion force. Both boats were used by the army, because its missions were normally against ocean-side beaches, such as New Guinea or the Philippines, where coral reefs were limited. Unlike the atolls, the landing beaches were against the lagoon side of the island, which were ringed by barriers of coral. The Higgins Boats often got stranded out on the reef, and the troops would have to wade ashore several hundred yards under enemy fire.

The other recognizable landing craft to gain fame in the war was the AMTRAC or LVT. These "names" are interchangeable and are respectively known as the Amphibious Tractor and the Landing Vehicle Tracked. The LVT was generally the name used with its modification number list to the right, such as LVT-2. The craft got its start as a civilian rescue vehicle in Florida in the late 1930s. The Navy and the Marines took interest in the machine and realized the military potential of transporting troops and cargo from ship to shore. The LVT-1 first saw service in Guadalcanal in 1942. They were unarmored, carried 20 combat troops, and mounted .50 and .30 caliber machine guns. The LVT-2 was slightly reshaped by being extended approximately 5 feet and widened by nearly a foot and it carried 24 troops. The disadvantage to these two machines was that the troops were required to bail out over the top and expose themselves to hostile fire. By mid-1944 the LVT-4 was ready for the invasion of Saipan and later the LVT-3 for the assault on Okinawa in 1945. The third model was delayed getting into service because of production issues. These two were similarly armed with .30 and .50 caliber machine guns. However, to the relief of the troops being transported, they were reconfigured to have a rear-dropping ramp. There were two more LVT types worth mentioning. These are the LVT(A)1 and the LVT(A)4. They were classified as amphibious tanks. The former vehicle mounted a 37mm gun and the latter had a short 75mm howitzer and both were lightly armored.

The LVT vehicle series was not intended to be an inland fighting machine. The tracks were narrow and the underbelly ground clearance was small. The further inland it went the more debris troops would need to clear so it could advance. Also, they were not well armored and would become vulnerable to Japanese heavy machine gun fire. Their job was to get their Marines to a covered spot near the beach. This was a predetermined spot for releasing the troops. Once this was accomplished, they would return to the sea to make way for the subsequent assault waves. The amphibious tanks would remain and provide valuable cover fire until the heavier M4 Shermans arrived, which could be one to three hours away.

Invasion Tactics

It was the invasion of Tarawa in November 1943 that called into question amphibious tactics. The invasion was marked by mistakes and high casualty counts. Landings prior to that battle had been mild in comparison. They were not attacks on fortified atolls, but larger and more difficult islands to defend, with reefs that were relatively easy to bypass or destroy prior to the assault. One of the first problems encountered on Tarawa was the reef barrier. The Higgins Boats were unable to cross it and were forced to drop their ramps. The Marines had to wade ashore several hundred yards just to get to the seawall, all the while being fired on. Furthermore, not enough LVTs were used to deliver that first wave, which reduced the available firepower on the beach. Additionally, the pre-landing naval and air bombardments did not last long enough. Last, the need to completely remove the enemy's ability to put up an air defense at the time of the landing was not fully grasped. All this plus other errors made the battle a costly one. The Marines landed with 12,000 men and nearly 3,200 became casualties. The Japanese lost nearly all of the 4,500 troops defending the island.

With this experience behind them, Naval and Marine strategists began rethinking tactics to assault fortified islands with a determined enemy to fight to the last man. Ship-to-shore communications increased to provide better target information to naval gunnery and air support. As a result of the difficulties in getting men on the beaches, more LVTs participated in the initial waves. Also, the navy sought to add more demolition teams to blast larger gaps in the reefs to allow the Higgins Boats through unhindered. Finally, the troops obtained more firepower by providing them with additional machine guns, bazookas, flamethrowers, and demolition equipment to boost their ability to destroy Japanese pillboxes.

Landing troops on the beach was a hazardous task and required careful organizational planning. Regimental Combat Teams were organized depending on the mission. These were further broken down into Battalion Landing Teams (BLTs), where it was common to find a tank platoon attached. The tanks typically landed in the later waves of the assault. If the situation warranted more immediate needs for armored support, the amphibious tanks could be added to the first waves. The LVT battalions contained three companies of 30 tracks and each company could land an infantry battalion. The amphibious tank battalions were also made up of three companies but each company contained 18 vehicles. After loading the landing crafts with their troops, these boat teams would fight as one unit. Many times infantry platoons would be split between two craft. It was not until the fighting subsided that individual platoons could reorganize under their respective commands. The companies of the battalion would land abreast and if the beach was narrow the companies would have to land in columns. The incoming waves could be as little as five minutes apart. Thus, it required quick action on the beach to unload and get out as soon as possible. The landing beaches would range from 400 to 1500 yards wide and as close to the objective as possible. The first objective, called the O-1, had to be within reasonable distance to the beach for support but far enough away to make room for the troop buildup to occur without reducing the effectiveness of the Shore Party's job. Once ashore, the fighting would begin. But if the deceptions worked the landings might only run into light resistance at the beach. Also, by late 1944 the Japanese were withholding fire until the enemy came inland. Needless to say, machine gun bunkers, snipers, and counterattacks were a threat and were still encountered on the beach. The most feared Japanese assault was the dreaded Night Attack or the last ditch Banzai charge, which were just as lethal as they were mentally taxing on the G.I.s.

Wargame Implications

Perhaps the best place to review the Pacific War for wargaming purposes might be the landings, as it is a natural place to start the march inland to engage the dug-in defenders. The first thing to do will be to organize the landing force. From the perspective of the rules found in this book, each platoon will be split into two LVT models. This means a company of Marines, at full strength, would occupy 10 LVT-4s. If support teams, such as medium machine guns, bazooka teams, or additional squads are added as reinforcements, more LVTs will have to be supplied to the landing group. An advisable ratio of squads to models would be two squads per LVT or one squad and two support teams. For wargaming purposes, I recommend limiting the number of LVT(A)1s and 4s, again those amphibious tanks armed with the 37mm anti-tank gun and 75mm howitzer. The ideal amount would be no more than two of each per infantry company landing on the beach. If LCM(3)s are used for delivering tanks to an active beach, it would be best to have them arrive at turn 4 or later. This will help simulate the fact that they were not in the first waves. However, for a wargame it may not be feasible to have such a large landing force as to have them arrive in wave 5 or 6. But the gamer should have to wait some amount of time proportional to the number of turns the game is expected to be played. As a reminder, the number of tanks being delivered to the troops should be 1 or 2 per company and no more than 5 to a battalion. Though it would be permissible to have tanks and amphibious tanks on the same game board because they serve different tactical purposes.

Prior to the landing, a system of simulated bombardments will have to be mutually arranged. The simplest and fastest way to do this is to divide up the board into 12 squares after the Japanese player has completed his setup. If he has forces hidden, it should be noted as to which squares those units occupy. The invading player should roll a 4-sided die to see how many squares have been neutralized. The player then rolls a 12-sided die the number of times indicated by his roll of the 4-sided die. The number rolled on the 12-sided die indicates the numbered square. The infantry and soft-skinned vehicles in those squares are considered knocked out and are removed from play. If a bunker or tank was in the square, a roll of a 1 on a 4-sided die means it was destroyed. For example, the invading player rolls a 2 on the 4-sided die. He gets to roll the 12-sided die twice. Those rolls are a 3 and a 7. This means the units in those squares are affected. If he rolls the same number twice, he does not get a re-roll of the dice. This method is just a recommendation, even though some simple system should be devised to replicate a bombardment.

Once the troops have landed, it is important to have a point at which the Amtracs will halt, unload their troops, and exit the board via the ocean side of the table. Preferably, if a company or more of troops are assaulting the beach, there should be at least two waves separated by 1 or 2 turns and the landing space per company should be no greater than 25 inches. This will represent 250 yards of landing space. It is imperative for the invading player to experience a congested beach assault, as this would be the case in real life. The amphibious tanks will remain on the board and there should be a clearly marked or expressed area through which is it forbidden for them to enter or cross. The landing troops should have a defined O-1 for the game; this should be at least 40 to 60 inches away from the demarcation line. The Line of Demarcation in this case is an objective just inside the beachhead which allows the troops to reform and push on toward the O-1.

In terms of a wargame, the objectives that define victory for either side should be in line with historical accounts. The Japanese were never able to repel an American invasion. Therefore, it would be unrealistic to have as an objective to drive the Marines off the beach. Conversely, it would not be wise to have the invaders completely wipe out all the Japanese. The best way to handle this is to lay out the objectives in terms of the number of turns to meet the goals. The O-1 for the attacker will of course be the objective, and for the Japanese it will be their mission to prevent them from securing it. The recommended amount of turns for this will be based on the terrain and the distance from the demarcation line. By calculating the infantry movements to reach the O-1 and allowing for combat delays, the players can settle on the number of turns for the game.

As the U.S. Marine or Army player maneuvers forward, he will experience the Japanese player's defenses. The defender should think in terms of laying out a chain of bunkers and dug-in Japanese troops, with machine guns making up to a quarter to a third of the positions. This does include those light machine guns found at the squad level. There should also be hidden snipers accounted for in the terrain. Also, it would not be unheard of for the Japanese to have a dug-in tank as part of the defense. The knee mortars may be the only indirect fire allotted, and the range should be remembered as very limited. In this book, it is 18 inches. For a beach landing scenario, the use of a charge or large-scale counterattack should be avoided, as it would be uncharacteristic for invading troops to be hit by it in the initial hours of the invasion. This was typically reserved for the first night counterassault.

As the troops move inland, it will be necessary for them to concentrate their firepower on dug-in positions that the Japanese player has laid out. If tank support is available, HE should be used in conjunction with machine gun fire to allow flamethrowers to get into position to destroy the bunkers. Alternatively, they can attempt to bypass these positions in favor of heading to the O-1, assuming subsequent waves will take out the enemy strongholds.

Moving the battle past the beach to a scenario inland can suffice for any engagement with the Japanese in Burma, New Guinea, or the Philippines, in the latter part of the war. The troops would have to be prepared for a potential Banzai charge that would usually occur in the early predawn hours. For gaming, this would mean setting up the allied soldiers in small units; perhaps each platoon or company would provide its own perimeter security by deploying in a circular manner. This is somewhat dependent on the density of the jungle being used. The less dense it is the more linear the defensive position can become. But it is necessary that the units or platoons are mutually supporting one another. In heavy jungle this may mean being within 10 to 12 inches of each other. In the center of the defense should be some element of reserve to be ready to plug any gaps that develop as a result of the Japanese breaking into the defense. In a gaming situation, some tactical standards might be forgone. For instance, placing out observation posts or forward machine gun positions may be unnecessary. In practice, commanders placed those soldiers there for early warning of an attack. But with gaming, the players generally can see the attack forming and do not need to expose more troops than needed. For that matter, the Japanese can dispense with the need to send out small units before an attack to find a weak spot in the defense. Last, the players should decide on a method for determining the direction of attack. For example, by dividing the board into cardinal directions (and presumably not the rear unless it is to be part of the scenario), they can roll a die to indicate the path of attack, but this should be done after the allied units have set up.

Gaming the Japanese Rush tactic is a rather simple affair. There are only a few matters to keep in mind. Though it is similar to a Banzai charge, it is characterized by having two distinct waves in the assault, as opposed to the charge being one large wave of screaming soldiers. The objectives should be clearly defined and success should be in terms of securing those objectives. The number of turns necessary to complete the task will also be important in assessing the victory conditions. For this particular tactic, the Japanese troops ought to be allotted some measure of additional movement over their opponent to simulate their quickness of foot and the fact that they have been trained for this specific maneuver. The troops running to capture the first objective will need to halt after securing it. The second wave will need to be held back and kept moving at a normal pace until it is called up to advance to its objective. The reserve element can be part of one platoon and a few of the support units within the company. If the first wave is needed to secure the second wave's goal, then its movement should revert back to normal. It is assumed that they have expended their exuberant energy in the first assault. When contact is made, flanking the enemy should always be attempted. For that matter, flanking an opponent is always a key tactic. Troops should not just blindingly assault in a linear manner straight at the enemy. By flanking him, it is much easier to force him to fall back and to start the process of dislodging him from his positions.

If the Scorpion tactic is to be gamed, it too has a few issues to bear in mind. First, the scenario should be limited in scale and designed around the first successful attacks made by the Japanese. The game should somewhat be centered on the Allies holding a road with minimal defenses deep in the jungle. Because the battle board is only so large, it is not possible to have a "stinger" movement played out in its entirety. The best way is to allow the Japanese to enter from one of the flanks, while they are moving up the road to engage their enemy. Victory for the Allies can be defined as fighting a successful withdrawal without being cut off and destroyed.

The last major tactic to simulate is the Australian jungle drill. As they make contact with the enemy, the platoons of the company maneuver into predetermined positions in relation to one another. The first platoon should halt and begin firing as it spreads out and finds whatever cover is nearby. The second platoon will move to the right to flank and or secure a predominate piece of terrain. The third platoon will rush to the left for the same purpose. Of course, in a wargame the Japanese position may already be visible. If it is, the Australian player should begin formulating his attack and look ahead as to the possible escape routes the enemy may use to flee off the board. This is important because the flanking platoons can move in, capture, and block these paths. Also as the units are moving forward, they should not be in a linear formation, but in platoons by column. The squads should be several inches from one another and the platoons should be separated by 10 to 20 inches.

To counter this, the Japanese player should have employed snipers and small teams in front of the defensive line. Here again, these troops are not intended to defeat the enemy advance but to slow it and break it up before hitting the main fortified position. Imagine a player having a small defensive line with a reinforced platoon covering a turn in a road or trail with a few forward deployed light machine guns and a few snipers. Hopefully, the players will have worked out some simple methods of concealing these types of units and if so maybe the whole Japanese defense can lay hidden. The Australian player would be forced to deal with these challenges while trying to accomplish his mission, especially if there is a time limit to the game. If the enemy is hidden, then he may be compelled to prematurely deploy his troops and occupy positions he might otherwise not.

Amphibious Operations of the Western Theater

As the world was becoming more and more embroiled in the war, the United States found itself having to come to grips with the reality that it would have to use amphibious invasions not only in dealing with the Japanese threats but in tackling the Axis forces of Germany and Italy. The main difference between these two theaters of war was their logistics. In the Pacific, the Navy and Marines were dealing with the prospect of handling limited invasion forces. In other words, they only had to be able to deliver a specific amount of materials to accomplish one mission. The

Atlantic and Mediterranean theaters, however, dealt with how to transport not just the invasion troops and equipment but the follow-up men and material to sustain a protracted offensive.

After the U.S. entered the war, the European and Mediterranean theaters would see several invasions by American and British forces, although it started with the Allied powers debating the best strategy for bringing the war to Germany. The Americans believed the best way was to mount an invasion of Northwest Europe by mid-1943. The British remained unconvinced and would not consider it. They persuaded the untested Americans to focus on the Mediterranean first. By late 1942, the Axis forces in the Atlantic and Mediterranean were unable to put up an effective naval force to counter the Allies. This helped pave the way for the attacks on North Africa, Sicily, and Italy. The first invasion in the West was Operation Torch, in French Morocco. Despite being lightly resisted, it did offer some valuable lessons for the Allied war planners. They had to deliver over 80,000 men with all their material at three different landing zones. The next test for them came with the invasion of Sicily in late July 1943. The landings themselves went well. It was the paratrooper drops that went horribly wrong. Due to wind, dreadful planning, enemy anti-aircraft fire, and general combat confusion, the paratroopers landed all over the southwest portion of the island. Very few were close enough to seize their objectives. Most of them had to link up with other units and commands to achieve the designated targets laid out by General Harold Alexander. Once the invasion forces moved inland, the Germans put up stiff resistance until it was decided by the German High Command to abandon the island, which was never in doubt but only a question of time because of the collapse of the Italian Government under Mussolini and the general disintegration of the Italian Army. The next seaborne assaults for the Allies to land were at Salerno, Anzio, and, of course, Normandy, and later the attack on Southern France.

The most heavily defended landing sites were the beaches of Normandy. It was here that the Allies used their full knowledge of assaulting and clearing beaches. Although there were tactical differences between the British and American forces in the methods of clearing beaches, they did a great job in doing so. The British organized and employed units specifically tasked to handle obstacles. They used tanks specially fitted with bridging equipment to cross anti-tank ditches. Tanks were also fitted with flails to clear minefields. Other units were used to remove and destroy obstacles. The Americans had similar types of units. However, these were formed from regular army forces and trained for specific missions. After accomplishing the mission, the teams were broken up and reorganized back into their pre-mission units. This was all needed to battle the largest seawall fortress in history, the Atlantic Wall, which was hoped would repel any attempt to get at Germany itself. The Americans finally got the chance to strike at her over two years after entering the war. They were successful in bringing down the vaunted "Wall" within hours after hitting the beach.

In terms of the beach landings, there were differences and similarities to those being performed in the Pacific. One of the main differences was that many of the beaches were not as heavily defended and they contained fewer manmade obstacles. (Naturally, this description is contrary to the Normandy Landings. It must be remembered that it took the Germans several years and numerous conscript laborers to achieve what they did from early 1942 until June 6, 1944, and they had still not completed the task.) Therefore, the landings were a little less hectic and unloading was made easier, as was supplying reinforcements. This is not to suggest the landings were unopposed. They still encountered enemy infantry and dangerous mines, anti-tank ditches, tank traps, and barbed wire. The point is that the Allied war planners had many options to choose from to deceive the enemy unlike the concentrated defenses at the Atlantic Wall.

The landing intervals varied from 10 to 30 minutes depending on the anticipated level of opposition. If the planners suspected strong resistance, LCMs would ferry tanks in as early as the first wave and sometimes leading the infantry. The Army did not have amphibious tanks like the Marines in the Pacific and therefore they needed to have some form of large caliber direct assault weapon beyond a bazooka. The first waves had two primary missions: get a foothold and start clearing obstacles.

These waves were organized in a manner similar to the soldiers in the Pacific. The men were assigned to boat teams and they were armed as self-sufficiently as possible. They would contain men armed with Browning Automatic Rifles (BARs), a .30 caliber machine gun, a bazooka team, a 60mm mortar team, Bangalore torpedoes, and other weapons for specific tasks. Once a lull in the fight occurred, the men would be reorganized back into their platoons and companies.

The landing craft used were generally the same. They used LCP(L) (Landing Craft, Personnel Large), which held 36 men, the LCVP (Landing Craft Vehicle or Personnel), LCM(3) (Landing Craft, Mechanized, Mk.III), and LCM(6), to name a few. The LVCPs were the principal landing craft and not the LVTs. A of company G.I.s had a reduced number of craft to arrive on shore. It occupied seven landing craft instead of the ten needed in the Amtracs. The LVTs were not used in the West because there were not enough of them to fulfill all the needs of both theaters. There were a few used in Operation Torch for cargo duty and some used by the British toward the end of the war to cross various rivers, including the Rhine, but these were not used in large numbers. Another reason for not seeking to expand production to fill the needs in the Atlantic was that the surf conditions were different. The Marines and Army using them in the Pacific typically attacked the lagoon side of an atoll, which had relatively calm waters. The open seas of the Mediterranean and Atlantic had much rougher water, which made the low waterline of the Amtrac susceptible to overlapping waves, resulting in flooding the crew compartment.

The other equipment seen on the beaches were the DUKW and tanks fitted with special devices to wade through water. The DUKW (not an acronym but a General Motors vehicle designation), often called the Duck, was essentially a waterborne cargo truck. Its mission was to ferry badly needed supplies, such as munitions and medical provisions, to the shore in the first hours of the attack, before the shore parties could get in and unload the major supply ships. Many of the tanks that were coming in the first waves possessed fording kits that would allow them to traverse in water up to their turrets. The other system was to fit the M4 and M5 tanks with collapsible rubberized canvases and rear rotor blades to propel them through the water. These tanks could be launched as far away as 5000 yards from the landing site. These types of systems had mixed success in the invasion of Normandy.

The divisions participating in the invasion landings had a similar organization to those fighting the Japanese. Regimental Combat Teams (RCTs) were broken down into Battalion Landing Teams. Each of the RCTs, depending on the mission or assignment, were allotted tanks, engineers, anti-tank guns, and anti-aircraft equipment, which were in turn attached to specific BLTs for their respective objectives. A Battalion would land two companies abreast with the weapons company trailing behind. The third would take on the reserve role and land in the next wave. The weapons company was also organized in self-sufficient boat teams because they were sometimes called upon to fill a needed gap on the beach. The landing zones for battalions ranged between 250 and 1000 yards.

One of the largest contrasts between the two theaters of war was the use of paratroopers. The Pacific did see several airborne drops to reinforce and secure key points. But due to the nature of the terrain, large-scale operations could not be performed. In the West, the paratroopers were a key component to nearly all large landings. Their tasks ranged from taking bridges to seizing crossroads. The chief objective was to disrupt the enemy's ability to consolidate and deliver an effective counterattack in the areas surrounding the beaches. Many of the aircraft inadvertently scattered their paratroopers all over the drop zone areas, requiring the troopers to make their way to their objectives through hostile territory. This had an enormous psychological impact on the enemy. From their point of view, they believed the numbers of troops involved in the drops were much larger than they were. This alone made good use of the airborne infantry because it prompted the enemy to tie up far more troops than they otherwise might have.

Wargame Implications

The invasions against the Germans and Italians will be different from those done to depict attacks against the Japanese. The main issue the gamers will face is gathering up enough landing craft for the job. The LVTs and the amphibious tanks will have to sit this one out. The gamers will need to assemble at least four LCVPs per company, which both Airfix and Pegasus Hobbies manufacture. Another kit made by Airfix is the LCM(3); I suggest not more than one per company of infantry, if it is transporting a tank. When simulating a battle in the Mediterranean or Atlantic, the landings should not involve more than a battalion. The reason for this is two-fold. First, the wargamers will need at least 60 inches of shoreline for a landing. Second, they will need a minimum of 8 LCVP and 2 LCM(3) to visually represent a landing in force. Going beyond this will require a small investment of time and money to prepare for one large battle. Naturally, as the landing craft are removed after they disgorge their troops, they can be reused for the subsequent waves.

It should be noted that sometimes wargaming is a balance of time, money, and taste. Therefore, other devices can be used to substitute for a landing craft. The small kit boxes that house 1/72 scale tanks or other models make good landing craft provided they are not larger than 4 by 8 inches. Boxes that are larger than this begin to fit the role of those carrying tanks. Other good makeshift craft are the tins that contain smoked fish snacks or sardines. Putting a little olive drab spray paint on these types of craft will go a long way in camouflaging their origins and create a little needed realism for a game. These suggestions may seem a little strange to bring up. But when battling an invasion in the Western Theater, it may be a one-time or very seldom event, which does not warrant spending the time and money necessary to create a landing force for one afternoon. Most games simulating Northwest Europe, Italy, or the Desert Campaign are certainly land battles with tanks slugging it out. The kits needed could prevent some wargamers from ever experimenting with landing games. The Pacific is another matter, for many of the popularized aspects of gaming it are related to invasion tactics.

Those gamers going into that theater expect and want to have a landing force to fully enjoy their games.

The first landing type to mention is D-Day, June 6, 1944. The gamers playing or developing a scenario will first need to determine which nation and beach to represent. The British attacked the Sword and Gold beaches and the Canadians assaulted Juno. The Americans took on Omaha and Utah beaches. Each of these landing sites had their own specifics to challenge the invaders. It was the American troops that faced the greatest opposition to their attack. Any wargamer wanting to accurately portray a piece of beach ought to do some quick reading to find out the unique aspects related to that section.

The first place to start is with the beach defenses. The beach obstacles can range from barbed wire to tank traps. If minefield segments are to be used, the players should lay out templates that are approximately 3 inches by 8 inches. The pillboxes should be of concrete construction armed with machine guns and anti-tank weapons. These should be placed about 30 to 40 inches apart and there should be no more than 3 hardened bunkers on the game board. Trench positions can zigzag throughout the beach line. For defense in depth, a few rear trenches or pre-dug foxholes should be deployed. If recreating the British sector, a few beachfront buildings should be placed toward the mid-section of the board. The buildings should have some elements of prepared defenses. German tanks should be restricted to a few self-propelled guns. The Germans had held their armored reserves in the rear until it was clear where the Allies were making their "true" invasion. OKW, the German High Command, had anticipated the "real" invasion to be at Pas de Calais, the narrowest point between the European Continent and England.

The troops defending the beaches should be of standard quality. It was not until the Allies made it off the beaches that they ran into elite SS units. The number of Germans occupying the defenses can range from 20% to 35% of the invading force. Some German reinforcements can be brought in, but they should be very limited. Small localized units were rushed in because of their proximity to the fighting, but were not of an organized nature until several hours after the invasion had begun and many of them faced the challenges presented by the paratroopers.

Indirect fire support should also be kept to a minimum. It must be remembered that the game is representing a small section of the D-Day invasion and not the entire beach. The defenders would be competing for fire missions with other beach sections and may not be given as high a priority as another beach. This can be turned into an interesting aspect of the game by creating a simple chart with the types of indirect weapons that are available for the game in question. A roll of a 1 or 2 on a 6-sided die is for "no available support." The roll of a 3 or 4 means they have an 80mm mortar platoon support and a roll of a 5 or 6 means a powerful section of 150mm howitzers. Another approach is to have the support already predetermined. For example, an 80mm mortar platoon is in support of the section of beach. The German player should roll a 1 or 2 during the indirect fire phase to see if he can get a fire mission. Once he does, he gets to complete the mission in subsequent turns. However, when he determines it is necessary to change targets, he must reroll the 1 or 2 on the 6-sided die to get the second fire mission. Whatever indirect fire weapons are allotted to the defender, they should be considered "off board." Naturally, they would be in the rear anyway. But this helps alleviate some room in the rear of the board where maneuvering is already difficult.

The first issue to settle before the game starts is how to determine the pre-invasion bombardment effects on the game board. Unlike the Pacific, where the islands endured a bombardment for several days, the great secrecy that surrounded the invasion prevented a large-scale first hit up until the last few hours. Therefore, any one battalion's invasion beach might not reveal significant damage. One quick way to manage this is to have the attacking player roll one 6-sided die to see the number of attempts he gets at destroying something. Once the number is assessed, let him roll a 1 on a 6-sided die for destroying his chosen targets. To be sure, if a larger target is on the board, such as an extensive bunker, some modifications should be made to this approach. Perhaps it can take two or three hits to be totally destroyed. The point is to make it as simple and as playable as possible.

Switching over to offense, the gamer playing the Allies will need to assault the beach in a fairly aggressive manner. He should land two companies abreast and get moving to cover as soon as possible. Of course the units will need to leapfrog each other to provide cover fire. The craft exiting the board should not linger about in the hopes of laying down machine gun fire. They need to be cleared to allow the weapons company to come in and get set up to provide additional fire support from the extra machine gun sections and mortars. Next to land will be the reserve company of the battalion, or the tanks can land before their arrival. Landing the tanks can give extra support by firing high explosive and smoke rounds for the infantry making their way forward. Allowing them a few turns to do their work might provide the needed space to make a breakthrough in the enemy's defense. As this is going on, it will be important to coordinate attacks on the fixed installations, especially if the gamers are playing the rules contained within this book. The reason for this is that the Allied player will have an opportunity to gather some units around a pillbox. If the player wins the initiative, he stands a good chance of blasting a gap for trailing units.

The goal for a landing invasion depicting D-Day should be breaching the defensive line and holding it for several turns within a prescribed timeline. Obviously, the players can have the Allied units punch through to the other side of the board as an objective. Though it should be remembered that it is a battalion landing on presumably a 6 ft. by 8 ft. board and that this may not be enough to pour through a hole in 12 to 15 turns. Also, it may be tempting to have a grand landing, because it is D-Day after all. It is critical to take into account the amount of time available to the players before creating the scenario. Nothing is more frustrating than setting up a great game, only to get half way through it and have to call an end to it because time is up.

The defending player's objective is to prevent any holes from opening in his defensive line. If they are opened, he must seal them immediately or watch his position get destroyed. Hence, it becomes important that the Germans have some form of reserve and it should probably contain an assault gun, like a Stug III or a few Hanomag 251s to rush a few squads into action. It must be reiterated that the total German forces should be limited. Therefore, the reinforcements must be within the total units on hand for the Germans.

Turning to the invasions that were not as spectacular as D-Day, these games still possess some fun and interesting challenges. It will be necessary to do some quick research before setting up a game to get a feel for the defenses of a selected beach landing. In the broad sense, the defenses will be certainly less built up. The composition can be barbwire entanglements covered by a few bunkers or simply a minefield with a few sentry positions. To the rear, a defense in depth should be applied. This will necessitate that the game board be set up lengthwise with the invasion force attacking the narrower portion of the table. The types of items to be placed in the rear should be mobile troops that "happen to be in the area." The defensive force might contain a few tanks or armored vehicles and motorized infantry entering the board from the rear. Most of the pre-D-Day landings were against weaker and less organized opponents. The Axis forces expected invasions but exact time and locations varied greatly. For example, the Germans thought that Sicily might be invaded but equally believed there was a chance the Allies would strike somewhere in the Balkans. Also, the Germans relied on the Italians for preparing to meet any invasion in Sicily, which was inadequate to say the least. The troops the Allies can attack can be Vichy French, Germans, or Italians, depending on which battle will be played.

The attacking troops to land can be a modified battalion or a reinforced company with a modest mission. Of course, all of this is dependent on the size of the board and the time set aside to play the game. The landing craft are the same as the D-Day ones and still no LVTs are to be used. Tanks can still be slated to arrive early in the scenario to provide the needed firepower. For these invasions, the use of one or two aircraft providing a pass over the battlefield to strafe enemy position can be useful.

The overall objectives for the attacking and defending players should be limited. Somewhere on the board should be a coastal road to act as one of the objectives. The farther away from the beach, the better it is for this role, as an objective. The coastal road can also include a crossroad or a bridge. To add to the greater campaign, the Allies can have a platoon of paratroopers holding a bridge, with its mission to link up with the beleaguered troopers. Considering the terrain of the Mediterranean and the invasion spots during that theater, a few hills and a small village would be in order. These too can act as good goals for the mission. Although the more complicated the objective, the more consideration that needs to be given to the defending troops in terms of unit placement on the board and how reinforcements will arrive. The defending player can use a standard objective such as to deny an enemy a key point in a given time frame or to have its reinforcements capture and hold a key point for a specified time. This action might represent buying time for another sector of the invasion shore to be counterattacked.

Airborne

One of the great tactical achievements of the Second World War was the creation of the airborne arm of military forces. The new tactic gave birth to the idea of the vertical envelopment. Even though the concept had been around since the latter part of the First World War, it had no chance of being developed. The technical skills and equipment were years away from being possible. It was not until the 1930s that several nations began to truly test the soundness of dropping parachutists in any sizable numbers. The strategic vision was to drop regimental or larger-sized units behind enemy lines to create havoc, while the main attack pushed forward on the ground. Their task was to seize bridges, roadways, or key points of terrain in an effort to disrupt enemy counteractions. However, the traditional military establishment shunned the idea as being too unrealistic. Their mindset was focused on using airborne troops for simple raids and sabotage missions. In their defense, the transport capabilities and logistical means of support did not exist to facilitate anything but small incursions behind enemy lines.

In the early development, there were few means to carrier combat infantry to a drop site. The first transport aircraft were bombers. The troops had to exit the planes by crawling and jumping from wings or climbing out the dorsal machine gun post to jump. Civilian planes were also commandeered to test as platforms for paratroopers. Later, as the feasibility to drop paratroops developed, the need to ferry larger equipment for their support was recognized. Many of the current transport aircraft had to be modified to carry motorcycles, jeeps, and small howitzers. In addition, rigging was set up to attach heavy equipment under the fuselage of the aircraft to parachute in motorcycles and anti-tank guns. Gliders, too, had to be produced to augment the number of infantry that would have to be landed to form an effective assault. They ranged from small 8-to 10-man aircraft to large transport gliders that could hold light tanks or armored vehicles, like the British Hamilcar that participated in the Normandy invasion by carrying the Tetrarch tank into battle.

In the beginning of its formation, the limited resources in air transportation had a significant impact on the fighting strength of airborne units. They were slightly scaled down in comparison to their regular infantry counter parts; i.e., squads, platoons, companies, and battalions were all smaller in size. It may seem logical that companies and battalions would be affected. But the reduced squad size helped leave their fighting cohesiveness intact, particularly when the unit had to fit on one glider or plane. This meant they would drop together and fight together. This was also important because the men trained for a particular mission and needed to stay together as much as possible to complete their objective. This resulted in fewer men with less firepower to accomplish the operation, which in turn meant the men had to be better trained, more aggressive, and in superior physical condition relative to regular infantry. Man for man, they would be called on to carry more gear and weapons and be placed in greater harm. It was these factors that gave rise to the elite status afforded to those who belonged to the airborne, which still carries on today worldwide.

The Soviets were the first to expand their concepts past the drawing board and create actual air-landing forces. It was in the late 1930s that they could claim having several brigades dedicated as airborne troops, and they were the first to practice large-scale operations. It was these operations that captured the attention of the military world and in particular their growing rival, the Germans. During the war, they performed limited airborne operations that were within range of friendly artillery support. The Russians were not confident to send in large-scale missions because the Germans' defensive expertise was such that they could not guarantee reaching their troopers in a timely manner.

The Germans first started to form paratroops in the mid 1930s with the appointment of Kurt Student, an infantry officer, by Hermann Goering. The first unit organized was the First Aviation Division in 1937. The name's intent was to mask the true nature of the unit. Under the leadership of Generaloberst Student, the Germans increased a few trained parachutists into a fighting regiment. They also activated the first operational glider unit. In addition, as their operational awareness increased, it was recognized that regular infantry would need to be flown in by transport and assigned to the airborne force to boost the fighting prowess of the paratroops. It was these forces along with the paratroopers that shocked the world with their lighting actions in Belgium, Crete, and the capture of Fortress Eben Emael.

When German paratroopers so effectively opened the way for the advancing ground troops of the Wehrmacht, it amazed the British and Americans. They realized the seriousness of the potential use of this arm of the military. The result was a rushed program to enhance their equipment and make ready their own forces for action. However, it would be more than a year before either one could claim a reasonable readiness to carry out a mission larger than a battalion.

The morning of May 20, 1941 marked the first invasion by means of airborne troops, with the attack on the island of Crete by German paratroopers. The first waves landed at three points. The mission at first went terribly wrong. The intelligence was woeful as to the enemy's morale and readiness. When the men jumped, they were only armed with pistols and hand grenades. Only some of the NCOs (non-commission offices) had submachine guns. All their main weapons were dropped in containers, which landed 100 yards or more away. This meant the men had to fight with what they had as they made their way to the drop containers. This fact was not lost on the enemy, who blasted away at the nearly unarmed paratroopers. The reason for this was that the jump harnesses and straps were not designed to handle personal weapons. It was also believed that carrying rifles and additional gear would increase the chances of injury to the paratroopers during the drop. Many of the heavy weapons, such as the Gebirgskanone 15 cm mountain howitzers, had to be airlifted in after the airfields had been taken. The JU52s did manage to air drop a few 37mm anti-tank guns. But the Kettenkrad and motorcycles had to be transported by aircraft. During this operation the Germans introduced the first combat-efficient recoilless rifle. It was a 75mm gun that fired high explosives shells to an effective range of 3500 yards, though its maximum range was 6800 yards. They did go on to develop a 105mm, but it was not used until Sicily. The main saving grace for the troops on the ground was the fact that the German Luftwaffe had total control over the sky in Crete. This meant that Stuka drive bombers could readily swoop down in support of their comrades on the ground. It took three days for the Germans to subdue the island at a cost of nearly 30 percent in casualties.

The effects of the Crete invasion had a devastating impact on the future role of the German paratroops in the course of the war. The losses were so frightful that Hitler would never again be persuaded to mount another large-scale attack via the airborne troops. Afterward, the troopers would only perform a few minor jump operations in Sicily, Italy, and Northwest Europe. For most of the remainder of the war, the Fallschirmjaeger (German Paratroopers) took on the role of an elite ground force. Toward the end of the war, only a fraction of the total strength of the paratroopers had actually earned jump qualification status. Yet they still retained their uniforms and badges for the purpose of maintaining morale and their reputation. Also, they fought in virtually all theaters of action from North Africa to the Eastern Front. They gained their real fame for their defensive actions at Monte Cassino, in Italy. The paratroops stood up against relentless attacks and bombardments from the British and Americans for several months before withdrawing.

The Allies, having learned from the Germans, were able to pick up the pace where the German paratroopers left off. They created better ways of providing their troopers with more personal weapons. The Americans made the M1 carbine with a folding stock. The bazooka was able to be broken down into two separate parts. Those carrying rifles were able to suspend them beneath them by a long strap while floating down to the ground. The British Sten submachine and the American Thompson submachine gun were also carried on the jump. The large weapon sections were split up in transports to avoid wiping out the entire team, thus reducing the combat effectiveness of the mission. Their glider planes were large enough to carry a Willy's Jeep or a 57mm anti-tank gun. Some were even large enough to carry Bren Gun Carriers. Because the Allies were able to land jeeps and universal carriers, they were able to supply greater amounts of ammunition for mortars and machine guns, which could be thrown at the enemy shortly after landing. This translated into a more powerful airborne force than the Germans had just a few years earlier. Furthermore, they were able to dominate the sky in all their missions. This was critical because in the absence of indirect fire support like artillery, the main weapon system on which they relied was the fighter bomber. These knocked out dangerous threats to the paratroopers and glider-borne infantry. The Allies did perform some airborne missions in the Pacific Theater, but they were small in comparison to the West. These were mostly raids or reinforcement efforts; dropping a regiment was about all that could be achieved. The overriding reason was the nature of the terrain being fought over. It did not lend itself to large formations of paratroops, considering one squad could be dispersed over 200 to 300 hundred yards.

The Japanese and Italians also developed airborne troops, though their energies produced very little when compared to the other belligerents. The Japanese were also influenced by the actions of the Fallschirmjaeger in 1940. But they were only able to produce a few small units for limited actions. They lacked the transport abilities, and shortly after the start of Pacific War they lost the all-important air superiority to effectively deploy their men. They did manage to successfully land troopers in January and February 1942 to capture the Netherlands East Indies and Sumatra. The Italians built up a meager force in 1940 and 1941. However, the war was rapidly turning against them in North Africa, which diverted attention away from further developments. What troops they did have were sent into battle as infantry to fight the British and many of the units did not survive intact.

Defensive measures to oppose paratroopers were very difficult to plan out. The threatened areas had to be assessed by intelligence officials to determine the probable missions or objectives. Once this was done, the most likely drop zones had to be analyzed. The next obvious step was to figure out if those areas could be sabotaged by flooding or constructing obstacles. This was done by the Germans in the lead up to the Normandy invasion. Although some troopers were killed by such measures, the preparations did not stop the success of the Allied airborne in securing their objectives. The other action to take was to position rear forces to counterattack the landing zones once they were revealed. The unfortunate consequence of this was to pull forward troops back from the expected main attack, resulting in a weakened front.

Wargame Implications

Wargaming an airborne operation drop can be broken down into two types of general games. The first is to simulate a drop on an enemy position with the enemy present or very near. The premise of the game is to allow the paratrooper player an opportunity to experience a game in which the assault opens in a scattered manner, and require him to form his attack while under fire. The second is a more traditional match between two opponents that are already prepared to meet each other for combat. In the case of the former, the main issue to address is the appropriate method to deploy paratroopers or glider infantry on the ground. In the rules chapter, the matter is addressed, but it is worth repeating here:

"For each platoon or section landing on the field, the player will select his landing sites and the direction of the landing. Once the spots are marked, an 8-sided die is rolled to determine each 'flight's' dispersion between squads. For instance, a 5 is rolled. Then each squad will be set out 5 inches apart from each other in the direction of the flight path. The first squad will overshoot the mark by 5 inches. If some troops are forced off the board, it will take two turns for them to reenter from the spot they were forced off. Should that point be overrun by the enemy, the troops are cut off and removed from play.

"Glider troops may also be called upon for action and they will follow a similar procedure. The player using gliders will have marked the proposed spots for each glider in the direction they are to land. In this case a 10-sided die is used to determine the number of inches from the marker. If the glider should overshoot the target and land off the board, the same two-turn rule applies. The typical German glider for this game will hold one squad and the typical allied glider will hold one squad and one support element. Players who want to dig deeper into the exact glider load capacity are encouraged to do a little research on the subject. It is always important to keep the size, scope, and mission of the game in perspective, especially when developing a glider-based attack, particularly when most glider and airborne operations landed some distance from the target. Of course the German assaults on Eben Emael and Crete are the exceptions to that statement.

"Further, all jumps and glider assaults are not without initial injuries, as Generaloberst Kurt Student could attest. To simulate this fact, the airborne player will roll a 10-sided die for each company landing or gliding into action. The number rolled will be the number of hits the company takes. The player will distribute the hits to his units as he sees fit, to include any units that have 'flown' off the board. These hits are exempt from any morale checks, but not a sergeant's casualty."

Once the infantry are on the ground, they will have to wait one turn to fire or move. This is done on the assumption that the troops would not be ready to fight instantly upon landing on the ground. The troops would be somewhat disoriented and disorganized, nor would they land with their respective squads intact with weapons ready to shoot. By waiting one turn, the troopers can be said to be forming under the nearest NCO, untangling themselves from their chutes, loading and assembling their weapons, and preparing to move out. Here again quoting an earlier segment, *"If the defender wants to have forces on the board, not all of them will be activated. Only one in four units can be in prepared positions. The remainder must be in a "bivouac" area, at least one move away. There is some assumption that the airborne assault comes as a surprise. To complicate matters more for the defender, he will roll a 6-sided die to determine the number of turns it takes to alert his forces to action. The alternative is to still roll the number of turns it takes before the defender rushes into the area but this is with the whole or most of the forces entering in via defined routes.*

"It is important to remember that most initial airborne assaults occurred in the early hours of the morning. If the attack occurs at dawn or earlier, the maximum shooting range will be 18 inches with a –2 for all firing. It will have to be declared at the start of the game at what turn the sun is fully up and these modifiers go away."

There are various ways to replicate airborne troops landing in the drop zone. The most important thing to bear in mind is to keep the method simple and have it well thought out before the game beings. The same can be said for the defending player's troops reacting to the assault. For the early airborne attacks by the Germans, it should be remembered that they did or could parachute in 37mm anti-tank guns, though their use should be limited to one and certainly no more than two per game. The 2.8cm tapered bore anti-tank gun can also be parachuted in and the limit should be kept to two as well. These will have to be dropped separately from their crews. An easy way to account for this is to place markers on the board for each piece and their crew. The player can draw out a simple 5-point star with the five points representing the different directions of a miss. The center of the star signifies landing on the target. Then the player will need to roll a 6-sided die to determine the direction the crew and piece drift in. He will then have to roll a 20-sided die to determine the number of inches they land from the intended target spot. Initially, the gamer will have to set his two markers apart from one another. As a general rule of thumb, the two marks cannot be closer than six inches from each other. This procedure could mean the two separate by as much as 46 inches, though it is unlikely this will happen. Yet if it did, the purpose of the game is to allow the gamer the experience of landing under stressful conditions and bringing order out of chaos, which this situation would definitely fall into.

Once the attacking player starts to move, it may be easy to get carried away and forget sound wargame tactical doctrine. The player might find himself moving his troops to the objectives without thinking through the issues of concentration, command, fire, and maneuver. With troops scattered all over the board, it will be necessary to gather as many troops as possible into defined groups to begin assaulting their objections. This will increase their firepower and their ability to leapfrog to the target. In the "Blood and Guts" rules, squads under direct command of a platoon leader or company CO have their morale values increased by one. This helps in beating a morale test while working toward the objective.

The defender in this game has two tactical choices to make. He can use what troops are present and activated to counterattack the paratroopers while they are organizing. This can mean coming out from behind cover and assaulting through the disorganized troopers. This can certainly set back the timetable for the airborne infantry to achieve their goal. Unfortunately, this can result in weakening the defenses and leaving the objectives vulnerable until reinforcements arrive. The other choice is to start concentrating on the objectives by moving as many forces as available to the *suspected* goals, while waiting for the reinforcements to enter the game. However, this has the likelihood of dividing the defending player's troops and reducing his combat strength at each point.

This brings up another matter. If the players are making up their own scenario, there should be at least two possible objectives. The important point is that the defender should not know the exact details regarding which is the ultimate mission. It is critical that the defender have to do some guessing. The best example of this is Operation Market Garden. In the opening stages of the battle, the Germans were clueless as to the purpose of the paratroopers' task.

The next type of game is the traditional match between organized enemies. In this case, the paratroopers are one of the opponents and it is assumed they have already dropped, organized, and have begun advancing on their objective. When creating a scenario, the primary concern is how to equip the paratrooper or glider-borne infantry. If the troopers are going to be used as infantry, like the 82nd Airborne was at Bastogne or the actions of the Fallschirmjaegers against the Allies in Normandy, then this section is not applicable. In these kinds of games, those troops can be equipped with nearly any type of weapon or support units that regular infantry can be assigned. What is of concern here are the types of munitions and equipment that the airborne units would have shortly after taking the field, either from parachuting in or by glider landing.

Having said this, there is always the exception to the rule. There were those instances in which the German paratroopers did receive their motorcycles, field guns, and anti-tank guns once the airfields were captured, as was the case in Crete. Similarly, if they jumped as the lead elements in a reinforcement action and friendly airfields were nearby, like in Sicily, then more equipment can be present. Moreover, the action may not be a jump at all but a reinforcement mission by air transport, which occurred in Italy.

Starting with the Germans, these infantry units would be armed with standard weapons and some minor field equipment. It is reasonable to assume that they would have their light and medium machine guns, mortars, and light anti-tanks guns. However, the latter two items would require the assistance of a Kittenkrad or motorcycle with a sidecar, to not only provide transport but to carry the ammunition. Therefore, a little homework may be in order to get exact details of what was at the scene. Unfortunately, not many books are written with the wargamer in mind. Thus, the gamer might be forced into making a judgment call on history. As stated above, there should be limits on how many heavier pieces are used by one or two companies of troops.

For the American and British airborne infantry, their weapon pool will be larger, especially if the scenario is D-Day and thereafter. Prior to the D-Day landings, the Allied paratrooper arsenal was similar to that of the Germans. The transport and glider developments were still in the beginning phases. Subsequently, the paratrooper drops were not as large or as well-armed as the D-Day missions. These troops can certainly be armed with machine guns, bazookas, and light mortars. In the Northwest Europe Front, they would have jeeps, 75mm and 105mm pack howitzers, 57mm anti-tanks guns, and a few Bren Gun Carriers. The latter assumes the large transport glider, the Hamilcar, was nearby.

One extra feature to the weapons and equipment issue that should be reviewed for the wargame is the prospect of captured enemy gear. This can be far-ranging, particularly if the scenario is historical fiction. It may be tempting to allow the paratroopers of both sides to come rambling into the game in some captured tanks! Even though that may have happened, the documentation on such events is pretty slim. I have only read one account of American paratroopers outside Bastogne recapturing a Sherman and using it in a static defensive position. Therefore, it is possible to have such weapons but it is pretty unlikely. The nice part about historical fiction wargames is that the word fiction is in the title and a game is just that, a game. For those a little less enthusiastic about letting their British Red Devils ride into battle with Panther G tanks, there are some more realistic alternatives. It was common for the troopers to commandeer enemy jeeps and trucks for transport to the objective. Sometimes even armored cars and half-tracks were taken over and marked with aerial markings such as national flags to avoid being attacked by friendly fire. When deciding to use enemy equipment, it is best to have limits on how many captured vehicles the airborne may have, because the gamers are most likely only dealing with one or two companies of infantry. The recommended amount is two, but no more than three. It may also be possible that the paratroopers captured anti-tank guns or similar weapons, especially if the scenario is about their defense of a captured position. The troopers may have been familiar with certain enemy guns but were not likely to be as proficient as the intended crew, and firing modifiers should be placed on the new "crews."

This brings up the scenario in which the airborne are on the defensive while occupying a key terrain feature. Many times a ridge overlooking a road or a specific objective such as a bridge was the target of the airborne troopers. These scenarios are relatively easy to research because many of their clashes within the first hours of the drop or glider landing were at their appointed objective. One of the most famous actions was the defense of Pegasus Bridge on June 6, 1944. Another interesting action was the German Paratrooper defense of the Cretan prison. They had taken refuge within the first hours of the attack and came under assault by New Zealanders supported by two Mk.VI tanks.

Airborne games are relatively simple to create and set up. The most important aspect is to keep the scenario basic. It must be remembered that most airborne ventures were chaotic. The troopers landed all over the countryside and sometimes managed to land on the drop zone. Thus, the troopers that initially took the objective were from a smattering of units and were not up to full strength. This might translate into a gamer using a company or less of paratroopers securing the objective. Additionally, the counterattacking enemy force would have been limited to the soldiers in the area. This would further mean that they were rear echelon troops perhaps with minimal to no combat experience. (Of course, this cannot be said of the German troops in the Arnhem area. Hence, that is why the mission ended in ultimate failure.) The troops in the rules of this book should have their morale made up of ones and twos. The enemy might have a few trucks or half-tracks to act as their transport vehicles. But heavy weapons and tanks should be avoided. The half-tracks should only be armed with machine guns, though it is entirely reasonable to have anti-aircraft guns brought into the game. Being rear troops, they would have access to those weapons, or the counterattacking force might be a Luftwaffe anti-aircraft battery.

CHAPTER 10

Tank Development of World War Two

The development of tanks and the associated anti-tank guns of World War Two were not equal across the different belligerent nations. Each country took different paths and had different levels of long-range thinking that influenced their nation's armored forces. This chapter focuses on the development of tanks and their armament in World War Two. At the end of the chapter, I lay out several tables that present general specifications for the most common tanks and their variants that were used by the different countries. These specifications include armor thickness, type of gun, sub-armament, crew, and speed. There is also a chart that shows the different anti-tank guns and their armor penetration capabilities at various ranges. These are not intended to be an all-inclusive work on the subject. The intention is to give the wargamer an easy reference tool, when he is assembling his forces and wanting to compare the strengths and weaknesses of the different vehicles and the comparative strengths of varying guns.

At the conclusion of the First World War, the British held the lead in the development of the tank. They were the world's foremost producers and held the greatest collection of experts on the subject. However, due to the drawdown from a wartime economy to one of peace and prosperity, the British government shelved most of their talent and resources. Intermilitary feuds also meant that the tank's future was not taken seriously. The British War Office further hampered the technological development by not giving clear direction as to the intended use of the tank. The English favored mobility and crew protection over firepower, even though they expected that one of the main tasks of tanks would be fighting other tanks. Unfortunately, the War Office allowed anti-tank gun development to fall under the domain of the Royal Artillery, which meant little time was devoted to creating effective anti-tank guns. The Royal Artillery spent its shrinking budget on current weapon upgrades and new artillery developments. This helps answer why Britain was so underprepared in this area by the time war broke out and why it took several years to overcome this handicap.

Throughout the 1920s and 1930s, military theorists universally agreed that tanks needed to fulfill three primary roles and that their design should be changed from their predecessors in the First World War. The first class of tank, the heavy tank, would provide the armor support for infantry attacks and would accompany the infantry to their objectives. The medium tank would form the traditional cavalry role by punching holes through the enemy line and disrupting communications and supply lines as well as hitting weak points in the enemy's rear. Light tanks performed the task of reconnaissance. They were lightly armored and lightly armed to increase their relative speed and mobility. In addition, the tank's interior and exterior were altered to meet the new tasks being created. Across the world, tanks started taking on the look they have today. In World War One, tanks generally had a fixed firing platform and an open interior that encompassed the engine. By the 1920s, tanks were broken down into three primary components: the driving compartment, the engine section, and the fighting compartment. They also took on the turret for the main fighting function. It would be the turret ring and the distance between the tracks that would later prove vital to a tank being fitted with a better anti-tank gun and a larger turret to meet the new tank threats offered by the enemy. The British were one of the first to incorporate these changes in their Medium Mk I, which was one of the first serviceable tanks of the interwar era. It was armed with multiple machine guns. Its top speed was 14.8 mph and it was constructed of riveted armor plate eight millimeters thick. But it was obsolete by the time of the Second World War.

In the run up to the war, the British did have several classes of tanks already well in development. Many of the light tanks were produced in collaboration with Vickers. This produced the Universal Carrier or Bren Gun Carrier, the Light Mk II, and the Mk VI. The carrier was the only one to serve continuously throughout the war. The Mk II and VI, though fast, were too underarmed. Their role was eclipsed by the introduction of the American M3 Light tank known to the British as the Honey. It got its nickname because of its relatively superior mechanical reliability to that of the British tanks. The Cruiser class of British tanks was a respectable line of armor that was originally known as the A series of medium tanks. It started with the A9 Cruiser Mk I. It was armed with a 2pdr. anti-tank gun and two small forward turrets equipped with Vickers .303 machine guns. The track and suspension were borrowed from the ill-fated Matilda Mk I. The maximum speed was a fair advancement for that size vehicle, but the armor protection was poor with only a maximum thickness of 14mm. The A10 dropped the twin machine gun turrets and increased the armor plating to 30mm. The A13s and later models adopted a new track and bogie system similar to that of the famous desert Crusader II, though they still retained the 2pdr. as the primary anti-tank gun. The line continued to grow through the A27 Cromwell and the A34 Comet. The British did not start arming their tanks with a 6pdr. anti-tank gun until the latter half of 1942, which was given to the Crusader III. The Cruiser class was somewhat sidelined by the infusion and adaptation of American tanks into British tank formations. It may be tempting to add the Sherman Firefly into the Cruiser series. However, it was never produced in the volume needed to equip full formations. The tanks were allocated piecemeal to British tank companies, usually one tank per troop. (The troop was equivalent to the American armored platoon.) Its purpose was to be able to successfully engage the heavier German Panther and Tiger tanks with some level of armament parity.

The British also produced a line of heavy tanks originally denoted as "infantry tanks," starting with the development of the A11 (or better known as the Matilda I). This odd armored vehicle sprang to life as a result of the confused state of the British War Office in 1930s. Although it had respectable armor protection of 60mm thickness, it was only armed with a Vickers .303 machine gun and its cross-country speed was a horrendous 5 to 6 mph. At the time of its production, it was not envisioned that infantry tanks would encounter enemy armor. The need for a better alterative was quickly pursued, and the Matilda II was put into production by 1937. Even though its speed was only marginally better, it was still armed with a 2pdr. but with increased armor protection. At the start of the war, this tank was arguably one of the best tanks in the world. While the Matilda II was getting its start, Vickers began designing another heavy tank. It adopted the A11's track system, but the A11 hull was upgraded to create the Valentine. It too was equipped with a 2pdr. Unfortunately, the small turret size only allow for two men to operate the main gun. This design flaw hindered the tank's rate of fire. The Valentine went on to have many modifications including the Archer and Bishop.

The most famous English tank to serve in the war was the Churchill, which began entering service in June 1941 with only a modest number of vehicles. The reason for its unique elliptical track design was that some theorized that the coming war would be similar to the trench warfare of the last war. Therefore, the army should have a tank with solid trench-crossing abilities, which it did at 10 feet. The Matilda II and Valentine could only cover 7 feet by comparison. It was not until 1943 that its combat value was put to the test in Tunisia. It was initially armed with a 2pdr. and a 3-inch howitzer in the hull, which was soon dropped in favor of a hull machine gun. The Churchill went on to be up-gunned and up-armored throughout the war.

Before concluding the discussion on British armor, a brief mention should be made of their weaponry. The 2pdr. was a 40mm anti-tank gun. The 6pdr. was a 57mm and the 17pdr. was a 76mm gun. The early guns, the 2pdr. and the 6pdr. were not equipped to fire high explosives (HE) in support of infantry. The reason for this was that during the early tank development years in the post–World War One era, the British focused on tanks fighting tanks. Hence their early tanks had relatively decent amour protection for the time but had no HE to support their infantry in the attack. If HE was needed, it was reasoned that the artillery batteries supporting the attack would be sufficient. It was not until early 1943 that the 6pdr. started receiving HE rounds. However, by that time the 17pdr. was beginning to make its appearance, and it was capable of firing high explosive shells. To cope with the need to have close support for the infantry, the British reconfigured several of their tanks to be able to fire HE only. These included the Cruiser Marks I and II, Crusader II, and Matilda II. The designation is denoted by a CS (Close Support) following the tank's name, for example the Cruiser Mark I CS.

The Versailles Treaty concluding the First World War restricted the Germans in developing tanks and other armaments. However, by the mid-1920s, Germany started rearming itself and by 1939 they had the most powerful armored forces in the world. They initially started secret developments under agricultural pretenses as early as 1921. In the late 1920s, the Soviets allowed the Germans to test their "tractors" at the Kazan training grounds. The Germans, like the Russians, prized firepower above all else in their tank development programs. This may seem a contradiction when one looks at a Panzer I, which was lightly armed. The Panzer I initially served as a training tank but because the Panzer IIs and IIIs had not been produced in sufficient numbers for the early campaigns of the war, it was forced to act as a combat vehicle. All things considered, it proved itself well in the role of a light tank, despite only being armed with machines guns. (Hitler and the High Command had not anticipated going to war in 1939. They had assumed that the Allies would continue to acquiesce to German demands to include the Polish Campaign.)

The German designers had also picked up on the concept of producing the three primary classifications of the tank: light, medium, and heavy. The Panzer II was produced on the heels of the first Panzer Is being delivered into service. The need for an anti-tank gun in a turret was obvious, so the Panzer II was armed with a 20mm cannon. It is worth noting that the early German tanks were not the mythical monsters the later German tanks became. They were by comparison equal to their British counterparts in terms of speed and armor, but the British by the mid 1930s had the advantage of the 2pdr, which was still superior to the 37mm used in the early version of the Panzer III. When these early models became obsolete, the Germans had the foresight to upgrade them with heavy caliber weapons, like the Czech 47mm and the Pak 40 75mm mounted on the Marder II. Another insight they had was that all German guns carried high explosive rounds, something the British had omitted with the 2pdr. The Panzer III took on the role of the medium tank. Its design started in the late 1930s and was accepted for service in September 1939. There were less than 100 available for the invasion of Poland and by May 1940 some 350 were ready for the French Campaign. Although it was produced with a 37mm, plans were already being made to upgrade the turret with a short 50mm (kwk L/42), which started production in 1940. Because of the size of the tank's turret ring, the tank was able to be up-gunned several times. By 1943 it was being armed with the kwk L/60, the long version of the 50mm. It was also armed with a short 75mm howitzer for infantry support. In addition, by the late 1930s, the Panzer IV had started production as Germany's heavy tank. It was first armed with a short 75mm howitzer. Its role was to provide HE and smoke support for the advancing tank columns, though later it underwent numerous upgrades as the war progressed. It holds the title as being the only tank of the German army that was produced throughout the entire war. One of the more successful models was the Ausf H. It was armed with a kwk L/48, 75mm anti-tank gun. Of course in terms of a heavy tank it was eclipsed by the development of the Panther, Tiger, and Tiger II, which essentially made it a medium tank.

The procession of German tanks and their innovations could fill volumes of books, and certainly many books have been written on the subject. What is important to recognize is that the German tank designers had placed great forethought into tank development. They started with the training model, the Panzer

I. Models II, III, and IV were in design development roughly at the same time in the late 1930s, when other nations were still trying to understand the tank's strategic and tactical role. This, coupled with creating Panzer armies gearing up for Blitzkrieg warfare, made the German war machine invincible in the early days of the war.

The Russians, like the Germans, took an early lead in their tank development programs and they regarded firepower and speed as the key ingredients for tank production. After their civil war, Soviet industrial capacity was left in ruins. It was not until 1928 that they could produce a copy of the French FT-17, known as the T-18. By investing in some of the Vickers' designs, they began producing the T-26s in the mid 1930s. The important note here is that the Soviets included a 37mm anti-tank gun in the tank's turret. Although it was not the equivalent of a British 2pdr., it was an advancement in Soviet tank fire power. Another such vehicle that surprised the military world was the creation of the BT series, which had incorporated the American Christie Suspension. The BT 5 was armed with a 45mm gun and served the Communists well in the Spanish Civil War. The BT 7 was an upgraded version of its predecessor. It too was armed with a 45mm gun and its speed was about 50 mph even though it was upgraded in armor thickness.

Seeing the success of having a well-armed and fast tank, the Russians began designs for a new project. The famed T-34 was on a prototype drawing board as early as 1937, under the A-20 name. It was finally ready by June 1940.When the Germans invaded, the Soviets had approximately 1200 T-34s. It was this tank that changed tank design concepts with its sloped armor, speed, and armament. The sloped armor allowed the tank designers to minimize the armor's thickness without jeopardizing the quality of protection relative to the current tank technology of the day. With reduced armor thickness, the mobility of the tank could be increased. Also, the tank's treads were wider than other contemporary models and this gave the T-34 better cross-country performance, which the Germans would discover in the winter counterattack of 1941 outside

Moscow. If there were any design flaws, it was the fact that the turret design was small. It carried a powerful 76.2mm gun, but the size of the turret meant that only two men operated the tasks of loading, aiming, commanding, and firing. Also, the turret did not have a rotating floor base to turn with the gun. This meant that the turret crew had to climb over objects on the floor of the tank to keep up with the turret's rotation.

The Soviets were the first to master heavy tank designs and started producing them in the 1930s. An early example is the T-35. It was a multi-turreted monster with a 76.2mm serving as its primary armament. Amazingly, by 1939, the Soviets departed from the T-35 design style in favor of the more successful KV tank series. This demonstrated incredible insight into what a heavy tank would need in the coming war. Its armor protection was over 100 millimeters thick, and it could still claim a top speed of over 20 mph. It came armed with a 76.2mm anti-tank gun, which would later stun the Germans. The first prototypes were available to be engaged in combat in the Russo-Finnish War of 1940. This tank also laid the foundation for the later heavy tanks of the Soviet arsenal in the JS I and II. These tanks housed an 85mm and 122mm gun, respectively. Throughout the war, the Russians showed great resilience in constantly being able to upgrade their tanks with greater armor and firepower. This fact put the Germans ever more on the technological defensive in their struggle to stay ahead of the Russians.

Perhaps the most interesting aspect of Soviet tank history is what might have been. M.N. Tukhachevsky was a leading figure in Russian tank tactics in the early 1930s. He was instrumental in the early formations of the country's mechanized armored forces. By 1935 Stalin's factories had produced over 10,000 tanks, and by June 1941 German intelligence estimated that they had produced some 24,000 armored vehicles. Unfortunately, he and his subordinates were executed as a result of the purge trails, along with many other military commanders. This negatively impacted the state of readiness of the Soviet Army. After his death, the mechanized brigades were broken up and dispersed to the infantry, similar to the French strategy. Had he not been sentenced to death, one wonders what condition the Soviet Tank

Corps would have been in at the time of the German invasion. Also, would they have produced and equipped their formations with their superior tanks prior to 1941? Naturally that idea is irrelevant to history, but for a wargamer it stimulates some interesting ideas for gaming Operation Barbarrosa.

By comparison to the other major powers of the Second World War, America's tank development was very slow in coming and was initially very limited. In post–World War One America, military spending was drastically cut. It suffered initially from the political feelings of isolationism and the traditional American mindset of having a limited peacetime army. The remaining tanks after the war were organized into 4 battalions and placed under the control of the infantry. Later, in the wake of the Great Depression, further restrictions were placed on weapon advancements. With tank development, by order of Congress under the control of the infantry, General Douglas MacArthur placed the light tank's development under the U.S. Cavalry and called them "combat cars." The Americans, like the Europeans, were interested in developing tanks according to international standards. That is having light and medium tanks. However, heavy tanks at the time were beyond the means of the Army war planners. The Army had already stipulated that development would consist of only 5-and 15-ton vehicles: light and medium tanks. By 1939, America could only muster about 112 newer tanks or "combat cars." With German victories in Europe in 1940, the United States could still only claim a meager 464 tanks. Fortunately, the political winds had shifted and Congress poured massive amounts of money into tank production. In 1941, there were over 4000 tanks built and by the following year nearly 25,000 rolled off the assembly line. In total, America built over 88,000 tanks and 43,000 self-propelled guns and tank destroyers. With these kinds of numbers and the Soviets producing a similar amount, the Germans stood no chance of victory. They were only able to produce about 50,000 tanks during the course of the war.

The most famous U.S. tank of the Second World War is, of course, the Sherman M4. It was certainly not the best tank of the war, but it did have several endearing qualities. The overall size was larger than other tanks in its class. This not only gave a bit more comfort to the crew but allowed for better maintenance because access to components was easier. This characteristic also favored eventual upgrades in armor and anti-tank gun armament. Another factor, though not unique to the Sherman as other American tanks had it too, was that it had a gyroscopic gun stabilization system that stabilized the gun in elevation while the tank was moving. These characteristics and the sheer production numbers led the British to adopt and fit their tank formations with the U.S. Sherman.

The American approach to armored tactical developments differed somewhat from the European nations. The U.S. military believed that the main battle tank should have a dual-purpose gun. They wanted a gun that not only fired an armor-piercing round but could effectively fire high explosive and smoke rounds. This explains why the Sherman retained its 75mm for as long as it did despite having a usable 76mm anti-tank gun. The 76mm gun was turned over to the tank destroyer battalions and mounted in the M10s. The American tacticians believed in having the medium tanks support the mechanized troops and to have the tank destroyers engage enemy tanks from a distance. This notation stemmed from a lack of appreciation and farsightedness into the tank's ultimate role: that tanks should be designed to destroy other tanks and armor-piercing firepower should be placed as a top priority. Toward the end of the war, American tanks were up-armored and up-gunned. The U.S. did produce a heavy tank known as the Pershing, but it did not arrive until February 1945 and it saw limited service in the war.

It is true that other nations were building tanks prior to World War Two and brought them into battle as the war broke out. France, Italy, and Japan were the contributing secondary powers producing such vehicles. However, they lacked the industrial capacity to muster the quantity needed to be effective over the long term. Also, their military planners were stuck in the infantry support mindset. It is known that France had some of the best tanks at the start of the war, such as the Somua, Char

B, and H39. Unfortunately, they were deficient in grasping what the Germans had already learned and that was to concentrate their tanks. Had they done so from the start, the German invasion would have met armored formation with armored formation and perhaps things might have ended differently.

German Tanks

Tank Type	Max. Armor Thickness	Main Armament	Sub Armament	Crew	Speed in M.P.H.
Panzer Ib	15mm	2 MG 7.62mm	NA	2	25
Panzer Ib Command	30mm	1 MG 7.62mm	NA	2	20
Jadg Panzer I	13mm	47mm Pak 36(t)	NA	3	25
35(t)	25mm	37mm kwk L/43 34 (t)	1 MG 7.62mm	3	18
38(t)	25mm	37mm kwk L/40	2 MG 7.62mm	4	26
Marder II	35mm	75mm Pak 40/2	1 MG7.92mm	3	25
Marder IIIm	25mm	75mm Pak 40/3 L46	1 MG 7.62mm	4	30
Panzer IIc	20mm	20mm kwk 30	1 MG 7.62mm	3	25
Panzer IIf	35mm	20mm kwk 30	1 MG 7.62mm	3	25

Panzer II Luchs	30mm	20mm kwk 38	1 MG 7.62mm	4	40
Wespe	30mm	105HE leFH 18m L28		5	25
Panzer IIIe	30mm	37mm kwk 36	2 MG 7.62mm	5	25
Panzer IIIj	50mm	Short 50mm kwk 42	2 MG 7.62mm	5	25
Panzer III L	50mm	Long 50mm kwk 39 L60	2 MG 7.62mm	5	25
Stug IIId	50mm	Short 75mm HE kwk L24	NA	4	25
Stug IIIg	80mm	Long 75mm AP Stuk 40 L/48	1 MG 7.62mm	4	25
Stug IIIh	50mm	105 HE Stu. H 42 L/28	1 MG 7.62mm	4	25
JgPz 38(t) Hetzer	60mm	75mm Pak 39	1 MG 7.62mm	4	25
Panzer IVb	30mm	Short 75mm kwk L24	1 MG 7.62mm	4	25
Panzer IVe	80mm	Short 75mm kwk L24	1 MG 7.62mm	5	25
Panzer IVh	80mm	Long 75mm kwk 40 L/48	1 MG 7.62mm	5	25
Nashorn	30mm	88mm Pak 43	NA	5	24

Hummel	30mm	150mm HE sIG 33	NA	6	24
Grille	25mm	150mm HE sIG 33	1 MG 7.92mm	5	21
JgPz. IV/70	80mm	Long 75mm Stu. K L/70	1 MG 7.62mm	4	25
Stug Pz. IV Brum-mbar	100mm	150m StuH 43L/12	NA	4	24
Panther D	100mm	Long 75mm kwk 42 L/70	2 MG 7.62mm	5	28
Panther G	110 mm	Long 75mm kwk 43 L/71	2 MG 7.62mm	5	28
JgPz. Panther	80mm	88mm Pak 43/3	1 MG 7.62mm	4	25
JgPz. Elefant	200mm	88mm Pak 43/2	NA	6	12.5
Tiger I	100mm	88mm Pak 36 L/56	2 MG 7.62mm	5	24
Tiger II	150mm	88mm kwk 43	2 MG 7.62mm	5	24
JgPz. Tiger	250mm	128mm Pak 44 L/55	1 MG 7.62mm	6	23

Armored Fighting Vehicles
(German)

AFV Type	*Max. Armor Thickness*	*Main Armament*	*Sub Armament*	*Crew*	*Speed in M.P.H.*
SdKfz 231 (6 rad.)	14.5mm	20mm kwk 30	1 MG 7.62mm	4	37
SdKfz 232 (8 rad.)	14.5mm	20mm kwk 30	1 MG 7.62mm	4	53
SdKfz (222)	14.5	20mm kwk 30	1 MG 7.62mm	3	46
SdKfz (251) Hanomag	12mm	NA	1 MG 7.62mm	12*	31

SdKfz (251)/9 Hanomag	12mm	75mm Short HE kwk L24	NA	3	31
SdKfz (251/22) Hanomag	12mm	75mm Pak L/46	NA	3	31
SdKfz (250/10)	12mm	37mm Pak 35/36	NA	3	31
SdKfz (250)	12mm	NA	1 MG 7.62mm	6*	37
SdKfz (250/8)	14.5mm	75mm kwk L24	1 MG 7.62mm	3	37
SdKfz (250/9)	14.5mm	20mm kwk 30/38 L/55	1 MG 7.62mm	3	37
SdKfz 234/2 Puma	100mm	Long 50mm kwk 39/1 L60	1 MG 7.62mm	4	53
SdKfz 234/3	30mm	Short 75mm kwk L24	1 MG 7.62mm	5	53

*Assumes the troops being carried.

Italian Tanks

Tank Type	Max. Armor Thickness	Main Armament	Sub Armament	Crew	Speed in M.P.H.
CV33	13.5mm	(2) 8mm MG	NA	2	26
M11/39	30mm	37mm	(2) MG	3	20
M13/40	40mm	47mm	1 MG	4	20
M15/42	50mm	47mm	1MG	4	25
L.6/40	30mm	20mm	1MG	2	20
Semovente 75/34	42mm	75mm HE/AP	1MG	3	20
Semovente M40/41	30mm	75mm HE/AP	1MG	3	20

Italian Armored Fighting Vehicles

AFV Type	Max. Armor Thickness	Main Armament	Sub Armament	Crew	Speed in M.P.H.
Autoblinda 40	18mm	(2) 8mm MG	NA	4	46
Autoblinda 41	18mm	(1) 20mm (1) 8mm	NA	4	46
Autoblinda 43	22mm	47mm	NA	4	46
Lince	25mm	8mm	NA	3	53

Japanese Tanks

Tank Type	Max. Armor Thickness	Main Armament	Sub Armament	Crew	Speed in M.P.H.
Light Type 94	12mm	7.7mm MG	NA	2	25
Light Type 95	12mm	37mm	7.7mm MG	3	28
Light Type 97	16mm	37mm	NA	2	28
Medium Type 97	25mm	37mm	(2) 7.7mm MG	3	24
Medium Type 97 New Turret	33mm	47mm	(2) 7.7mm MG	4	24
Ho-Ni*	25mm	75mm HE	NA	4	24

*The 75mm had a muzzle velocity of 2260 feet per second and constituted the only truly effective anti-tank gun.

British Tanks

Tank Type	Max. Armor Thickness	Main Armament	Sub Armament	Crew	Speed in M.P.H.
Mk1 Matilda	60mm	7.7mm MG	NA	2	8
Light Mk. VIb	14mm	12.7mm MG	(1) 7.7mm MG	3	35
Light Mk. VIc	14mm	15mm MG	(1) 7.92mm MG	3	35
Cruiser Mk. I (A9)	14mm	2pdr.	(2) 7.7mm MG	6	25
Cruiser Mk. IIa (A13)	38mm	2pdr.	(1) 7.92mm MG	5	16
Cruiser Mk. IV (A13)	30mm	2pdr.	(2) 7.7mm MG	4	30
Crusader Mk. II	49mm	2pdr.	(2) 7.7mm MG	5	26
Crusader Mk. III	49mm	6pdr	(2) 7.7mm MG	5	26
M3 Lee	51mm	37mm & 75mm	(2) 7.7mm MG	6	26
Stuart	51mm	37mm	(2) 7.7mm MG	4	37
Valentine Mk. II	65mm	2pdr.	(1) 7.7mm MG	3	15

Bishop	60mm	25pdr. HE	NA	4	15
Archer	60mm	17pdr.	NA	4	15
Churchill Mk. I	102mm	2pdr. & 3 inch Hwtz.	(1) 7.7mm MG	5	15
Churchill Mk. III	102mm	6pdr.	(2) 7.7mm MG	5	15
Churchill Mk. VI	102mm	75mm	(2) 7.7mm MG	5	15
Churchill Mk. VII	152mm	75mm	(2) 7.7mm MG	5	12
Cromwell	76mm	75mm	(2) 7.7mm MG	5	32
Comet	102mm	17pdr.	(2) 7.7mm MG	5	30
Universal Carrier	10mm	Bren Gun	NA	4	30
Tetrarch	14mm	2pdr.	(1) 7.7mm MG	3	40

British Armored Fighting Vehicles

AFV Type	Max. Armor Thickness	Main Armament	Sub Armament	Crew	Speed in M.P.H.
Morris CS9	7mm	AT Rifle	1 MG	4	45
Humber Mk II	15mm	(1) 12.5mm MG	1 MG .30 cal.	3	40
Humber Mk II	15mm	37mm	1 MG .30 cal.	3	45
Scout Car MK I	30mm	1 MG	NA	2	55
Daimler Mk II	16mm	2pdr.	1 MG .30 cal.	3	50
AEC MkII	30mm	6pdr.	1 MG.30 cal.	4	41
Morris Mk II	14mm	MG	NA	3	50

American Tanks

Tank Type	Max. Armor Thickness	Main Armament	Sub Armament	Crew	Speed in M.P.H.
M2A4 Light	19mm	37mm	3 MG .30 cal.	4	37
M3 Light	51mm	37mm	2 MG .30 cal.	4	37
M5A1 Light	67mm	37mm	2 MG .30 cal.	4	37
M22 Light	25mm	37mm	1 MG .30 cal	3	39
M24 Light	25mm	75mm	2 MG .30 cal.	5	35
M3 Grant/ Lee	51mm	37mm & 75mm	2 MG .30 cal.	6	26
M12 GMC	25mm	155mm HE	NA	6	19
M4A1 Sherman	51mm	75mm	2 MG .30 cal.	5	23
M4A3	63mm	76.2mm	2 MG .30 cal.	5	29
M26 Pershing	101mm	90mm	2 MG.30 cal.	5	29
M10 GMC	37mm	76.2mm	NA	5	29
M36 GMC	50mm	90mm	NA	5	29
M18 GMC	12mm	76.2mm	NA	5	49
M7 GMC	62mm	105mm HE	NA	7	24

M8 HMC	67mm	75mm HE	1 MG.30 cal.	4	37
LVT(A)1	13mm	37mm	1 MG.30 cal.	4	24 land /6 sea

American Armored Fighting Vehicles

AFV Type	Max. Armor Thickness	Main Armament	Sub Armament	Crew	Speed in M.P.H.
M8	19mm	37mm	1 MG.30 cal.	4	55
T17 Staghound	32mm	37mm	1 MG.30 cal.	5	55
M3 ½ track	16mm	.50 cal	1 MG.30 cal.	12	45
M3 Scout Car	12mm	.50 cal	1 MG.30 cal.	6	55

Soviet Tanks

Tank Type	Max. Armor Thickness	Main Armament	Sub Armament	Crew	Speed in M.P.H.
BT-5	13mm	45mm	(1) 7.62mm MG	3	44
BT-7	22mm	45mm	(2) 7.62mm MG	3	53

T-26	25mm	45m	(2) 7.62mm MG	3	18
T-60	20mm	20mm	(1) 7.62mm MG	2	27
T-70	60mm	45mm	(1) 7.62mm MG	2	27
T34/76	45mm	76.2mm	(1) 7.62mm MG	4	34
T34/85	90mm	85mm	(1) 7.62mm MG	5	34
KV-1	75mm	76.2mm	(3) 7.62mm MG	5	21
KV-2	110mm	152mm HE	(2) 7.62mm MG	6	16
IS-1	160mm	85mm	(1)7.62mm MG	4	24
IS-2	160mm	122mm	(3) 7.62mm MG	4	22
SU-76	35mm	76.2mm	(1)7.62mm MG	4	27
SU-85	45mm	85mm	(2) 7.62mm MG	4	29
SU-100	45mm	100mm	(2) 7.62mm MG	4	29
SU-122	45mm	122mm HE	(2) 7.62mm MG	5	34
SU-152	90mm	152mm HE	(2) 7.62mm MG	5	22

Soviet Armored Fighting Vehicles

AFV Type	Max. Armor Thickness	Main Armament	Sub Armament	Crew	Speed in M.P.H.
BA-64	10mm		(1) 7.62mm MG	2	31
BA-10	14mm	45mm	(1) 7.62mm MG	4	54

Armor Penetration Tables:

Range in Meters/Penetration in Millimeters

Range	100	200	300	400	500	600	700	800	900	1000	1250	1500	2000	2500
German Guns														
PzB 39 ATR			25											
2.8cm S. Pz. 41	69	65	60	56	52	48	44	41	23	11				
Pak 37 37mm		56		51	48	46								
Pak 40 37mm	68	61	55	49	48	40	37							
Pak 41 47mm	100	83 @250m			72		62 @ 750m			53				
Pak 38 50m	120	109 @250m		98	86		69 @ 750m			55	44			

Range	100	200	300	400	500	600	700	800	900	1000	1250	1500	2000	2500
Pak 40 75mm	137				115					96			66	53
Pak 36 76.2mm	152				118					92		71	55	43
88 Flak L56	127				117					106		97	88	
Pak 43 88mm	265				226					192		162	136	114
Pak 44 128mm					215					202				
2cm KwK L55		33	30	26	21	17								
3.7cm KwK 45L	64	50	45	36 @ 450m	30	32								
5cm KwK L42	94			56 @ 450m						36		28	22	

Range	100	200	300	400	500	600	700	800	900	1000	1250	1500	2000	2500
5cm KwK L60	73			61 @450m	59				50	48	40	38	29	
7.5cm KwK L24	45			41 @450m	38					35				
7.5cm KwK L43	99			89 @450m						81			64	
7.5cm KwK L48		105	97	90 @ 450m	89	87	85	83	80	74	70	62		
7.5cm KwK L70	138			141 @ 450m	124				121			99	88	
8.8 cm KwK L56	120			110 @ 450m						90			84	80
8.8cm KwK L71	198			182 @ 450m					167		153		132	115
Pz.schrk 88mm		150												

Range	100	200	300	400	500	600	700	800	900	1000	1250	1500	2000	2500
Pz faust 30 Klein		100												
Pz faust 30		150												
Pz faust 60/90		150												
British Guns														
Boys ATR 14mm			21											
PIAT	100													
2 pdr.		56	53	50	48	42	39	35	30	26				
6 pdr.		93	89	85	81	79	77	69	64	60	50			
75mm (Grant Tank)		66		61	58	55		49						

Range	100	200	300	400	500	600	700	800	900	1000	1250	1500	2000	2500
17 pdr.					186									
Polish Guns														
Polish Anti Tank Rifle 7.62mm	30													
Bofors 37mm L45					40									
French Guns														
SAL 1937 25mm					30									
SAL 1937 47mm					57									
Italian Guns														

300

Range	100	200	300	400	500	600	700	800	900	1000	1250	1500	2000	2500
47/32Model 47mm					55					26				
90/53 AA Gun 90mm										101				
American Guns														
Bazooka	100													
37mm					48					42				
M2 (75mm Lee Tank)		66		61	58	55		49						
M3 (75mm Sherman)					70									
76mm M1A1										88				
76mm M1A2										133				

Range	100	200	300	400	500	600	700	800	900	1000	1250	1500	2000	2500
90mm				126/APC*						120 APC			105 APC	
Japanese Guns														
Type 97 ATR			30											
37mm Type 97					35									
47mm Type 01										40				
Soviet Guns														
45mm M1937										38				
45mm M1942					52									

Range	100	200	300	400	500	600	700	800	900	1000	1250	1500	2000	2500
57mm M1943					93									
100mm M1944					181									
PTRD 1941 ATR			25											

* Armor-Piercing, Capped.

CHAPTER 11

Childhood Reflections

I thought I would share some reflections of my childhood of playing and collecting toy soldiers and developing into a wargamer. This last chapter is dedicated to all those would-be wargamers and those still throwing dice in hopes of the perfect roll. My hope is that I can reinvigorate some burned out gamer souls, arouse some distant memories of the reader, and provoke a few folks to tap into that lost child who enjoyed his toy soldier collection.

Toy soldiers entered my world when I was very young, though when, I am not exactly sure. I must have been between four and six years old. The reason I say that is because the usual toys of that age were still an active part of my wooden toy box. I had small plastic dinosaurs, racing cars, and regular nondescript Legos. As I mentioned at the start of the book, I got interested in "gaming" with soldiers sometime after the Christmas vacation of my fourth-grade year. I know my older brothers had little troops and played regularly. Admittedly, I do not recall ever seeing them setting up toy soldiers. They were older by the time I arrived. Greg has me beat by ten years, and Zack has me by close to five years. My earliest memory with either of them was watching Greg place 1/72 scale Airfix British 8th Army troops, the ones holding the mine detectors, in the flames of the fireplace and watching them melt away. After that, it gets hazy. I know I started to play with the ubiquitous green soldiers with M16s by the time I was in kindergarten. I think my class even had a few in the toy box section. But mostly the figure toys were red fireman, blue policemen, and white astronauts. I do not recall when I got my first bag of green soldiers. Yet I do remember going to Kmart with my parents and looking at all the tanks, trucks, armored cars, and cannons lined up in the toy section at the bottom of the aisle in small bins. Of course they were all in green and meant for the green American troops. It must be about that time that I pestered my mom or dad into buying me something. I do recall having several of those tanks, a couple of trucks, one jeep, and a cannon. I used to play in the backyard on the side of the house. The backyard used to have a small spot at the rear of the dog-run where no bushes were planted and there was dirt built up next to the wall and the house. The way it was situated left a nice little valley for the soldiers to fight in. I would sometimes run the hose and let the water form a "river" between two groups of infantry. I would then assail them with rocks and whichever side emerged with men still standing was declared the winner. I cannot remember how the tanks fared. I just know they were difficult to topple over with a rock. Sometimes my middle brother, Zack, would play and he seemed quite capable of doing it. Naturally, he beat me every time!

At about this time in my childhood a neighborhood boy and I became friends and he too had toy soldiers. Terry was given some gigantic 6-or 8-inch green soldiers. I have never seen or read about these figures since. We used to battle in his sandbox, leading his squad of troops on maneuvers. Unfortunately, that is all he had in the way of true soldiers. So there was not much we could do with the 10 or 12 men he had. Later, he did receive a castle fort to play with and it had a couple of dozen knights to man the walls or breach the fortress door. If my memory serves me correctly, the men were made of different-colored plastic and snapped together. The set was provisioned with a white and red tent. The castle walls were made of padded plastic with cardboard sheets inserted in between the inner and outer walls to keep the walls erect. We had great fun setting them up and fighting each other's warriors.

I suppose I hit a milestone when another neighborhood boy got a Christmas gift one year of blue soldiers. Although they were a bit smaller than my green guys, these troops were a fantastic enemy for my soldiers. Their poses and weapons were different and that is precisely what mattered. We would set them up and play for what seems like hours.

It is not until I was in the fourth grade that things start to come into focus. I guess my brothers figured I was old enough to enter the world of the little guys. I had received that Christmas several boxes of Airfix figures: one set of Napoleonic British Infantry accompanied by one set of French Infantry, one set of U.S. Marines, and one set of German Afrika Korps. They had also given me a tank with a metal top and a plastic bottom. My first battle took place that morning. My brother, Zack, had set up the figures in our atrium, with lines of men facing each other. He then commenced to knocking them over with a small pebble or some such thing. Sadly, the tank did not last long. I think within a week my brother blew it up with firecrackers. Somehow the thought of the plastic belly meeting his makeshift mines and not surviving the repeated blasts never crossed his mind. If it did, he paid no attention to it. He handed me my tank in several pieces and kept on walking.

Interestingly enough, I was fascinated by the small figures, and I never took to battering them with rocks or anything that would damage them. It somehow seemed an injustice. The big soldiers were another matter. I had no problem pounding them with rocks. If I had to guess why, it would have to be the mesmerizing box art. Each one of the Airfix boxes depicted a fabulous battle scene full of action. The Napoleonic cavalry were always charging gallantly toward the enemy. The Napoleonic infantry were ready to fight for their lives, amidst smoke, dust, and gunfire. The World War Two boxes were full of great battles from the 8th Army to the Russian Infantry. It was enough to light up my imagination and inspire me to recreate battles of my own. I cannot say I had a favorite. They were all so brilliant. I later went on, to my mother's dismay, to cutting up the boxes and using them as wallpaper on the wall next to my bed. I have to hand it to her for not immediately ordering me to take them down. If one of my boys decided to cover one of his walls in his room with Lego boxes, I would probably tell him to take them off. Of course, upon recalling this I might just refrain.

From those first boxes of soldiers, my collection grew. I used to beg my older brother, Greg, to take me to the hobby store. I would save up my quarters I earned for keeping my room clean and for pulling weeds in the backyard. I can still see the circular rack filled with boxes of figures. The Napoleonic British Hussars come to mind with a price tag of $1.69 sitting at my eye level. As I purchased more sets, I placed them in a large shoebox. I think it used to hold about a dozen or so boxes of figures. I remember it clearly because it was about the time my parents divorced and I recall bringing it to my dad's house very weekend.

As this collection grew, my interest in the big soldiers faded. I did manage to get a few sets of the 1/32 scale Airfix soldiers. However, only the German Mountain Troops and British Paratroopers come to mind. I used to have ski races with the Germans. The British never got much play. For some reason, I had it in my mind they were modern troops, and I did not want them intermingled with my other figures. My last great venture with the larger soldiers came when I decided I was going to ride my bike several miles from home to an old toy store called Toy City. I went there on a mission to buy a box set that contained two large plastic tanks, a jeep and a truck. How I managed to ride home with it, I will never know. It was a very large set. It must have taken me a long time. The store bag kept twisting with the wind as I gripped it while holding onto the handlebars. Later that evening, I watched *Too Late a Hero* while playing with my new soldiers. What a great night, new soldiers and a war movie to watch all in the same day! Those soldiers along, with my other big ones, ended up in a large grocery paper bag in the storage closet. Occasionally, I would take them out for a battle in the backyard. During grade school, I placed a handful in my desk to play with at recess. The playground had a lower level and a higher level, with a slope in between. On the slope were gopher holes that I used as foxholes. Sometimes the other boys would gather around, and we would play a small battle. Unfortunately, these soldiers met an untimely demise. As I mentioned in the beginning of the book, one of the older neighborhood boys, the brother of a friend, had asked to borrow them for his ninth grade film-making class. He wanted to film a war movie in miniature. Naively, I let him have them. In a few weeks, he returned them. I was shocked and sadden to find them in charred ruins. I do not think there was a soldier unaffected. I must say I was never compensated for this crime against plastic humanity and I learned a valuable lesson that day. *No one will ever treat my stuff like I will.*

Sometime after the 4th grade, I was introduced to another childhood friend, Tony. I got to know him through another chum. He was like me. He collected soldiers and built models as I was just learning to do. I recall he had numerous small plastic containers that his father had given him from the restaurant he owned, and Tony had filled them with little soldiers. I was astonished by the number and types of soldiers he had. He had soldiers and model kits I had never seen before and I was certainly envious. These soldiers were from Atlantic. He had the Schwimwagon jeep with the motorcycles, the odd looking Kettenkrad, and the oversized quad anti-aircraft gun. In addition, he had the Atlantic Russian, German, Japanese, and Afrika Korps infantries. He also had numerous Matchbox kits and soldiers. Even though I did like the tanks and planes, I never developed the affection for the Matchbox figures like I did the Airfix. I think I was already well attached and biased toward the latter.

Those Atlantic sets do bring back memories of some of my first kits. At some point, my oldest brother took me to another hobby shop in town, Frank's Hobby Shop, which has since closed. Half of the store was dedicated to trains. The owner had a large-scale train set up to run all over the store suspended just below the ceiling. The other half was the typical model stuff. In one aisle he had 1/72 scale figures and tanks. One of those shelves had the Atlantic tanks and miniatures. The first tanks I ever purchased were the Tiger Is. I can still see myself opening them on the couch in front of the television and assembling them. The box art is still clearly implanted in my mind. I later bought the Leopards and the tank with the giant missile attached, which looks like a Scud Missile launcher! I did buy only one or two boxes of the figures. They were the tiny box sets with about 20 or so figures. The shop only carried the helicopter pilots, policemen, and navy personnel. I bought the policemen. Although I thought the motorcycles were fun, the set did not impress me. Therefore, I resisted spending my precious few dollars on the other boxes of figures. I do not think the owner got much else in stock, because by this time it was the early 1980s and Atlantic was on the way out (or it had already folded), and these were the last remaining kits in the shop.

Somewhere along the way, in those early years, I did manage to get my hands on the Atlantic World War Two box sets. I vaguely remember Tony asking me if I wanted to mail order one or maybe I found one or two at Frank's Hobby Shop. Either way, I eventually got the Monte Cassino, the Ardennes, and the Stalingrad sets. Each one contained infantry, tanks, or the German Schwimwagon, Kettenkrad, and motorcycle kit. The play sets had a photographed paper base about 24 inches by 24 inches. The so-called base was a photo shot from the top view. It contained trees, bushes, and houses in rubble. The set did have some basic rules to form a game, though I cannot say I ever gave them much thought. I might have tried it once or twice, but I discarded the notation of using those rules rather quickly. I still have two of the boxes with the bases stored in my garage. I even have the original tanks, infantry, and vehicles within my collection.

The greatest kit I ever purchased came from that hobby store. I was too young to have ever gotten my hands on the *Airfix Historama* kits or the other battle sets Airfix sold. Nor did I ever find the MPC/Airfix battle sets. The only one I ever purchased in my childhood was the *MPC Attack: Normandy* set. It was absolutely fabulous, from the box art to the contents. It had a set of American and German infantry, plus a Sherman and Tiger. It also came with a house in ruins and small other knickknacks to dress up the battlefield. (These kits were all from Airfix.) I immediately went to work on building the kits. Once I finished it, I played with it continuously despite the unpainted near purple color of the base! I believe I still have the original Sherman and the house, both having several layers of paint, within my collection.

The next major revelation to hit me in my toy soldier youth was going to my standard hobby shop next to the Catholic Church I attended and finding something unusual. One day, maybe after church, I discovered that a new set of figures had arrived. These were the ESCI kits. The store owner had stocked a whole aisle with new stuff. I was absolutely delighted. The first set I purchased was the Big Red One American infantry followed by the British, French, and German infantries. I would eventually go on to collect them all. It was the ESCI brand that captured my interest in Napoleonic figures. Even though I had some of the Airfix sets, their three-piece cavalry troopers never quite stood up in playing and my own lack of Airfix artillery kits turned me off to collecting more boxes of figures. The ESCI cavalry troopers were still three pieces, stand, horse and man, but their assembly was well-fitting and playworthy. I collected all the cavalry sets. My favorite kit was the Polish Lancers. The manufacturer also introduced four artillery cannons to one boxed set. That was like having a whole battery ready to go. They also produced several infantry sets that ended up in my collection. The Napoleonic battles that later followed on my friend's dining room table were fabulous spectacles, not only for the pageantry of the figures lined up on the table but for the painstaking time that went into setting them up individually. It never occurred to my friend and I to use stands. Whole battles were destroyed if the table was bumped too hard.

ESCI also went on to produce their famous Historic Battle Sets. I collected a number of them. My first set was Rorke's Drift. It contained two sets of Zulus and British infantry, and the battlefield accessories kit was in soft plastic. The accessory set allowed for different options from creating fieldworks to barricades to a lookout tower. In the center of the vacuum-formed base was a ruined building. Those little Englishmen fought many a day in those ruins struggling for their plastic lives. Later, I went on to gather several of the World War Two series dioramas ESCI manufactured. Most of them contained two sets of opposing infantry, two tanks or vehicles, and a hard plastic accessories kit. Most of the vacuum-formed bases were different. But over time they began to show up in different period sets. For instance, the second set of the Battle of the Bulge had the same vacuum-form as the Gettysburg battle kit. I think by the time I was collecting them ESCI had sold or licensed its products to another company and that might have been the issue. I can claim to have had at one time or another, the following sets: Anzio, Okinawa, Tarawa, Iwo Jima, Gettysburg, both Battle of the Bulge sets, and El Alamein. (As for the last one, though, I am not exactly sure of the name. It was a North African set to be sure.) Yet I never retained any of the original sets. They all eventually disappeared over time.

While growing up, I would occasionally come across odds and ends that would fit in with my soldier collection. I remember finding birthday blister packs with Airfix knockoffs at a local toy store in the party section. I think I only got those once because the quality was so bad. Once, after reading a *Sgt. Rock* comic book, I found an advertisement in the back for a box of soldiers with tanks, aircraft, and ships. So I promptly ordered it. I was so thrilled that I was going to receive the *be-all and end-all* of soldier sets that I promised a neighbor kid I was going to give him my other soldiers once it arrived in the mail. Of course, I was referring to my retired big green ones. I still had not separated from my green troops. For six to eight weeks, I daydreamed about this set. I imagined the look of the hundred or so soldiers listed to come in the box. I fantasized about having enormous battles spread across my bedroom. I could not have been more disappointed when a small 6-inch box arrived in the mail. When I opened it up, I found 1-inch flat plastic soldiers and tanks mounted on stands. Everything was as flat as a nickel, even the ships and planes. I felt I had suffered a cruel joke. I broke the news to my friend, and he graciously understood my plight.

The best set I found came from an old pharmacy store that was down the hill from my dad's house. While I was browsing the toy section, I came across two *Capitan Courageous* sets. They were blister packs that had, not surprisingly, Airfix knockoff Marines in 1/72 scale. The sets also contained large World War One–looking cannons. The cannons fired little red projectiles. Also in the sets were 1-inch-high redoubts for the cannons to sit behind. Mounted on the redoubt was a little green and red searchlight. This was a fantastic find. I now had artillery for my little soldiers and something for them to hide behind instead of a crumpled sock. I am pretty certain those redoubts were the first terrain pieces I had as a boy.

Sometime after this, I was wandering the toy aisles of Kmart and found a battle train set for the U.S. Army. The train was HO scale. It had a rail gun like Anzio Annie and a boxcar with two 88mm flak guns built in. To reveal the guns, the sides of the boxcar fell open. There were also two flat cars. One carried a M47 tank and the other held an 18-wheel tractor trailer. There was also a cargo car where men could be placed and a storage car with a lit searchlight. I was somehow able to persuade my dad to get this for me for Christmas. Upon receiving it, I managed to scrounge up a piece of plywood large enough to hold the circular train track and I left it set up in my bedroom for months.

Across from the Kmart I used to ride my bike to, there was a Pic-n-Sav. From time to time I would find small die cast tanks and planes in the toy section. Once, it had a number of Sgt. Rock figures with a base that would allow the top half of the figure to twist, as if spraying machine gun bullets. They sold for 99 cents. So I bought three or four over the course of a few weeks. On one grand occasion, the store had 1/72 scale Aurora/ESCI Panzer III and Wespe tanks for a dollar. I think I was only able to buy two. Subsequently, I can remember lying in bed thinking, "If I could just do enough chores and wash a few cars, I could buy five or more models." Sadly, I went back the following week and they were all gone.

As time passed, my collection grew. My friend, Tony, met an older fellow. We were probably 12 years old and he was maybe 19 years old. I think he met him at Church. This guy had outgrown his model tanks and had moved on to a large collection of 1/285 scale micro-armor. He was selling his assortment of Roco Mini-tanks for 75 cents each. I must have just had a birthday because I had some money. I surveyed his collection and bought all I could. I do not know if he had many Allied tanks, but I sure ended up with a great collection of Tiger IIs and various German tanks. I can only remember getting a few Churchill and painted Cromwell tanks. By this time, I had amassed a nice mixture of armored kits; some sloppily built and most unpainted. In my preteen and early teen years, I was more interested in playing than painting. My mother allowed me to place them in a storage cupboard in our hallway. My collection took up two shelves, top and bottom, and that collection of Roco tanks maxed out what space I had left.

I also went on to build and dabble in other military model realms. For several years in my mid-teens, I decided to collect 1/700 scale ships for the Pacific Theater. I think I must have had the battle of Midway in my head. I built several of the aircraft carriers from that battle, both Japanese and American. I also had destroyers, cruisers, battleships, and submarines. I even went on to buy the little packages of extra airplanes, such as fighters, dive bombers, and torpedo bombers for the U.S. and Japanese. During this time, I found a D-Day 1/700 scale set. It had a vacuum-formed base and itty bitty Shermans and trucks. It had a Landing Ship, Tank (LST), a couple of troop transports, and a rocket barrage ship. I think it even had some landing craft. I did try to game with all this naval stuff, but the idea never grew on me. Tony and I had several battles in my living room. However, it got complicated with the size of the ships. The battleships really did not participate in the game other than being attacked by aircraft. Admittedly, the idea was better than the application.

Before the ship-building phase, I did build a modest air force of various nationalities to assist the ground troops. The first plane I built was a ME 262 jet fighter, which I purchased at a local grocery store. The store carried several different types of models from cars to planes. My collection ranged from fighters to a couple of bombers. I was all about adding firepower when wargaming entered my life. I went so far as to build a 1/72 scale B-29. Apparently, I was going to have my own Falaise Gap breakout on steroids. I did have a B-25 and B-26 to add and little extra help. The funny thing is I do not think I ever wargamed with them. Perhaps my opponents cried foul and I relented. The fighters, though, got plenty of use strafing the battlefield. We saw that in movies, and therefore thought it was a legitimate practice.

No collection of soldiers for a young developing wargamer would be complete without a try at creating some serious terrain to play on. My first endeavor was making a dirt box to put in my room. I got another piece of plywood from somewhere and tacked 4-inch cardboard walls around it and filled it with dirt from the backyard. Now, I was ready to play soldiers in style. I could make foxholes, bomb craters, trenches, and roads. I cut some Evergreen tree clippings to stick in the dirt for real trees. It lasted about two days. When my mom saw this, she went ballistic! I can still hear her ranting about the carpet, the dirt, and the vacuum cleaner. Now, in retrospect, with children of my own and two of them boys, I am in full agreement with her. It was a bad idea.

One thing that did get tolerated was my second attempt at an indoor war-board. I took that same 3 ft. by 4 ft. piece of plywood (dusted off, of course) and punched small holes into it. I then jammed more tree clippings from our Evergreen in the front yard as miniature trees. The tree was not the typical long-needled type. It had thick, funny-looking leaves that worked for my purposes. This war-board allowed me to set up great battles in a forest or jungle. This was the first time I got to use my Japanese infantry in anything that resembled a South Pacific island setting. I am not sure how long this board lasted in my room. Frankly, I do not think it lasted all that long because the trees kept dying out on me.

The next project was a little different; it was an actual table. My grandfather had given me a small wooden toddler table to play on when I was about 4 years old. By the time I was 7 or so, it lay dormant in the corner of the garage. At about 12 years old, I had a flash of insight to build a permanent terrain model. I grabbed some spare chicken wire that was lying around. My older brother had to use some of it to keep our little dog from escaping out our back gate. I bent it into shape and tied it to the table. It was essentially two hills with a river valley down the center. Under the chicken wire, I stuffed crumpled up newspaper. I created my own papier-mâché with water, flour, and strips of newspaper. I covered the entire surface and within a few hours it hardened enough to paint. We had some tawny colored paint in the garage, so I used this as dirt color for the hills. My brother, Zack, had some blue model paint that I used for the river. Thus, by the end of a long day, I had a battleground. Yet I went a step further. After all, what is a river valley without a bridge? I took some small strips of wood and cut them into 3-or 4-inch pieces and I assembled them without glue in the center of the valley to form a bridge. I did not want the bridge to be a lasting structure. My Airfix and Matchbox commandos had to have something to blow up, not to mention the battles that needed to be fought over it. The only drawback was that the little bridge was not the sturdiest configuration. On several occasions the bridge collapsed in mid-battle, upsetting the entire combat scene. It was fun nonetheless.

The last great adventure in creating a functional board for toy soldier combat was in the mid-1980s. I got my hands on a 4 ft. by 6 ft. piece of plywood. It might even have been 8 feet long. (Honestly, I have no idea where I kept getting these plywood boards from.) This time I tried the papier-mâché without the chicken wire and placed it over crumbled paper. It did not really hold its shape that well but it was good enough to play on. At one end, I recreated the hills and river like my previous work, which included the same fall-apart bridge. The other end contained the river and a flat plain leading up to those hills. I spent probably more time playing solo battles with my different historical periods than gaming with my friends. I had a splendid time with my World War Two stuff. I truly loved setting up my tanks and infantry all over the board and playing with or without dice, especially after watching a war movie on TV.

I cannot overestimate the affect the great Hollywood war films had on my young life. In a time before cable television, I had only a few stations to watch. As I recall, one of the three local networks would broadcast *War is Hell* week at varying times of the year, though I remember them mainly in the fall after school had started. The station would show one film each night, Monday through Friday. The titles were of the great films of the 1950s, 1960s, and 1970s: *The Guns of Navarrone, Anzio, Force 10 From Navarrone, The Big Red One, The Longest Day, The Sands of Iwo Jima, The Green Berets, The Battle of the Bulge, The Devils Brigade, Merrill's Marauder, The Dirty Dozen, A Bridge Too Far, Too Late a Hero, Bridge on River Kwai, Kelley's Heroes, Patton,* and *To Hell and Back*. Although I am sure there were others, these inspired my imagination. After watching one, I would immediately start conjuring up ideas for my next battle as soon as I finished my homework after school the following day. One time after watching the *Battle of the Bulge*, I decided to recreate the scene of the Tigers assaulting the town of Ambleve, or so I think that was the name of town in the movie. It was where Charles Bronson was ordered to lead the rearguard fight against the advancing Germans. The battle scene has a wave of Tiger IIs (really M-47 American tanks) crashing through the walls of the town, blasting and smashing the Americans. I used my Tiger IIs I bought from Tony's friend to lead a charge over a white sheet (my rendition of snow) to the Americans holding the other side. I think I had some old HO railroad buildings and miscellaneous junk to serve as the blown out town. Even though I cannot remember the exact outcome, I am pretty sure the Germans won. Certainly, one of the most rousing movies to watch as a kid was *A Bridge Too Far*. Unlike most war films that revolve around one battle scene, this movie was jam-packed. There was the initial fight with 30 Corps pushing up the road, the river crossing at Nijmegen, and the combat scenes in Arnhem. I am pretty sure I tried them all. I do remember using a bunch of the Airfix Marine rubber boats to cross a river and assault the other side with disastrous effects to the Americans.

I must confess the war movie that I still watch today like it was the first time is *Kelley's Heroes*. I think I have watched it over 20 times and I still love the theme song, *Burning Bridges*. The movie still gets me in the mood to game. More importantly, however, it makes me laugh and reminds me of a simpler time in my life. My favorite scene is when Carroll O'Connor comes running down the stairs in his morning red general's robe asking why he has broken through the entire front and is unaware of it. He is directed to the radio to listen to the ensuing battle that Clint Eastwood is engaged in while trying to get to the bank with the gold. He then hears the Gravediggers Registration unit over the radio stating they have a stake in the advance too. It ends with him getting up and shouting for his uniform.

As I got older, my collection continued to grow. The Atlantic figures and tanks took on new emphasis. By the time I left for the Marine Corps, I had a sizable collection. But sometime during a tour in Okinawa, a mail order hobby shop was selling numerous Atlantic kits dirt cheap. Of course, I bought them and stuffed them in my sea bag. I was able to get their mortar kits, anti-tank guns, and numerous infantry sets. After the service, I still continued to collect them. I now have about a dozen each of the Tiger Is, Jag-Tigers, Shermans, Chi Has, and T-35/85s. I also have several Leopards, M113s, Ontos, German SdKfz. 7 half-tracks, U.S. 6 Ton Cargo trucks, and six very special SdKfz. 232 armored cars. The latter were starting to go brittle, as sometimes the plastic does. So I painted and based them for my games. Actually, the armored cars are very close to 1/72 scale. The only thing that makes them bigger is the exaggerated radio antenna, which is larger than the scale size. Naturally, I have numerous miscellaneous infantry. My favorite infantry set is the World War Two Indian infantry. They are complete with the Sheik Turban. I have painted up a company of these troops to battle in the Burma Campaign.

Finally, as a "mature" man playing with toy soldiers, I take great pride in my collection. I have not only collected the Atlantic miniatures but have been fortunate to be able to purchase old diorama sets of ESCI from Stalingrad to Operation Husky, with several in between. I have even expanded my unopened box sets of figures and tanks, which include Airfix, Matchbox, Revell, and ESCI. I did eventually reduce my gathering activities. I had enough to open my own hobby shop. I did persuade myself to sell off portions of it because I was running out of room, though I have some treasures that will stay with me for some time to come.

Turning to my start in wargaming, I can point to my good friend, Blake Meech. He had learned it from some other kids that I did not know well. Those boys were into fantasy gaming, like Dungeons and Dragons. (Even though I was young, I saw there was a difference between the two gamers, historical and fantasy.) Blake and I found a small clearing between some bushes in the entryway to my home's atrium and set up a small game. I think I was the Americans and he was the Germans. The tanks I had at the time were from Atlantic. The only ones that come to mind, however, are the modern Leopard tanks. The game was simple. We each had about 50 soldiers and a few tanks. The forces were set up a few inches from each other. The rules were rather basic and modest. We each had a red 6-sided die to roll and we each took turns declaring our fire. I can only remember that 1, 2, or 3 meant something killed or destroyed. How exactly we determined casualties produced from machine guns or tank firing at infantry absolutely escapes me. I do remember that it launched me down a path that has lasted decades and hopefully decades more.

I do not think it was long before our games took on a bit more sophistication. I would spend the night at Blake's house, and we would set up small games on a piece of plywood that was painted dark brown with a blue river painted down the center. There was also a 1-inch dark brown bridge painted across the river at the center. We would set up our sides with our soldiers. There were to be no borrowed troops in these games. Our forces were treated like our own armies. At this stage, we started introducing movement after each side fired his troops and tanks. Every soldier or armored fighting vehicle that could fire at a target got its chance to fire. Naturally, this took a while. Fortunately, we had small forces. I think we even started on the concept of modifiers for troops behind cover. I seem to recall my Captain Courageous redoubts and the troops behind them being somewhat safe from enemy fire. At some point, we added casualty assessments. We would point to a particular spot that an HE round was to land or the burst of a machine gun was going to spray its plastic death. Assuming a hit was rolled, we would roll a 6-sided die to determine the number of men that were knocked down. Movement was confined to a few inches regardless of the vehicle or personnel. We always tried to get to the bridge, but it usually ended in hand-to-hand combat. Resolving that was nothing more than each of us rolling a 6-sided die per man and seeing who rolled the highest number. The highest naturally won the contest and the poor victim was knocked over.

When Blake introduced me to Tony (the friend I described before), I discovered that he too was starting down the wargaming trail. Where he picked it up, I am not sure. It might have been his older brother. He did have a friend named Allan that was an "advanced" wargamer for his age. I had met him through Tony and I remember playing a few games with him, one World War Two and the other a U.S. Civil War. His games were governed by some system of rules that he kept stored in his head. But I recall Allan's style of gaming had a nice order about it. Though how his system worked is beyond my brain power to bring to mind. Nevertheless, Tony immediately picked up on what Blake and I were doing. The three of us gamed in the same fashion for several years. The games were set up at each other's homes on large blankets with pillows underneath to form hills. Occasionally, paper buildings were placed on the battlefield to serve as cover as were a few model trees. (The buildings were a nice invention of mine. I had taken cardboard strips and folded them over to make right angles. Two right angles were placed together to form a square structure. I then placed a thin cardboard square on top to form a roof. The buildings were given the essential doors and windows by cutting them out. I added floors by cutting slits into one side of the right angle and wedging another roof square into the gap.) Mostly, the games were large tank battles with infantry struggling to keep up. They were fun and gave me some of my best childhood joy.

I think I was about 12 or 13 when our wargames started to really change in favor of actual rules. I discovered *Rommel's Panzers*, a small bookcase wargame. I found it in a game shop in Fullerton, California. It was a small board game that had a paper map as the board. There were small counters representing tanks, trucks, infantry, and anti-tank guns. It was then that I realized that more intricacies could be added to my gaming. The greatest of which was that tanks could be given armor ratings and each had different rates of speed. From this, I set upon creating my own rules. I went to the local library that was a block from my house and checked out a few books on tanks. From this, I commenced to setting up my own armored charts. In addition, I learned about turn sequences and adding artillery and mortars as a separate phase. This further introduced me to the idea of using ranges for different weapons. I spent the next several months working on these rules.

What emerged was a functional set of rules that laid the foundation for my development as a wargamer. The rules allowed for two phases per turn: movement and firing. It was at that time I cemented the belief in rolling for initiative in both phases. Not that I was persuaded from other means. It would be years before I discovered that gamers wrote down orders. It was the flow of the game that mattered and rolling to see who would take the lead seemed the best. I think I might have challenged one of my friends on the idea of rolling to see who gets a full move; in other words, the winner of the roll moves and fires before the other player can do anything. That was out of the question; it was too punitive to the poor guy who rolled badly a few times in a row. Therefore, it was settled that each side in the battle would roll to see who moved first and who would fire first in each phase of each turn.

In those rules, movements were organized by type of unit, which was a first for our little wargame group. Different vehicles and tanks had different rates of speed as did infantry. The infantry was broken down into two groups; those troops carrying crew-served weapons and those that were not. There were also some basic modifiers that slowed down movements, like streams, walls, hills, and off-road travel for AFVs. Of course these were basic, but the list of modifiers grew as our experience level increased.

Once both sides completed movement, it was on to firing. The indirect fire phase of artillery and mortars was first. This was simply done by calling out the intended target, which was usually a tank, and rolling to see if a hit occurred. Misses were ignored. At the time, there was no such thing as rounds landing short or going long. They were assumed to have gone off-board. If a hit was scored, it was treated like before. That is, the target was destroyed pending a second roll for penetration. If the tank or vehicle was blown up, the player got to roll a 6-sided die to determine how many troops near the blast were killed. I do not think I actually wrote down how far away the troops had to be in order to be safe, though I think the unspoken rule was three to four inches. Interestingly, I do not remember any arguing about troops being too far to be affected. I drew distinctions between mortars and artillery. Artillery was naturally more powerful. My knowledge was still very limited. I was unaware of the different types of mortars. I had assumed they were the same and that idea came from how the soldiers were armed in the box sets. On the other hand, with artillery, I had my suspicions. Tony had built a *Hasegawa 1/72 Long Tom* and I knew that was bigger than the *Airfix 88mm* I had.

After the mortars and artillery were fired, the player then started firing his infantry and tanks. Originally, I allowed for all troops to fire provided they had a line-of-sight path to the target. As I mentioned, basing troops had not crossed the minds of our wargame group. Each of us would set up maybe 100 to 200 figures by hand on the battlefield. It quickly became a problem to say every soldier could fire. This sent me back to the drawing board to come up with a solution. I settled on the idea of assigning firing points to all units, including tanks and the indirect weapons. Anything that fired an explosive shell would cost 7 points, machine guns 5 points, submachine guns 3 points. Rifles were the cheapest to fire, at 1 point. Other weapons, like grenades, flamethrowers, and rifle grenades, were assigned 2 points. At the start of a game, the number of firing points was determined. Primarily, this was calculated by how many tanks and cannons each side possessed. To be sure, each side wanted to be able to fire off all its tanks. Next, we would add a few more points to make sure some infantry got a chance to fire. For scoring a hit, ranges were included, along with a few modifiers like hard or soft cover. Once a hit was scored, the different weapons had different effects. Pistols and rifles were one-shot one-hit weapons. Machine guns were allowed to roll two 6-sided dice to determine the number of men they knocked over. Submachine guns, flamethrowers, and hand grenades got one 6-sided die to roll. Tanks firing at infantry were treated the same way, with one 6-sided die for casualties. I did not know about the different types of ammunition the tanks could fire, let alone the basic distinction between High Explosive and Armor Piercing. To us it was all the same.

One of the greatest achievements of this new system of mine was that it gave us a better way for allowing different tanks from different nations to more accurately battle each other. The system had assigned weapons and armor classes on an easy-to-use chart. I had sized up armor thicknesses for each tank under review and had given it a relative value to other tanks. The same was done for gun sizes. I think the main benchmark in both categories was the Jagd-Tiger. This system is very similar to what is presented in this book under Table 8.3.

On other fronts, I made attempts to create easy rules for other periods, like the musket and ancient eras. I never found or created lasting methods or ideas until well past my adolescent years. The best I could come up with for the musket period was assigning distances for movement and ranges for firing. Movement was easy, that was already a standardized practice that could be modified from my World War Two rules. The trouble was in firing troops. I settled on rolling a given die for the number of soldiers represented and the number that appeared on the die or dice was the number of casualties inflicted on the enemy. For example, if 24 figures were lined up facing another group of soldiers, the firing player could choose his dice: four 6-sided dice, three 8-sided dice, or two 12-sided dice. If he rolled a score of 14, then 14 soldiers were toppled over. Given the fact we did not use a tray to mount our figures, numerous troops were needed to have a good game. But the time to move and maneuver hundreds of little men pretty much ended the enthusiasm to play more than a handful of games. The ancient period was not much better. Again, movement was not an issue. How to handle the inevitable slugfest, however, was a great challenge. At first, I resorted to rolling two 6-sided dice per contest between two individual warriors. However, this became a mind-numbing process if a couple of hundred Romans and barbarians were hacking at each other. I later proceeded to group the figures in clusters and rolled one die per group. The numbers rolled for each opposing group represented the number of casualties they took. Once more, battling ancients did not gather much attention in the wargame group. If these two periods did not get the consideration they deserved in gaming, they most definitely got it in my collection. I think I bought every set that came out multiple times. I figured someday I would crack the code on how to game these chaps in a proper format.

Later, when I joined the Marine Corps, I took my World War Two set of rules with me. One might have expected I would have found numerous willing participants for wargaming. Sadly, the answer was no, though I did find one, Cory. He and I spent many a night afterhours building up our forces and preparing them for combat. Of course we had to be very mindful about the size of our collections. We were in the same infantry platoon and we traveled quite a bit overseas. On more than one occasion, we had to send most of our stuff home before leaving garrison duty and shipping out to Okinawa.

While in the Marine Corps, I did get a few opportunities to participant in true miniature "wargaming." I was stationed in Kaneohe Bay and at the time the base had an indoor wargame facility. The table was massive. It had to have been 20 feet by 20 feet. It was a modular setup, with numerous spare 4 ft. by 5 ft. terrain pieces that could be arranged in any number of ways for a battlefield. The miniature pieces were 1/285 scale micro-armor. I cannot recall the details of the battles. I knew we were fighting the Soviets with their hordes of tanks. I seem to remember the Marines having missile launchers, and a few tanks with indirect fire support from mortars, artillery, and aircraft. The reason the details of these games are sketchy is that each time I participated I was placed in a room with my platoon commander, and he had the window seat. I was a lowly Lance Corporal of an 81mm mortar platoon, and my job was to listen to radio requests for fire support, as I was a member of the Fire Direction Center.

After I got out of the Marines, I went to college and started collecting and gaming once more. It was shortly after college that I met Larry Squire, Mike Creek, and Jim French, who formed the core of my wargame experience as an adult. When I met them, I started to realize that the hobby was something greater than my own activities. Both Larry and Mike have huge wargame areas. Larry has an entire enclosed patio with 6 folding tables set up on a nearly permanent basis. He has drawn out 3-inch hexes across the board, for easy range and unit facing determinations. Mike's two-car garage is nearly taken up by his permanent wargame table. He also developed his own very successful blog website: http://bunkermeister.blogspot.com. I was privileged enough to get to play games on their tables and see their splendid collections.

Unfortunately, the hobby still felt like a private endeavor, with a loose collection of people who enjoyed the same thing. At some point after the year 2000, I came across a magazine called *Military Digest* at a local hobby store. This started to clue me in on a much greater and larger wargame community. I found out that this particular issue was essentially a reprint of past articles from the 1970s and 1980s. It was not until I stumbled across Don Featherstone's book, *Battles with Model Soldiers*, that I fully grasped the full magnitude of the hobby, both past and present. From that point on, I discovered several more books for all sorts of historical periods. I collected and read books from all the great authors in the hobby: Don Featherstone, Charles Grant, Paddy Griffith, Terrence Wise, Bruce Quarrie, and C.F. Wesencraft. They have certainly influenced my perspective in wargame design. I owe them a great deal of gratitude for developing the hobby into what it is today and the fantastic fun and joy it has brought me. My childhood would not have been the same had they not had the courage to undertake writing to propel and expand the hobby.

CHAPTER 12

Conclusion

This book has certainly covered a number of topics. It has discussed wargaming to fundamental aspects of World War Two. Wargaming is a fun and exciting hobby, and I hope I have provoked some thought on wargame design and those ideas that help develop a good game. Gamers will not always agree on troop movements, weapon firing, and the other intricacies of a rule system. Nevertheless, if the intent and logic of the rules are examined, perhaps some arguments can be averted. The *Blood and Guts* rules are not meant to be the final say on wargaming the Second World War, but are instead intended to be a balanced wargame approach to the period. I do not pretend that I have designed a perfect system that will meet every wargamer's expectation, which would be impossible. Rather, I want gamers to have a relatively easy set of rules to use and be able to game any theater of action with a fair degree of realism, in a miniature sense. Moreover, I hope that players will find that the mounting of figures is a flexible and inexpensive system. By adjusting the tactical label details on the figure stands, players can get far greater use of their troops. This allows the player's figures to be used in different scenarios. Also, by using this system one box of plastic soldiers or a few packs of metal figures can easily be formed into an infantry company. Furthermore, the tactical details are what tell the player what the stand represents. This means that a player can use any figure to represent a medium machine gun team or mortar section. This alone helps reduce the cost of collecting figures. Finally, I suspect players will find the game moves along at a good pace. Getting to the all important battlefield result in a few hours has always been my chief concern.

Although I only wrote nine historic battle scenarios, there is an endless array of battle games that can be researched. I wholeheartedly encourage gamers to write a few scenarios of their own to game with their friends. Doing so is a phenomenal way to increase one's knowledge of history and get a better grasp of what men in warfare have had to endure. The process of creating a scenario transforms a distant and impersonal conflict into an object of personal involvement.

In the latter half of the book, I set out to create a modest tactical and AFV reference guide for wargamers. I wanted to write a set of rules with material to assist in developing wargame armies and provide tactical information for the use of those armies. I hope gamers will find the *Wargame Implications* useful in their fields of play. If anything, I trust I have spurred some thought about how to better employ a wargame unit at the company level. This should not be overlooked. The player who has a war plan prior to a game is more likely to win that game and have a much more enjoyable time. The tank development chapter is designed to give the reader a quick understanding of how tanks evolved in the war and what were the basic highlights of those developments for the major combatants.

Finally, I hope the last chapter brought back a few memories and smiles to the reader. Sometimes it is good to reminisce about our childhood and to recall our fondest memories. For some it may be Hot Wheels, comic books, or baseball cards. For me, it was my toy soldiers and I am very grateful it was. I hope that this book will inspire other would-be authors to pull up a keyboard and start clicking away. I earnestly believe that by writing more books on the subject of wargaming this community can add a new generation to the ranks.

The End

BIBLIOGRAPHY

Aclaide, Jose Antonio. *Unternehmen: Merfur*. Spain: AF Editores, 2008. (English Edition)

Bull, Stephen. *World War II Infantry Tactics Squad and Platoon*. Oxford: Osprey Publishing, 2004.

Catton, Charles. *Tanks and Armored Fighting Vehicles Visual Encyclopedia*. London: Amber Books, 2009.

Chamberlain, Peter and Ellis, Chris. *British and American Tanks of World War II*. New York: Arco Publishing,1969.

Daugherty III, Leo J. *Fighting Techniques of a Japanese Infantryman 1941–1945*. St. Paul: MBI Publishing Co., 2002.

Edwards, Roger. *German Airborne Troops*. Garden City: Doubleday & Company, Inc., 1974.

Featherstone, Donald. *Battles in Miniature Vol. 1 A Wargaming Guide to the Western Desert Campaign 1940–1942*. Lexington: John Curry, 2010.

Forty, George. *World War Two AFV's Armoured Fighting Vehicles & Self Propelled Artillery*. London: Osprey, 1996.

Foss, Christopher. *World War II Tanks and Fighting Vehicles.* New York, Arco Publishing, 1981.

Gailey, Harry. *MacArthur Strikes Back, Decision at Buna: New Guinea 1942-1943.* Novato: Presidio Press, Inc., 2000.

Gander, Terry J. *Collins Jane's Tanks of World War Two.* Rome: Harper Collins Publishers, 1995.

Gudgin, Peter. *Armoured Firepower: The Development of Tank Armament 1939-45.* Gloucestershire: Sutton Publishing, 1997.

Hoffschmidt, E.J., Tantum, W.H. *German Tank and Antitank.* Old Greenwich: WE Inc., 1968.

Hogg, Ian. *Artillery in Color 1920-1963.* New York: Arco Publishing, 1980.

Macksey, Kenneth. *Tank Tactics 1939-1945.* London: Almark Publishing Co, Ltd., 1976.

Mesko, Jim. *Amtracs in Action Part One.* Carrolton: Squadron/Signal Publications, Inc.1993.

Mesko, Jim. *U.S. Self-Propelled Guns in Action.* Carrolton: Squadron/Signal Publications, Inc.1999.

Rottman, Gordon. *U.S. World War II Amphibious Tactics Mediterranean & European Theaters.* Oxford: Osprey Publishing, 2006.

Rottman, Gordon. *U.S. World War II Amphibious Tactics Army & Marine Corps, Pacific Theaters.* Oxford: Osprey Publishing, 2004.

Rottman, Gordon. *World War II Airborne Warfare Tactics.* Oxford: Osprey Publishing, 2006.

Rottman, Gordon. *World War II Infantry Anti-Tank Tactics.* Oxford: Osprey Publishing, 2005.

Rottman, Gordon. *World War II Jungle Tactics.* Oxford: Osprey Publishing, 2007.

Weeks, John. *Men Against Tanks.* New York: Mason/Charter, 1975.

Online Sources

Kennedy, Gary. "Battalion Organization During the Second World War." (Online) Available. www.bayonetstrength.150m.com, 2000–2010.

"Airborne Operations A German Appraisal" Pages 1–43. (Online) Available. www.history.army.mil/books/wwii/104-13/104-13.htm

http://www.history.army.mil/html/bookshelves/resmat/ww2list.html

http://www.ibiblio.org/hyperwar

http://www.wwiivehicles.com

ABOUT THE AUTHOR

David Hall currently resides in Albuquerque, New Mexico, with his wife and three children. He proudly served in the United States Marines and is a Veteran of Desert Shield and Desert Storm. He graduated from California State University, Fullerton, in 1996, and miniature wargaming has been his passion since childhood.

INDEX